Bible Theology

by

W.B. Godbey

First Fruits Press
Wilmore,
Kentucky
c2018

Bible theology. By W.B. Godbey.
First Fruits Press, © 2018

ISBN: 9781621717706 (print), 9781621717713 (digital), 9781621717720 (kindle)

Digital version at http://place.asburyseminary.edu/godbey/13/

First Fruits Press is a digital imprint of the Asbury Theological Seminary, B.L. Fisher Library. Asbury Theological Seminary is the legal owner of the material previously published by the Pentecostal Publishing Co. and reserves the right to release new editions of this material as well as new material produced by Asbury Theological Seminary. Its publications are available for noncommercial and educational uses, such as research, teaching and private study. First Fruits Press has licensed the digital version of this work under the Creative Commons Attribution Noncommercial 3.0 United States License. To view a copy of this license, visit http://creativecommons.org/licenses/by-nc/3.0/us/.

For all other uses, contact:

First Fruits Press
B.L. Fisher Library
Asbury Theological Seminary
204 N. Lexington Ave.
Wilmore, KY 40390
http://place.asburyseminary.edu/firstfruits

Godbey, W. B. (William Baxter), 1833-1920.
  Bible theology / by W.B. Godbey. – Wilmore, KY : First Fruits Press, ©2018.
  419 pages ; cm.
  Reprint. Previously published: Cincinnati, Ohio : God's Revivalist Office, c1911.
  ISBN: 9781621717706 (pbk.)
  1. Theology, Doctrinal. I. Title.
      BT75.G62 2018   230.7

Cover design by Jon Ramsay

asburyseminary.edu
800.2ASBURY
204 North Lexington Avenue
Wilmore, Kentucky 40390

First Fruits Press
The Academic Open Press of Asbury Theological Seminary
204 N. Lexington Ave., Wilmore, KY 40390
859-858-2236
first.fruits@asburyseminary.edu
asbury.to/firstfruits

BIBLE THEOLOGY

By

REV. W. B. GODBEY, A. M.

Author of

Seventy Books and Booklets on Holiness and Travels, Among Which the Seven "Commentaries on the New Testament," "Translation of the New Testament," "Footprints of Jesus in the Holy Land," "Life of Jesus and His Apostles," "Tour Around the World," "Autobiography," "Incarnation of the Holy Ghost," "Glorification," "Christian Perfection," "Holiness or Hell," "Sanctification," "Baptism," "Demonology," and "Work of the Holy Spirit," are the Most Prominent.

GOD'S REVIVALIST OFFICE,
"Mount of Blessings,"
Cincinnati, O.

COPYRIGHTED, 1911, BY GOD'S REVIVALIST OFFICE.

Contents.

	PAGE
Exordium	5

CHAPTER I.
The Divinity	9

CHAPTER II.
The Trinity	15

CHAPTER III.
Total Depravity	24

CHAPTER IV.
Conviction and Repentance	28

CHAPTER V.
Justification, Regeneration and Conversion	35

CHAPTER VI.
Sanctification, Holiness and Perfection	50

CHAPTER VII.
Christian Baptism	70

CHAPTER VIII.
The Pentecostal Experience	84

CHAPTER IX.
The Divine "Agape" and Spiritual Graces	95

CHAPTER X.
Election of Grace and Reprobation and Foreknowledge	133

CHAPTER XI.
Spiritual Gifts.................................... 150

CHAPTER XII.
Glorification..................................... 207

CHAPTER XIII.
Our Lord's Return and Glorious Reign on the Earth 221

CHAPTER XIV.
Signs of His Coming............................. 255

CHAPTER XV.
The Post-millennial View of our Lord's Second Coming Untenable......................... 279

CHAPTER XVI.
The Eucharist.................................... 296

CHAPTER XVII.
Symbolic Baptism................................ 300

CHAPTER XVIII.
Apostasy... 331

CHAPTER XIX.
Matrimony....................................... 354

CHAPTER XX.
The Church...................................... 369

EXORDIUM.

Theology is a compound from *Logos*, "Word," and *Theos*, "God"; therefore it simply means, "the Word of God." Like many other words, it has been literally perverted by that awful demon—sect-idolatry,—until it has utterly lost its true meaning, and in current parlance now means creedology. In most of the theological colleges dispersed throughout Christendom, the curriculum is ingeniously selected, and adjusted directly to conserve the creed in which the doctrines of the sect or denomination which it represents are formulated, *e. g.*, if it be a Methodist institution, the great work of the faculty, in the use of their curriculum, is so to instruct the students as to qualify them to bend the Bible to the Methodist creed; if it be Baptist, the great work is to so bend the Bible as to conserve their creed; if Presbyterian, or Congregational, their assiduous study is to bend the whole Bible to the Westminister confession of faith; if Campbellites, the whole Bible must conserve the water-god, whose majesty puts all other gods into eclipse.

The adoption of the Nicene Creed by the first great ecumenical council of the Christian Church, A. D. 325, over which the Emperor Constantine presided, sitting in a golden chair, was the greatest mistake in the history of the Church. It was all right to formulate it as a book of simple erudition, auxiliary to Bible study, at the same time unequivocably recognizing the Word of

God as the only authority, especially the New Testament (not depreciating the Old, which is identical with the New, giving the same truth in symbolism), because we are under its dispensation. The normal attitude of Christendom recognizes no leader but Jesus, no guide but the Holy Ghost, and no authority but the New Testament. The Bible Schools and Holiness Colleges, which already illuminate Christendom and are multiplying rapidly, are a veritable sunburst on the forlorn hope of the world. I say forlorn, because human creeds have so dominated the religious mind as to fill the world with bewilderment and actually open a wide door to popular skepticism and infidelity. This great Holiness Movement, girdling the globe, has proved the precursor of many independent churches, founded on the New Testament as their only creed and authority.

In my peregrinations in all lands, I find many of the Holiness people have a book of discipline in which doctrines, rules and regulations are formulated; but am happy, thus far, to find no case in which this book is recognized obligatory, but simply instructive and thus convenient auxiliary laws in the management of the Church. It is pertinent on the part of all, diligently to guard this point and never tie ourselves to anything but God's plain, simple and unsophisticated Word, as we are so fortunate in His merciful providence to have it in the inspired originals; the Old in Hebrew, and the New in the beautiful incorruptible and unmistakable Greek.

If the Holiness Churches ever tie themselves to a creed, other than God's simple Word, they are already fallen and gone in the track of their denominational predecessors in the awful downward trend to dead churchisms and idolatry. The only security is walking alone with the Unseen God, midway between formal churchanity on the one side, and wild fanaticism on the other. They are both the ambuscaded hell-traps of Satan, who gives you the utmost freedom in making your choice, as in either case his black lasso drops around your neck, gradually tightening in the Lethean slumber of an unconscious Antinomian death, the awful prelude of swift damnation. While this walk along the narrow path of holiness to the Lord is so delicate and precarious, that constant vigilance is the price of success; yet it is so plain and easy, that "way-faring men, though fools, shall not err therein." There is but one qualification demanded by the King of Heaven, and that is purity; as He has decreed that "the unclean shall not pass over it," hence, none but the wholly sanctified can walk therein. Dead profession, and wild fanaticism, both turn all their artillery against the real, genuine sanctification, i. e., perfect humility, love and purity; the Holy Ghost our Sanctifier, incarnated in the heart, King Jesus reigning without a rival in the heart and life. This book you now read is the gift of the Holy Ghost, with but one end in view and that is to teach you this great and wonderful salvation revealed in God's precious Word. Therefore, you should so study it, as to not only receive, but appropriate it, and assimilate it and make it your own unseparable gift of God. I trow it is in one respect unlike any other theological book you have ever seen; in the simple fact that it is perfectly free from humanisms in every form and phase and conserves no creed, sect or denomination: I am satisfied the reader will unequivocally corroborate this conclusion.

Bible Theology.

CHAPTER I.

THE DIVINITY.

The Apostle Paul defines the attitudes of the heathen, "*For the invisible things of Him are seen from the creation of the world, being made known by His works, both His eternal power and Divinity: so that they are left without excuse: because, knowing God, they did not glorify Him as God, nor were they thankful; but they became vain in their reasonings, and their foolish heart was darkened.*"

The translators of the English Version in this passage have translated the word *theiotees*, "Godhead," which is not its meaning, but *Divinity*. It is a universally recognized fact that the heathen know the God of creation; but it is everywhere obviously patent that they are utterly ignorant of the Trinity, *i. e.*, they know nothing about the Saviour. "The untutored savage in his primeval wilds, sees God in the clouds, and hears Him in the winds; whose soul proud science never taught to stray, as far as the solar walk—the milky way."

In this chapter Paul describes the sad apostasy from God, as in the family of Noah, the second father of mankind. Therefore, the Pagans are the apostasy of the Noachian church; the Jews, and Moslems, that of the

Mosaic; and the Oriental Greeks and Latins, that of the Apostolic; while the Protestant Churches are also in spiritual delapidation.

Paul here certifies this gradual trend away from God, the light of Satan and then into darkness. They first went into intellectualism, where the Protestant Churches are now vainly substituting intellect and learning for the Holy Ghost. Then they went on into idolatry, where we now find the Oriental Christians, Jews and Moslems. Finally they degenerated into brutality, where we are now shocked to find the heathen nations. Mid all this terrible apostasy, they are still very religious, verifying the philosophical maxim, that, "Man is the religious animal."

The Bible nowhere gives us a formal argument to prove the existence of God. It would be superfluous; whereas the Bible has no superfluities, but is pre-eminently practical. The material universe everywhere incontestably reveals his Creator. The worship of the God of nature is not idolatry, that is Satan's counterfeit.

A. The sun, especially in Oriental skies, where he is so much more brilliant than in the Occident, leads the way in the capture of nature simple children to his adoration. In Egypt they worshipped him under the name of Osiris; in Phœnicia and Syria, Baal; in Assyria, Nisrock; in Armenia, the Veruna; in India, Paramatina; in Greece, Zeus, and in Italy, Jupiter. Cain seemed to have no apprehension of the God of redemption; but devoutly worshipped the god of nature. Without a Divine revelation, the intellect is utterly incompetent to apprehend the Divine attributes, Omnipotence, Omnipresence and Omniscience. Therefore, they resting in the conclusion that Divinity was under the necessity of utilizing subordinates in order to carry on the universe intuitively assigned Divinity to all of these agents and, consequently, multiplied gods of their own imagination illimitably. Confirmatory of the philosophical maxim, no nation has ever been discovered entirely destitute of any kind of religion. The most degraded savages are Fetichists. This strange religion consists in charms and diversified superstitions, which they worship, imputing to them supernatural power and influence, *i. e.*, snakes, bones, ostrich feathers and almost anything to which superstition may impute a charm, of course, developing into witchcraft, sorcery, necromancy and legerdemain. They believe a spirit is present, presiding over mountain, spring, river, rill, cave and thus they populate the whole world with supernatural beings, and pay to them more or less adoration. These divinities are both good and evil. They worship the latter, perhaps, nearly as much as the former, offering them not only their adoration, but sacrifices, in order to appease their wrath and avert calamities, which they are competent to send on them.

B. Not only does God reveal Himself in the stupendous and universal work of creation; but in His Holy Spirit, who is veritably the excarnate Christ. (Acts 16:6, 7.) (In all of my quotations, you will only find them reliably in my Translation, which you ought to have, as I use nothing but the Greek, and there are so many errors in the English Version that you would not always find the quotations in it correct.)

John 1:9: *"He is the true Light, which lighteth every person coming into the world."* 1 John 1:7: *"If we walk in the light, as He is in the light, we have fellowship one with another, and the Blood of Jesus Christ cleanses us from all sin."*

God does not require people to walk in light which He has not given. There is the wide open door for the salvation of the whole world, heathens, Jews, Mohammedans, and all sects and denominations of nominal Christians, if they only in the candor, honesty and integrity of their own hearts walk in all the light they have; not only will they be justified but in the finality sanctified by the expurgatory Blood of Jesus, dispensed by the Holy Spirit to every soul, responsive to His intercessions at the right hand of God. We will find, perhaps, to our surprise, multiplied thousands in heaven, who spent their lives in the dismal night of pagan superstition; but amid all did their best, humbly, faithfully and heroically walking in all the light they had. In the final judgment those who have lived under the light of Christianity will be judged by the whole Bible; while the generations antecedently to our Lord's incarnation will be judged by the Old Testament alone; whereas the multiplied millions of dark pagandom will be judged only by the laws of nature, as it was never their privilege to enjoy the revealed Word.

When I, for the first time, sailed for the Old World in 1895, I was entirely alone on the great steamer carrying two thousand souls, all strangers to me. Having sailed out of New York harbor, and reached the great ocean, soon a man with radiant countenance looked in my face and said, "You are God's man," to whom I responded, "You are another," and we mutually embraced, as if we had been comrades all our lives. We descended into the steerage and preached to the six hundred poor people of all nationalities. He was a citizen of London, homeward bound from a tour of seven years around the world, preaching the Gospel to all nations. He said, when he entered great old dark China, in the Pauline succession, he heroically passed the track of every predecessor, interpenetrating an interior province, whither no missionary had ever entered. Making his way to the mansion of the Mandarin with all expedition he received him with cordial welcome and proceeded to tell him that he was watching and waiting for his coming, as his father had prophesied with his dying breath, saying to him, "My son, in your time a man will come into this country, bringing with him the Jesus doctrine, which you must receive with all your heart and preach it to all our people, because it is the only true doctrine." Then closing his eyes, he left the government to his surviving son, who constantly looked for the missionary predicted by his dying father and joyfully receiving him, became his first convert to Christianity, turned preacher on the spot and went with him to tell the good news of salvation to his people, who had groped in heathen darkness from ages immemorial. You need not tell me that old Mandarin was not a Christian; he was not only a worshipper of the true God, but honored with the gift of prophesy, in which he blessed his people by the prediction of the coming missionary and thus threw the door wide open for the conversion of his people to Christianity. That old man had never seen a Christian, nor had any opportunity to learn a word in the Bible. In some mysterious way the name Jesus had come to him, and that was all he knew. I could corroborate this testimony indefinitely.

When Captain John Smith, of the Jamestown colony, the first ever planted on American soil, was a captive among the Indians, upon one attempt to teach the old chief Christianity, he was surprised to find that he knew more about God than himself, so he actually surrendered his commission, and sitting down at the feet of this venerable heathen saint, was delighted and edified by his testimony; showing plainly that he was acquainted with the God of the universe in a happy experience of personal salvation, whereas Smith only had the written Word, the religious form.

The flaming sun in his gorgeous glory, the silvery moon in her queenly beauty, and all the stars in their glittering constellation, corroborated by every towering mountain, whose snowy summit reflects the splendor of their golden brightness, with every swelling river, limpid lake, and crystal fountain, gladdening earth's millions with living waters, and every alluvian plain, invigorated by these prolific irrigations, unanimously and vociferously proclaim to all created intelligences that the Hand that made us is Divine.

CHAPTER II.

THE TRINITY.

The great Bible truth, in contradistinction to the polytheistical and pantheistical religions of the heathens, culminates in the unity of the Divinity.

This unity is perfectly compatible with the divine Trinity, though to finite minds upon superficial apprehension and investigation apparently incompatible and irreconcilable. This Trinity is not essential, but personal, accommodatory to the great plan of salvation; the Father bestowing the unspeakable Gift; the Son becoming our vicarious Substitute, and the Holy Ghost, the Omnipotent Executive.

Water is a trinity; solid in ice, liquid in its fluid, and vaporous in the atmosphere. In my evangelistic work, I am book editor in the morning, Bible teacher in the afternoon, and preacher at night; thus I exhibit three distinct characters, and yet I am only one man.

Our faith receives profitable testing in the reception of those great truths, which exhibit dilemmas and paradoxes. God has manifested His inscrutable wisdom and paradoxical mercy in so adjusting the plan of salvation as to make faith the condition of our salvaton. Our knowledge will always be limited; but there is no reason why there should be any deficiency in our faith, which is vitiated by nothing but doubts, which is the normal fruit of depravity, as well as the ejectment of evil spirits. Under the cleansing blood we altogether get rid of depravity; meanwhile it is our glorious privilege, also, to be delivered from all evil spirits; not that we will ever be free from temptation in this life; but that we can get out of gun-shot, so Satan will only waste his ammunition, when he shoots at us.

c. God the Father (1 John 4:8, 16) is defined to be love. John 3:16 tells us, *"God so loved the world that He gave His only begotten Son, that whosoever believeth on Him should not perish, but have eternal life."*

> "Oh, for this love, let rock and hills,
>   Their lasting silence break,
> And all harmonious human tongues
>   Their Savior's praises speak;
> Angels assist our mighty joys;
>   Strike all your harps of gold;
> But when you raise your highest notes,
>   His love can ne'er be told."

The incomprehensible love of the Father for this lost world He has created to enjoy His fellowship forever, was so unutterable as to superinduce the gift of His only Son to redeem every soul from sin, death and hell. Therefore, as you see clearly revealed in the precious Word, the love of God was the Archimedean lever that moved the uncreated Three in the heavenly synod to project the redemptive scheme. When the awful tidings of the fall reached heaven, the angelic millions were moved to profoundest sympathies, superinducing their spontaneous enthusiastic and unanimous espousal of the law's cause, but the infinite divinity forfeited out of the human organism by the fall, never could be restored by finitude, though involving the entire host of angels, archangels, cherubim, and seraphim. Amid this awful dilemma, every angel having suspended his golden harp on the weeping willows of Paradise sat down to weep over the irretrievable ruin. Meanwhile all hell is jubilant with shouts of victory, hailing the welcome accession of fallen earth to their restricted, gloomy dominions; when lo! the Son of God walks out on the celestial battlements and proclaims to the universe His espousal of the law's cause. Never in the history of the ages had Heaven been so astonished. When the news reached hell, oh how it paralyzed their jubilee, and sent panic through all the pandemoniums of damnation. They knew terrible issues were pending. Therefore, the battle-drums began to roar throughout all the realms of Diabolus. Poor old fallen Lucifer, who chose to reign in hell, rather than serve in heaven, now issues his royal mandamus to all his myrmidons and through them to all demons, fiends and imps, to prepare for war, as he is determined to hold the spoils he had won in Eden.

D. Thus the Son, the second Person of the Trinity espouses the law's cause and covenants with the Father to redeem that lost world by the substitution of His life, for that of every human being. Heb. 2:9: *"By the grace of God, Christ tasted death for every one."* The Greek here is *huper pantos, i.e., "in* the room *and stead of every* one," thus becoming our vicarious Substitute, and so redeeming us as to eternally sweep away the necessity of the damnation of a solitary soul, and not only to satisfy the law and precluding the necessity of the normal penalty; but to even magnifying the law, by doubly satisfying it, both actively in his sinless life, and passively in His meek and unmurmuring submission like the innocent lamb in the slaughter-pen, thus forever paying the penalty and disarming the law of all its vengeance, from the simple fact that the law is at perfect peace with a dead man.

Gal. 3:13, 14, 16. *"Christ hath redeemed us from under the curse of the law, being made a curse for us: for it is written, Cursed is every one that hangeth on a tree: in order that the blessing of Abraham might come on the Gentiles; and we may receive the promise of the Spirit through faith. For to Abraham and his seed, were the promises made. It does not say, Unto seeds, as of many; but unto thy seed, which is Christ."* Here you see the identity of the Abrahamic covenant with the Messianic, which was reiterated to Abraham, thus exalting him to the fatherhood of the faithful in all ages. That the redemption of Christ was summary and perfect, actually reaching every soul, in its vicarious substitutionary efficiency, we clearly learn from many Scriptures.

2 Cor. 5:14, 15: *"For the divine love of Christ constraineth us; judging thus, that one died for all, since all were dead: and He died for all, in order that the living may no longer live unto themselves, but unto Him who died for them, and is risen."* Here we have the strong preposition *huper* twice in this verse, which positively means that He took the place of every human being, and in the capacity of our substitute, met the law and paid the penalty.

Gal. 2:20: *"I am crucified along with Christ: and I live no more, but Christ liveth in me: the life which I now live in the flesh I live by the faith of the Son of God,*

Who loved me, and gave Himself for me." Here we have *huper emour*, whose literal meaning is, "in my room instead." What is true of Paul, appertains to every human being, as God is no respector of persons. Here you see most unequivocably and indisputably the vicarious substitutionary atonement of Christ for every human soul, thus copiously revealed in the precious word of God.

E. A great heresy has prevailed in the Church ever since the days of Arius in the second century, who denied the divinity of Christ, and said He was only a good man, used of God in His day and generation to give us all a perfect example, thus showing us how to live and to die. It brought a serious trouble into the Church, super-inducing the great division, developing the Aryan and Trinitarian Controversy, which racked the Church like a sweeping cyclone a thousand years. Though a general victory has perched on the Trinitarian banner; yet this day millions of nominal Christians are marching under Unitarian colors.

Confirmatory of its falsity, and establishing irreparably our Lord's divinity, we put John the Apostle in the witness-stand. Hear his testimony.

John 1:18: *"No one hath seen God at any time; the only begotten Son, the one being in the bosom of the Father, He hath declared Him."* Here you see the inspired Apostle pronounces Him the *"Only begotten God."* As God is Divine, here you see His Divinity is irretrievably revealed.

Now let us take John the Baptist, in response to the delegation of priests and Levites, asking him, if he be the Christ. Hear him.

John 1:23: *"I am the voice of one roaring in the wilderness, Prepare ye the way of the Lord, as Isaiah the prophet said."* (Isaiah 40:3.) Examine the prophecy, and you will find it said, *"Prepare ye the way of Jehovah."* Hence you see these two witnesses certify the identity of Jesus and Jehovah.

Now let us take Paul and Moses.

1 Cor. 10:9: *"Neither let us tempt the Lord, as some of them tempted Him, and were destroyed by serpents."* (Numbers 21:5.) Paul here certifies that they tempted Christ; and Moses says they tempted Jehovah. Now it follows as an inevitable sequence from these Scriptures, that if Christ be not Divine, the Jehovah of the Old Testament is not Divine, which would utterly demolish all the claims of the Bible to a Divine origin and bring it down to a level of the Koran of Mohammed and Joe Smith's Book of Mormons; because this dogma would repudiate the divinity of Jehovah and bring Him down to the level of Baal, Zeus, and Jupiter. While the vicarious substitutionary atonement which Christ made with His precious blood redeems every human soul from sin, death and hell; the great work of the Holy Ghost is the dispensation of that redemption to every lost son and daughter of Adam's ruined race.

F. The identity of the Holy Ghost and the Father is uniformly recognized throughout the Bible.

Acts 5:3, 4: *"Peter said to Ananias, For what has Satan filled thy heart that thou shouldst lie to the Holy Ghost, and keep back a part of the price of the land? ... Why didst thou put this thing in thy heart? Thou hast not lied unto men, but unto God."* Here you clearly see the synonym of the Holy Ghost with the Father.

THE TRINITY.

Acts 16:6: *"And they traveled through the Phrygian and Galatian country, being forbidden by the Holy Ghost to speak the word in Asia, having come opposite Mysia, they were endeavoring to go into Bithynia, and the Spirit of Jesus did not permit them."* In these two verses you clearly see the synonym of the Holy Ghost with the Spirit of Jesus.

Hence you see clearly, that the Holy Ghost is the Spirit of the Father, at the same time the Spirit of the Son. This fact gives you clear light on the complicated problem of the unpardonable sin, which Jesus says is blasphemy of the Spirit. (Matt. 12:31, 32.) Blasphemy means "contemptuous treatment of God applied to the Holy Ghost;" it means not only "contentious neglect," but even irreconcilable refellancy, culminating in grieving Him away, so He gives you up to the devil, whose service you have chosen; God saying to Him, "Come away, let him alone; he is joined to his idols, let him believe a lie, and be damned." Hence the amissability of this sin, *i. e.,* the blasphemy of the Holy Ghost, which does not attain to the Father or the Son. 1 Cor. 12:3: *"No one is able to say, Jesus is Lord, but by the Holy Ghost."* This arises from the fact that He is the only Revelator of Jesus. Just as He revealed Him to Saul of Tarsus, near Damascus, shining down on him in His transfiguration glory; so the Holy Spirit reveals Him to every true penitent believing soul, at the same time inspiring all the help he needs to receive Him. In a similar manner, the Holy Ghost in sanctification reveals the glorified Saviour within, setting upon the throne of the heart and reigning within, and without, every rival having been swept away by the cleansing Blood and consumed by the refining fire. Gal. 1:15, 16, 17: *"When He, who separated me from the womb of my mother, and called me by His grace, was pleased to reveal His Son in me; . . . I no longer conferred with flesh and blood; . . . . . but went away into Arabia, and after three years returned to Damascus."* There you have Paul's testimony to the second work of grace, after he had fought the old man of sin three years in the desert of Arabia; finally reaching utter desperation (Romans 7:24), he turns him over to the Lord Jesus Christ, who delivers him instantaneously and takes a seat on the throne of his heart, thus the Holy Ghost in regeneration reveals Jesus to the sinner, whereas in sanctification He reveals Him to the Christian, crowned and sceptered on the throne of his heart, reigning in this life forever. Thus the Holy Ghost is the Executive of the Trinity, the Convictor of the sinner, the Regenerator of the penitent, the Restorer of the backslider, the Sanctifier of the Christian, the Glorifier of every saint in the resurrection and the translation. Therefore, the Holy Ghost is veritably none other than the Omnipotent Jehovah and Victorious Saviour. When God executes the stupendous miracles of His grace in regeneration and sanctification, He does it through His agent, the Holy Ghost. When Jesus saves sinners, and sanctifies believers, He does these mighty works through His omnipotent agent, the Holy Spirit.

A prominent Roman law, *"Facit per alum, facit per se;"* (what one does through another, he does through himself;) was transferred to England, and thence to America, and still stands in the code of these two great nations in the original Latin, in which the Romans used

The Trinity.

it, those memorable thousand years, while they ruled the world. That law is significantly true in the divine administration, as well as the human.

What God does through His Spirit, He does through Himself; what the Saviour does through His Spirit, He does through Himself. He said, "It was better for Him to go away and send the Comforter." This is confirmed in the fact that His human body was not Omnipotent, neither is it now; the Holy Ghost in His inscrutable ubiquity is present everywhere at the same time.

In my boyhood, I heard preachers draw an obvious distinction between the Holy Ghost and the Holy Spirit. In this they simply exposed their ignorance, as there is no difference, never was, and never can be. The veracity of this bold statement, you see at once when I tell you, but in the original, there is but the one phrase, *pneuma hagion,* which the translator at his own option renders "Holy Ghost" or "Holy Spirit." It would be perfectly correct to leave either of those phrases entirely out of the English Bible, and retain the other in every passage. Hence it is a matter perfectly optionary with the translator.

I may here observe that a slight error appears in the spelling of the word, "Ghost," whose true etymology is "Ghest," in which it was originally written in the Saxon language. The idea is that He enters your home and becomes your Guest, to abide with you forever.

CHAPTER III.

Total Depravity.

While the truth of total depravity is fundamental in the revealed Word, and so important to the student, that denying it, he is in great danger of eternal wreckage; whereas if he is even skeptical, he is destined to suffer awful detriment in his experience and work for the salvation of others.

This truth was first repudiated by Pelagius a contemporary of Saint Augustine, the great theologian of the fifth century. It is now boldly preached by the Campbellites, who are rapidly spreading over the continent, especially in the West, repudiating depravity, and as a normal sequence the work of the Holy Ghost, whose personality they even deny; thus constituting the great western wing of Satan's heretical vampire.

Meanwhile the Unitarians, repudiating the divinity of Christ, constitute the eastern wing. Thus this cruel vampire fanning its victim with his soothing pinions into the lethean slumber of despiritualized churchisms, cruelly sucks away the last drop of spiritual blood, sealing the hopeless doom in endless woe.

G. At a great camp-meeting, thirty years ago, I heard a powerful sermon, delivered by a brilliant Methodist preacher to a vast audience, against total depravity. As he held them spell-bound, and soared on the pinions of his eloquence, O how he withered, blistered and blighted the doctrine of total depravity, lampooning everyone that preached it. I felt shocked because of its prominence in the Methodist creed, which he had professed to believe, and vowed to defend, when the Conference ordained him.

His grand hypothesis was the impracticability of our salvation, if total depravity were true; whereas the Lord from Alpha to Omega, offers it (salvation) free to all, and pleads with all to receive it, as an unmerited gratuity in the glorious Christ He in His condescending mercy has sent into the world. The preacher vociferously certified that if we are all totally depraved God would be destitute of resources, having nothing to work on, and the whole plan of salvation would in that case collapse, an eternal failure. When he wound up, I took him aside and looked him in the face and said, Brother— if you or I had to build a house, we would need a foundation on which to locate it, and material out of which to build it; but when God Almighty got ready to build this big world on which we stand He just made it out of nothing, and hung it upon nothing, and it has been shining and shouting ever since, so you have made an awful mistake comparing the Omnipotent God to feeble man. He dropped his head, then and seemed to drop into meditation about two minutes, then looking up, he said, "Brother Godbey, I see I have preached foolishness; please tell nobody and I will preach it no more." He made the great mistake, which the higher critics, whose name is "legion," are now making, to the wreckage of the popular pulpits, and the damnation of the people, *i. e.*, substituting his own fallible ratiocination for the plain Word of God.

H. The Word of God is clear, explicit, and unmistakably confirmatory of this doctrine of total depravity, so odious to Satan, and his deluded votaries. God said to Adam, *"In the day thou eatest thereof, thou shalt surely die."* Consequently we know he did die, that very day. God did not say, "Your mind shall die," in which case he would become totally idiotic; nor "Your body shall die;" as in that case he would have dropped a corpse in his tracks. Man is neither mind nor body, but an immortal spirit. After God had created him soul and body, He imparted to him, a scintilla of His own Spirit, when He breathed on him, and he became a living soul; having hitherto been destitute of Divine life, though in common with all creation, having animated life. This Divine life he forfeited, when he sinned; thus becoming a spiritual corpse, which is the real attitude of every sinner in earth and hell. God had created him, invested with the power to propagate his species. In his unfallen state, he had no posterity. God had created him in, "His own image and likeness," "which is righteousness and true holiness," (Eph. 4:24), the synonym of Divine life. After he fell, it is stated, that he begat a son in his own likeness, which was destitution of Divine righteousness and true holiness. Therefore in the realm of spiritual death, the human race was propagated and multiplied upon the face of the whole earth. Eph. 2:1: *"You hath He quickened, who were dead in trespasses and in sins."* This is eminent New Testament phraseology, uniformly certifying that the sinner is dead. It applies to the man himself; who is an immortal spirit in a state of death, *i. e.*, destitute of the Divine life.

Here you see the incontestable proof that every human being unregenerated is totally depraved.

The reason this doctrine is rejected so currently

TOTAL DEPRAVITY.

is because it is not understood, but misapprehended in the conclusion that it means wickedness in the superlative degree, which is a great mistake. In this sense, it does not even apply to the devil, because he is a progressive being, as well as all finites, and getting worse incessantly, like all sinners, both demoniacal and human.

We should always be careful to leave all Scripture precisely where God has put it; in that case you would find your Bible, not only all true, but the most sensible Book in the world.

Spiritual death does not mean wickedness in its superlative enormity; but simply *destitution of a Divine life,* which is the veritable condition of every sinner in earth and hell, human and diabolical. "Quicken," which is the current New Testament word for "regenerate," is a Greek compound, from *zooee,* "life" and *poieoo,* "to create." Therefore it simply means, "To create life in the dead human spirit." Regeneration is veritable spiritual resurrection; the Holy Spirit, the Creator thus administering the resurrection power to the dead human spirit, a *defacto* miracle.

Hence you see, the doctrine of total depravity is incontestably Scriptural and true. Among sinners, both human and diabolical, you will find an infinite diversity of wickedness; yet in one respect, perfect uniformity and that is their utter destitution of Divine life, and an experimental knowledge of God.

CHAPTER IV.

CONVICTION AND REPENTANCE.

Every sinner is a criminal against the Divine government, exposed to wrath and hell. The Holy Spirit is the Executive of Heaven, sent out, both by the Father and the Son, to arrest every criminal, and arraign him at the tribunal of his own conscience, which is a miniature of the judgment-bar. *Edeggkos* is the *writ Habius Corpus* issued in the Divine government for the arrest of every criminal, and his prosecution before the tribunal of his own conscience, in this world, and the judgment-seat of Christ in the great day. John 16:8, 9: *"And having come, He will convict the world concerning sin, and concerning righteousness, and concerning judgment: concerning sin, indeed because they do not believe in Me."*

When we have true faith in Him, He takes away all our sins, and delivers us from the terrible torture of conviction.

V. 10. *"Concerning righteousness, because I go to the Father, and you see Me no more."* This is the righteousness of Christ, which we receive, when by faith we receive Him, as our Atoning Substitute, and God for His sake, grants us a free pardon of all our multitudinous transgressions.

V. 11. *"Concerning judgment, because the prince*

CONVICTION AND REPENTANCE.

of this world has been condemned." As the devil is the great old criminal, who has already been justly condemned and consigned to hell; therefore all the citizens of his kingdom (human and diabolical), as an inevitable sequence are condemned with him, and consigned to the same awful doom.

1. The Sinai Gospel of hell and damnation is God's appointed engineery to superinduce conviction in the heart of every sinner. When faithfully and heroically preached with the Holy Ghost sent down from Heaven, it always fastens a nightmare conviction in the guilty conscience of the sinner.

When the Lord sanctified me in 1868, He made me a cyclone of fire. Everywhere I preached, conviction like an awful pall settled down on the people, and a glorious revival broke out. I have often seen people fall as though shot down on the battle-field, and literally prostrate, unable to stand on their feet.

The Gospel has lost none of its power. When Sinai is indefatigably preached to sinners, the Holy Ghost is sure to execute His office-work; serving as Heaven's Policeman, He will arrest and arraign them at the tribunal of their own guilty consciences; when an awful pall will settle down on them, as if the archangel of doom had descended and was blowing his mighty trumpet and calling the dead to life.

Conviction is fundamental in the Gospel economy and must precede every conversion. The Divine order is immutable and irreversible. When conviction does its normal work, so-called godly sorrow, which worketh repentance (2 Cor. 7:10), like an avenging specter, puts his heavy grapple on the hellward bound, and hell-deserving sinner.

J. Repentance is the normal consequence of conviction; yet not irresistable, like conviction, which the Holy Ghost at some time administers to every soul, as the inseparable antecedent of His redeeming grace, which is free, for all. The only reason why sinners make their bed in hell is because they resist conviction. and will not repent. While conviction is the foundation, repentance rears up the human side of the new creation, the glorious reconstruction of the dilapidated and ruined human spirit.

Repentance, *metanoia*, from *meta,* "change," and *nos,* "the mind," literally means "the exchange of the carnal mind," which Satan put in man, when he fell and transmitted to every human being by the law of heredity, for the mind of Christ, which the Holy Ghost creates in the heart in regeneration, and makes perfect in sanctification, when He utterly destroys the residuum of the carnal mind, which survives regeneration, and continues to antagonize the new creation, rendering our service to God but partial and superinducing a thousand mournful calamitious defeats in spiritual combat and incessantly exposing us to the awful liability of spiritual wreckage.

When man repents, God always forgives and saves, thus administering graciously and copiously His own blessed counterpart, *i. e.,* a new heart and a new spirit. (Ezek. 36:26.)

Among the many errors in the English Version, we find in the case of Judas, the statement, "He repented," which is not correct; if he repented, God would have forgiven him, and saved him, as he does all truly penitent sinners. The word in that Scripture is not *metanoeoo*, but *metamelomai*, "Was seized with remorse," which is a prelude of hell-torment; so awful as frequently to superinduce suicide. Therefore Judas, unable to endure it, ran away and hung himself.

The true repentance always superinduces contrition, as the word means actually, "Crushing the heart," and restitution, which delights to give back all ill-gotten gains; thus radically revolutionizing the life.

In '49 a young man was converted in San Francisco on the streets. In a few days he came and bade farewell, stating that when an orphan-boy, he was bound out to an Englishman, whose money he stole, fled away to a ship, became a sailor and roamed over the seas, until the gold was discovered in California, and he became a miner. So when God saved his soul he immediately departed, to travel half round the world, hunt up his foster-father, and pay him back his stolen money with large interest.

When repentance does not pay all debts and restore all fraudulent gains within the range of possibility, it is shady, and will not bear the test of the Judgment.

K. The practical definition of repentance is, "A giving up." The sinner gives up all of his bad things to the devil from whom he got them; bids him a final adieu, leaving him forever. People must get honest before they can get saved. In that case they pay all their debts. We all owe the devil all of our meanness. Therefore the first step toward God is to pay off our old master, giving him back everything we ever got from him, going out of business with him, we part to meet no more.

Consecration is but a continuation of repentance, modified by totally different environments. As in repentance we gave all our bad things to the devil and left them with him forever, we now give all of our good things to God to be used to His glory forever.

Our spirit, soul and body are all good things, (when divested of sin), which God created for His glory. So also our earthly possessions, education, influence, and reputation, and all enterprises available in this life are good things, and God will use them for His glory, if we will consecrate them to Him.

Satan, in his capricious and fallacious delusions hallucinates the sinner with pride, vanity, egotism and pomposity superinducing the hallucination that he is monarch of all he surveys. All this is a lying strategem in order to keep his black lasso round his neck and lead him down to hell. Feeble man is not an independency, as he vainly presumes; but a dependency, and in every case subordinate to Satan or God. With the former, sin, misery, disgrace, calamity, wreckage and damnation are the portion of his cup. With God, life, holiness, happiness, Heaven and glory forever constitute his felicitious birthright.

As we read in 2 Corinthians 7:10, *"A godly sorrow worketh out repentance,"* the reason why we see almost universal spiritual wreckage, whithersoever we turn our eyes, is because the repentance was professed and not possessed, neither was it characterized by its inalienable demarkations, *i. e.,* contrition and restitution. The solution obtains in the fact that it was not superinduced by godly sorrow, but when repentance is genuine, God for Christ's sake always forgives and the Holy Spirit exe-

Conviction and Repentance. 33

cutes the glorious work of the new creation, imparting the new heart, and new spirit. When the repentance is spurious, the new creation enterprise invariably collapses and spiritual wreckage follows. The great burden of Gospel preaching is born on Sinai's smoky, quaky, summit, when the thunder-bolts and lightning shafts of hell and damnation send panic to the trembling multitudes, and expedite their stampede from impending doom. This is the Gospel of conviction, and is fundamental in the salvatory superstructure.

Without this radical, genuine conviction, the repentance which is the fruit of godly sorrow, 2 Corinthians 7:9 proves a failure, and the pearly gates forever close, while the portals of the pit open wide to receive the wicked and ruined soul.

The great work of this radical repentance which is invariably characterized by contrition and restitution and always inwrought by the Holy Ghost, through the medium of godly sorrow, superinduced by the thunder-bolt conviction, which gives the sinner an awful panorama of a bottomless hell, a topless heaven and a boundless eternity, constitutes the human side of the salvation superstructure, which begins in conviction and culminates in that utter and eternal abandonment to God, which climaxes consecration, and puts the soul on believing ground for entire sanctification, whence it sinks eternally into the will of God, plunges beneath the crimson flood, that washeth whiter than the snow:

> "Rise to walk in heaven's own light,
> Above the world and sin,
> With heart made pure, and garments white,
> And Christ enthroned within."

While we lament the mournful departure of the Sinai Gospel from popular pulpits; we are grieved to recognize an obvious deficiency among the holiness people at this important point. The reason it is so hard to get souls saved in the churches is because popular conviction is so deficient, without which every sinner is a gone log, neither splittable nor revivable.

The normal effect of the Sinai Gospel is to make every sinner a chestnut, cyprus, or white oak, ready for the wedge and the fro. We should let patience have its perfect work, and stand heroically on old thundering Sinai till conviction like a nightmare settles down on the wicked, giving them an awful panorama of judgment, hell and eternity. Then the old-style heart-crushing, Satan-defeating and soul-regenerating, pentecostal repentance will come back superinducing the vociferous roar, *"What shall I do to be saved?"*

CHAPTER V.

JUSTIFICATION, REGENERATION AND CONVERSION.

There are four justifications ordinarily in the history of every saved soul, regeneration in every case being the normal concomitant. When the soul truly repents and in the profound realization of his meetness of hell-fire and utter desperation, casts himself on the mercy of God in Christ, He always freely forgives for Jesus' sake.

This word is from the Latin *justis*, "just," and *fio*, "to make;" therefore it means, "To make just."

The sinner is a criminal already condemned and deserving nothing but a place in hell. Because Christ has taken his place in hell, because Christ has taken his place under the law and redeemed him by His Blood, God willingly and gladly forgives every sinner when he truly repents and by simple faith receives Jesus as his atoning Savior. Then the Holy Spirit, the Executive of the new creation instantaneously creates the Divine life in his heart, thus raising him from the dead.

L. Adam and Christ are both representative of the whole human race. 1 Corinthians 15:22: *"As in Adam all die, so in Christ shall all be made alive."*

The question pertinently arises, "When does this revivification take place?" The Bible answers the question, Hebrews 2:9: *"In order that Christ by the grace of God may taste death for every one."*

The word here is not "man", as in the English Version, but *pantos, i. e.,* "every one."

The question now arises, "When do we become a human being?" It is in the pre-natal: whereas the fall was seminal in father Adam, who was the only creation, mother Eve being no exception to the rule, as she was simply a transformation of Adam's rib. Therefore, when God created Adam, He created the human race. Acts 17:26: *"Of one* (man) *God created every race of people to dwell upon the face of the whole earth."* Hence you see the unity of creation. Adam was created capable of multiplying himself indefinitely, and thus filling the whole earth with teeming multitudes. Psalms 51:5: *"I was shapen in iniquity; and in sin did my mother conceive me."* You see from these Scriptures that every human being is generated in sin. When Adam sinned, he forfeited Divine life, became a sinner; but retained the power to multiply himself indefinitely on the earth. He could not transmit what he did not have, therefore the whole human race are generated in fallen Adam, and sinful. But as Christ is his glorious parallel, all are regenerated in him by the normal grace, which He produced through His vicarious, substitutionary atonement.

"Now when does this new creation supervene?" Obviously, the moment personality obtains.

The fall was seminal; as we are all in Adam, when he fell man fell with him. Whereas we all sinned seminally in Adam; we are all redeemed personally in Christ. (1 Corinthians 15:22.) Hence you see the redemption reaches us the moment personality prevails: normally transpiring the moment soul and body unite.

JUSTIFICATION. 37

You should never say, *"Born again,"* from the simple fact that Jesus never said it; but, *"Born from above,"* as He said. (St. John 3:5-7.) *"Born again"* misleads and causes Jesus to contradict Himself. You must get rid of the errors in King James' Translation. It was a great blessing, when made, three hundred years ago, when the world was just getting out of the Dark Ages —a thousand years—during which not one man in a thousand, nor one woman in twenty thousand could read. Meanwhile so much error inevitably got into the Bible, as it was transcribed over and over. All this time God in His mercy was miraculously keeping the pure, original New Testament safe on Mt. Sinai, which He revealed to His faithful servant, Dr. Tischendorf in 1859, and the holiness people constrained me to translate it. In this you have the correct Scripture, which is worth more than all the gold that ever glittered.

In the English Version we have many contradictions, leading the people into skepticism and infidelity; whereas there is not one in the true Scripture.

Jesus everywhere took the babes in His arms, certifying, *"Of such is the kingdom of Heaven."*

You see plainly, *"Born again"* would send to Hell every one dying before the physical birth; whereas, *"Born from above,"* as Jesus said, is in perfect harmony with His uniform recognition of infantile citizenship in the kingdom.

M. This beautiful truth of pre-natal regeneration is irrefutably confirmed in the prodigal son and his elder brother; both of whom were born in their father's house, the one sinned out, thus forfeiting his infantile justification; while his elder brother retained his, till the prodigal returned. However, he much needed sanctification to take the residuum of firebrand jealousy, which cropped out, when he heard the jubilant shout over his brother, who had actually gotten a long way ahead of him though having sunk down to the filth of the hog-pen, when the father kissed him, thus sealing his justification, then in dressing him with a blood-washed robe and the ring of the marriage covenant, thus confirming his sanctification, giving him membership in the bridehood; then giving him the Gospel shares, confirmatory of his call to preach.

When God works, time cuts a very small figure either in the *modus operandi* or the *opus operatuni*, from the simple fact that He is not a God of time but eternity.

Here we see justification, sanctification and the call to the ministry chase each other in rapid succession.

Though the older brother had never forfeited his infantile justification as abundantly confirmed in his protestation to his father, *"I have never at any time transgressed thy commandment,"* which you see the father accepted as true; yet he abundantly evinces his need of sanctification to deliver him from worry and jealousy; as he evidently thought they ought to be shouting over him, as he had been so good, instead of his brother, who had been so bad.

The imperfect tense here used, leaves the father pleading with him to come in, when the curtain falls, and hides the scene from vision.

Inspired Peter says, *"No Scripture is of private interpretation,"* therefore, we legitimately conclude from this illustration that every human being is born in the kingdom of God, which is none other than the

JUSTIFICATION. 39

house of the father, where both were born, and reared.

These Scriptures and innumerable others confirm the great consolatory truth, that Bible redemption is of Christ and not native purity, (which is Satan's falsehood.) Every human being is born in the kingdom of God as illustrated in the prodigal son, and his elder brother, and only got out by sinning out, which is not a necessity but an awful abnormity, which has sent numberless millions to hell.

This deep theology appertaining to the infantile relation to the gracious economy is so little understood even by preachers and Sunday-school teachers and, much less, parents, and still of so vital and transcendent importance that it should be published to the ends of the earth, and if understood and faithfully conserved it would do more to save the world than anything else. Christ has so perfectly redeemed the whole human race by his precious blood, as to preclude the slightest apology for the damnation of any. The uniform trend of children born in Christian families to grow into sin is not only the swift precursor to their own personal ruin, but it is the nightmare of damnation, defeating the evangelization of the world and blighting the hopes of mankind.

N. The very fact that every human being is justified and regenerated antecedently to the physical birth, so they are all born Christians and not sinners (for if they were sinners, dying, they would drop into hell), if understood and intelligently utilized by Christian parents, teachers and preachers, would in a generation, bring on the millennium. It is a burning shame on Christendom, to let their children grow up in sin. Every child ought to be intelligently converted to God before the age of accountability, when it is so liable to forfeit its infantile justification, thus backsliding out of the kingdom, into Satan's common, where in case of death, it would drop into hell.

Even the babies born of heathens are not sinners and idolators, like their parents, but Christians. Hence the great importance of pushing the evangelization of all pagan nations with the great possible expedition, at the same time gathering up all the infants within our reach and bringing them up in the nurture and admonition of the Lord, so they may never sin out of the kingdom and from their parents learn to worship idols and go into every manner of sin.

God's time for conversion is during the period of infantile justification. Conversion is not as people generally think, synonymous with either justification or regeneration.

Justification means the removal of your condemnation, and making you just before the law, which God does for Christ's sake only. (Rom. 5:1.)

Regeneration is the new birth. Both of these take place antecendently to the physical birth. Really they supervene the moment personality obtains in the succession of the fœtal state. Consequently, every human being is born a citizen of God's kingdom, not by virtue of native purity, which is false, but by the redemption, which Christ has purchased for every human being, whether born in a palace or a hovel.

In case of actual transgression, justification and regeneration are absolutely necessary concomitants of conversion, but in the case of infants, who have not

JUSTIFICATION.

reached responsibility, neither is there justification nor regeneration in their conversion, as both supervened with the incoming of personal existence.

Now with these facts before us, you readily see that God's time for the conversion of every human being is before the forfeiture of justification and regeneration by the commission of known sin. Here you must guard against a very dangerous heresy, which is frequently preached in the pulpits, *i. e.*, the possibility on the part of Christian parents so to bring up their children in the nurture and admonition of God, that they will never need conversion. This heresy Satan makes so plausible that it is very dangerous. You naturally ask the question, "If we are all justified and regenerated in the pre-natal state, so that we are born Christians and not sinners (which is true), then where is the need of conversion?" Oh, it is most imperatively needed, and should by all means take place before we are old enough to know right from wrong, and liable to commit sin, thus forfeiting our justification.

N. B. Conversion does not mean "justification" nor "regeneration;" it simply means "a turning around." This can not take place, in cases where known sins have been committed, without justification, to break the devil's chain, which holds you tight, and regeneration, to resurrect the dead soul. But before the age of accountability, when the soul is not only free from condemnation, but actually enjoys the spiritual life it received from the Holy Ghost antecedently to the physical birth, and consequently needs nothing but to turn and receive an introduction to the Saviour and actually form His acquaintance, receive the delectable inundation of his sweet redeeming and adopting love. In that case, instead of going into sin, it will at the moment of responsibility start grace-ward, God-ward and Heaven-ward.

The hereditary depravity (Psalms 51:5), in which it was generated as the normal malady of the fall, turns its face away from God, so the very moment it reaches responsibility, starting off faceforemost, it goes directly out of the kingdom into Satan's common and becomes a sinner, exposed to wrath and hell.

In its conversion before the forfeiture of infantile justification and regeneration, it does not need either of these graces, which it already possesses, but only to be turned around and introduced to God, as it neither sees Him nor knows Him, because by reason of this inherited depravity, though born in his kingdom, God is behind its back.

The popular dogma, which Satan has hoisted on the Church, that the child has to become a sinner, and actually serve Him, fall under condemnation and be guilty of known transgression in order to a true conviction and genuine conversion superinducing a happy Christian experience, is an atrocious falsehood, hatched in the bottomless pit, and propagated by ignorant preachers, manipulated by intriguing demons throughout Christendom.

During the infantile justification, the child is so simple-hearted, loving and teachable, that it is an easy matter to introduce it to the Saviour, till it gets acquainted with Him, and receives into its innocent heart the consciousness of His sweet redeeming love, and into its pure mind unclouded by condemnatory sin, the bright illumination of His Spirit, responsive to which, actually

JUSTIFICATION. 43

talling in love with Jesus and taking up with Him, it gladly sets out for Heaven, getting the start of the devil, it begins to run up the shining highway, bouyant with hope, exultant in expectation of one day reaching Heaven. It should be the joyous work of Christian parents, brothers, sisters, and friends thus to preach the Gospel to the innocent child before its beautiful face has ever been darkened by the black shadows which follow in the wake of a guilty conscience, constantly augmented by the dark pinion of Satan.

o. During the non-development of the intellect, the child is easily tempted and liable to backslide quickly, get under condemnation and into spiritual darkness. If permitted to remain out of the kingdom, in Satan's dark, filthy common, it will soon get hard, and continue to grow harder and harder, till it becomes an obdurate sinner, every transgression only facilitating its swift damnation. Consequently, the parents and the older members of the family, who ought to be stronger Christians, should be on the constant outlook; watching the little one, like guardian angels, always ready to rally to its rescue; by their prayers and exhortations, to accelerate its restoration with all possible expedition.

I hope you will not simply be content to read these important Bible truths, relative to the infant relation to the Divine economy, but will do your utmost to impart them especially to parents and Sunday-school teachers, and all Christian workers.

> "'Tis education forms the common mind,
> Just as the twig is bent, so is the tree inclined."

Oh, how easy to straighten the tender sprout, so it

will grow straight, whereas it is an impossibility to straighten the great old tree.

While traveling in India, I gazed on those wonderful banyan trees, with several hundred trunks, as the limb drops down from great height, entering the ground, takes root, grows, and forms another trunk. It is very convenient to use the bamboo-pole which there abounds, growing a hundred feet high, straight as an arrow, and hollow as a trumpet; manipulate the descending branches, admitted into this pole, which will conduct it perfectly straight down to the earth, till it takes root and grows, forming a most beautiful timber tree.

Therefore God's time for the conversion of every soul is antecedent to the age of responsibility. Rest assured, He has made no provision for sin. If we would only be true to Him, Satan would never get his black lasso around the neck of another son and daughter of Adam's own race.

Romans 5:20: *"Where sin did abound, there did grace much more abound."* When Satan is chained; his myrmidons all driven from the earth, and himself incarcerated in the bottomless pit, millennial glory descending and filling the whole earth, as the waters cover the sea; then the happy nations having learned this wonderful secret of securing the happy conversion of the children before the forfeiture, of the infantile justification, will look back upon us, their progenitors with astonishment at our tardiness of apprehension and slowness of comprehension, thus permitting Satan to capture the children for whom we would heroically, if put to the test lay down our lives.

"When do our children reach the years of responsi-

JUSTIFICATION.

bility?" The old theologians pronounced it the age of seven. Suffice it to say, no rule can be given; as it depends entirely upon the amount of light shining around them. Of course, the brighter the light, the earlier they reach accountability. As already observed, there are four justifications, and of course, concomitant regenerations as these two great works of grace like Siamese twins, live and die together. Though experimentally synchronous; logically justification always precedes regeneration, and far from identity, as some suppose, they are actually heterogenous, justification always taking place in Heaven, when the sinner in utter desperation casts himself on the mercy of God in Christ; for the sake of Jesus only, He always cancels his sins from Heaven's statutory and imputes to him the righteousness of Christ.

Many normal Christians, yea teeming millions, as we awfully opine, are so manipulated by Satan as to content themselves with their own righteousness, which is but filthy rags in the sight of God, only expediating their awful condemnation. Such was the terrible estate of the Jewish Church in the days of Christ. While self-righteousness only insures our condemnation before God, the righteousness of Christ imputed to us, when in utter contrition for all sins, we abandon ourselves to God, hopelessly casting our souls on His unmerited grace and mercy in Christ; then He freely counts us righteous for Jesus' sake, because He has carried our burdens, borne our sorrows and paid our debts.

"Does not Christ still need His own righteousness? Then, why, will He give it to us?"

Oh, we have a most wonderful Christ. He has three

righteousnesses. He has a righteousness peculiar to His Divinity, and essential to it, which He will never give to you and me. He also has a righteousness peculiar to His humanity and essential to it; which He will never give to you or me. Yet, He has a third righteousness, which arises from His perfect obedience to the Divine law, both actively, perfectly obeying it, all is light, committing no sin in thought, word, or deed; and passively acquiescent before its thundering retribution, supervenient for all transgressions, taking our place, dying in our own stead, and thus perfectly satisfying the awful vengeance against every transgressor and forever redeeming us from the penalty of the violated law.

The moment justification in Heaven cancels all of our sins; the Holy Spirit executes the stupendous work of the new creation, giving us a new heart and putting a new spirit within us. (Ezek. 36:26.)

The first justification and its cognate grace, regeneration, takes place in the pre-natal state, without faith or works; simply responsive to the vicarious, substitutionary atonement of Christ.

The second justification, and regeneration, appertain to the adult-sinner, and are properly reclamation from a backslidden state, as you see illustrated in the case of the prodigal son, who, when converted, as we generally say, simply got back to his father's house, in which he was born; clearly demonstrating the fact that what we call the conversion of the sinner, is misnamed, as it is only his reclamation, as his justification and regeneration, the cognate graces of conversion, actually took place in the prenatal state.

The third justification appertains to the Christian

JUSTIFICATION. 47

who is justified. As James says, James 2:24: *"By works, and not by faith only:"* illustrating it by the justification of Abraham, when he offered up his son Isaac on Mount Moriah; which took place forty-one years after he was freely justified by faith only, when, responsive to the call of God, he left Chaldea, going out, he knew not whither, into the land which God would show him.

James also gives the case of Rahab, the tavern-keeper in Jericho, who was justified by works, when she received the spies of Joshua and sent them out another way. As the primary word *zonah*, means, "A woman keeping a tavern," which was certainly her employment, with no implication against her moral character, and you see afterward became the wife of the Hebrew Salmon, the mother of Boaz, the husband of Ruth, the Moabitess, who were the parents of Obed, the father of Jesse, the father of David. Hence you see she was one of the honored mothers of our Lord.

That the justification of the sinner must be by faith alone, is abundantly confirmed in the fact of his utter incompetency to work for the Lord while in the devil's kingdom, where he must remain, till justified and born from above.

This Pelagian, Campbellitish, Mormonistic and Papatistical dogma, justification by works, is none other than the notorious hell-hatched heresy of legalism, the sleekest plank which Satan has projected, over which to slide souls into the bottomless pit. The absurdity, and even the blasphemy of this dogma is patent to every reflective mind, when we contemplate the ostensible fact, that if this were true, the Son of God might have saved his life from the cruel cross.

The very fact that we could not be saved by legal obedience, constitutes the reason the Son of God had to either come and bleed and die, or let us all sink hopelessly into irretrievable woe.

These audacious heretics proclaim to the hellward-bound multitudes, as I have so often heard them; "Come join the church; let us immerse you in water, and then keep the commandments, and you are all right for Heaven;" thus treating the dying love of Jesus with proud disdain, and blasphemous contempt.

We have had the commandments since the days of Eden, and as much water in the world since the flood as hitherto. They had Noah's flood. Hence you see how the work of Christ is sheer gratuity, if this contemptuous heresy were true. Therefore, if the sinner is not saved through faith alone, there is actually no hope for him.

P. After you get saved, and thus become a citizen of the kingdom; you must not only obey the decalogue, the laws of the kingdom; but prove your faith by your works.

The fourth justification takes place, when we stand before the judgment-seat of Christ. This is by works alone. Revelation 22:12: *"Behold, I come quickly; and my reward is with Me, to give unto each one according as his work is."*

Whereas the normal justification takes place in the pre-natal state with concomitant regeneration and that without either faith or works; the second justification, generally called, "The conversion of the sinner," which is simply the reclamation of the backslider, and is

JUSTIFICATION.

received by faith alone, without works; the third justification, which has the signification of approval, must accompany every Christian to the end of life and is enjoined by faith and works, as revealed by James, in vivid contradistinction to the powerful Pauline arguments, confirmatory of the justification of every sinner, by faith alone, without works; whereas the fourth justification by works alone, when we stand before the great white throne, is in the sense of reward, as there are infinite degrees in Heaven; each one rewarded according to our efficiency in the salvation of others.

Though our works are not the condition of our salvation, and have nothing to do with it, for we are saved by Christ alone, yet our works constitute the measure of our reward in Heaven.

CHAPTER VI.

SANCTIFICATION, HOLINESS AND PERFECTION.

These words are all synonymous, in the fact that they mutually refer to the same work of grace, currently known in literature, sacred and theological, as the "Second work of grace." There is but one Greek word, *hagiasnos*, and the same word in a modified form, *hagiotees*, and translated indiscriminately, "Sanctification" and "Holiness," at the option and discretion of the translator.

Consequently they are precisely synonymous in the New Testament.

In the English language there is a slight modification; "sanctification," meaning, "The work wrought in the heart by the Holy Spirit;" while, "holiness" means, "The experience superinduced and the state enjoyed by the soul in the kingdom after the work of sanctification," has been received.

Sanctification is from the Latin, *sanctus*, "holy," and *faceo*, "to make." Consequently it means, "The work of making holy," as well as the state superinduced by that work.

As the Greek, *hagarossnos*, is from *gee*, "the world," and *alpha*, "not" therefore, it literally means, "The work which takes the world out of you, and develops a state in which the world is no longer in your heart and

SANCTIFICATION.

life," in vivid contra-distinction to regeneration, which takes you out of the world.

Throughout the Bible, we have two diametrical opposites always moving in vivid panorama before our spiritual eyes, *i. e.*, "The Church," *ecclesia*, and, "The world." *Ecclesia* is from *eka*, "out," and *kaleo*, "to call." Therefore it simply means, the whole body of human souls, who have heard the call of the Holy Ghost and came out from the world for ever; identifying themselves with God alone.

Whereas regeneration brings us out of the world; sanctification takes the world out of us. Hence the double work. The one to take us out of the world, and the other to take the world out of us.

Preachers frequently stultify themselves by certifying the unity and identity of conversion and sanctification. It is very strange of people enjoying Biblical education to expose themselves to the criticisms of all intelligent Bible readers. The truth of it is, these works of grace are both diametrically opposite either to the other in signification and exegesis.

In regeneration, a babe is born; in sanctification, an old man dies; hence they differ as widely as the noon-day and midnight; the one a birth, and the other a death.

No wonder spiritual culture is at a low-ebb in the Church, and worldliness at high-tide. Oh! how we need multiplied millions to go abroad to the sixteen hundred millions of people in the world and preach to them simple solid Gospel truth.

Perfection is from the Latin *faceo*, "to make," and *per*, "complete." Hence you see clearly its synonymy with sanctification; both originating from the same word, differentiating one from the other only in the prefixes, *sanctus*, "holy" and *per*, "complete."

You know Christ came to destroy the works of the devil. (1 John 3:8.) "What is the works of the devil?" Sin and sin only, and when that is eliminated out of humanity, we enjoy the complete work of Christ.

Holiness means, "Soul soundness;" having a sanitary signification, *i. e.*, "soul ailments all healed." Therefore, you see the perfect synonymy of sanctification, holiness and perfection.

The Bible reveals four distinct elements, all beautifully co-operative in this great work of entire sanctification or perfection complete. Jesus prayed, *"Sanctify them through Thy truth: for Thy Word is truth."* (St. John 17:17.) In Eph. 5:25, 26 we have the commandment, *"Husbands, love your wives, with Divine love as Christ loved the Church, and gave Himself for Her; that He might sanctify Her: purifying her by the washing of water through the Word."*

Here you see the "Word" is again mentioned as the medium of our sanctification. 1 John 1:7: *"If we walk in the light, as He is in the light, we have fellowship one with another, and the Blood of Jesus Christ His Son cleanseth us from all sin."*

There you see, in harmony with many other Scriptures, it is done by the Blood. 1 Peter 1:2: *"Elect according to the foreknowledge of God the Father, through sanctification of the Spirit."*

2 Thessalonians 2:13: *"But we ought to give thanks unto God in behalf of you, brethren beloved of the Lord, because God hath chosen you from the beginning*

SANCTIFICATION.

unto salvation through the sanctification of the Spirit and belief of the truth."

You see in both of these Scriptures and many others, the work is imputed to the Holy Spirit.

In Paul's commission, Acts 26:18: *"To open their eyes, to turn them from darkness to light, from the power of Satan unto God, that they may receive forgiveness of sins, and an inheritance among the sanctified by faith that is in me."*

In this, and many others, as you see, it is imputed to faith. These four agencies are in perfect harmony and compatibility, one with the other, and the glorious work of entire sanctification.

The Blood of Jesus is the glorious *elises* of purgation from the awful pollution of hereditary depravity, *i. e.,* devil nature, filthy and wicked as Satan; black and horrific as hell, which we all inherited from our fallen progenitors.

The Word is the inspired medium through which we receive the efficacy of this wonderful expurgater the Life-blood of God's only Son.

The Holy Ghost, the very Spirit of the Father (Acts 5:3, 4), and the Son (Acts 16:6, 7), is the Omnipotent Agent, who administers the Blood and cleanses the heart, and sanctifies our nature from all unrighteousness.

Meanwhile faith is God's receptive and appropriative grace by which we receive this mighty work of entire sanctification, which defeats Satan for ever, and brings heaven into the heart.

Q. The importance of sanctification is transcendent as well as climactive in the graces of economy. Heb. 12:14: *"Without sanctification, no one shall see the Lord."*

This is not said of any other grace, from the simple fact that sanctification is the key that locks up the safe of salvation, without which Satan and burglars are sure to get in and spoliate the gold. It is the lynch-pin, that holds every wheel that runs the salvation wagon, and without which the wheel would quickly run off and wreckage inevitably follow. 1 Thes. 4:8: *"He that rejecteth* (sanctification) *rejecteth not man, but God, Who giveth unto you the Holy Ghost."*

God gives the Holy Ghost to all Christians to sanctify them. If they will not let Him do the work of His office, by this disobedience they grieve Him away and finally make their bed in a backslider's hell.

God forever cast away King Saul, because he spared Agag. This is a laudable and alarming case. The symbolisms of the Old Testament all teach real and inevasible truths by which we will all be judged in the Great Day.

The Amalekites had fought Israel forty years to keep them out of Canaan, the Land of Promise, abounding in corn, and wine, and flowing in milk and honey, thus vividly symbolizing the sanctified experience, which is nothing but the Canaan of perfect love and heaven in the heart. Saul in his royal capacity represented all Israel and symbolized every individual Christian in our dispensation. God commanded him to go with his army and utterly exterminate the Amalekites. He made a loud profession of obedience; going into the wilderness, and to a large extent, performing the commandment of the Lord. Yet his obedience was not perfect, because he spared Agag. Consequently, God cast him away and utterly refused to hear him, and never more answered his prayers, either by dreams, or visions or Urim or Thummim.

In his bewilderment, he went off and joined the spiritualists, and sought the enchantments of Satan's *prestos;* finally ending his unhappy life by suicide. This awful doom did not supervene, because his conversion was not clear. You find no more inconstestable record of the great first work of grace recorded in the Bible. It positively says, that when Saul met the Lord's prophet He gave him another heart.

King Agag here means, "Old Adam," surviving in the heart of every Christian, till he is utterly destroyed. The Amalekites with their valuable herds and flocks, signify all sorts of worldly professions and emoluments, which war against sanctification and the fullness of God.

The truth of it is, if we do not destroy everything that ever did antagonize our sanctification, we will grieve away the Holy Spirit, and ultimately fall into a backslider's hell.

Samuel, God's Nazarite prophet by his example shows us just what we are all to do. *"He lifted up the sword and hewed Agag all to pieces."* The sword in the Bible constantly symbolizes the Word of God. Therefore, we are to take it, and actually destroy everything in us and about us that ever did fight against our sanctification.

We are now in a pitch-battle with dead churchisms on the one side, and wild fanaticism (especially in the so-called Gift of Tongues,) on the other side. It is truly a time, when every soul is being tested and tried on every side. The sanctified people and all who heroically contend for "the faith once delivered to the saints" (Jude 1:3), are truly between two fires; dead formality and worldly churchanity on the one side (doing their best to draw you in by the Siren Song of sinful pleasure), and wild fanaticism on the other, crying, *"Lo! here and lo! there,"* but the Lord says, *"Go not after them."*

The stern question we always meet is simply, "Will you be content to walk alone with an unseen God?"

People claim to be sanctified wholly and doing their best, actually, to gobble up the Holiness Movement and boldly claiming to have all the miracles of the Apostolic Age (this I have heard with my own ears), at the same time lamentably deficient in the fruits of the Spirit, and really exhibiting the works of carnality to an alarming prominence. Thus, while professing everything that ever did take place, they flatly contradict the Word of God, cunningly perverting, twisting and subsidizing it to their own sectarian enterprises; laying under contribution all their wits to rob sanctification of every Pentecostal cannon and turn it aside with pop-gun batteries, thus minifying it to its geometrical point, and at the same time, multitudes of people who are notorious for having not so much as a clear experience of regeneration, much less sanctification, now under this loose teaching, boldly claim to be sanctified wholly, having hitherto never exhibited any of the fruits of the experience, *i. e.,* perfect love, purity of heart, and the fulness of the Spirit, now claiming all of these transcendant graces, and that we have nothing to do, but seek the gift of tongues; thus exalting one of the smallest out of the nine, to pre-eminence above perfect love, positively contradictory to God's Word. 1 Corinthians 12: 31. *"Yet I show unto you a more excellent way."* God has put entire sanctification at the top of the grace's curriculum, certifying that *"Though we*

SANCTIFICATION. 57

speak with the tongues of men and of angels, and have not perfect love, we are sounding brass and tinkling cymbal."

This bold assault of sanctification from the rank and file of the Holiness Movement, *i.e.*, by people aspiring to lead the movement, and throwing out their advertisements in big letters, publishing themselves as "the Apostolic Holiness people," at the same time thrusting a dagger to the heart, and clandestinely seeking the life of the beautiful angel of perfect love, without whose guardianship we will never pass the pearly portals and see the Lord, claiming to be her true conservators, give her no place to put down her feet, and take away all her panoply, constituting her invincible palladium, with which she proposes to conquer the world. Meanwhile, they turn away their votaries to follow a strange divinity, that never bled and died to redeem a lost world.

When we exalt the gifts above the graces, we violate the Word of God and grieve the Holy Spirit. When we divest Him of His sanctifying office, as the heretics are now doing, we awfully imperil our own souls, incurring the awful jeopardy of sinning against the Holy Ghost.

Multitudes of so-called holiness people are now running after these *phantasma-goria,* yet a remnant of Israel is left, who have not bowed the knees to Baal. O Soul, where do you stand? *"Watch and pray, lest you enter into temptation."*

R. Since God in the Bible has so positively revealed the absolute indispensability of sanctification, we must take heed and beware of everything that minifies it. *E.g.* The Power Heresy was the first among us to teach a third work of grace after entire sanctification. It is still among us. I heard it very recently preached and practiced in a great holiness meeting. It has prevailed extensively in the East, especially New England. Its great support and almost only proof-text is Acts I:8: *"You shall receive power after that the Holy Ghost has come upon you;"* an error in the English Version, which has done much harm. It reads, *"You shall receive the power of the Holy Ghost having come upon you;"* *i.e.*, the Holy Ghost Himself is the power, and if you seek any other power, you will go into fanaticism.

The Fire Heresy has prevailed extensively in the South and West, teaching a baptism of fire, apart and distinct from that of the Holy Ghost, and constituting a third blessing. I have known many people lose their sanctification by seeking this third blessing, and many go into wild fanaticism. Remember Nadab and Abihu who lost their lives by offering strange fire to the Lord. The original word means "other fire," *i.e.*, other than the Lord sent down from Heaven. The young men endeavored to imitate their father, offering incense to the Lord and when the fire did not fall on it, they ventured to facilitate the sacrifice by putting common fire on it, which not only consumed it, but flamed up in such a conflagration that it burnt them to death. This stands for everlasting warning to seek no fire but that of the Holy Ghost Himself.

When you seek other fire or power, Satan is ready to give you wild-fire, while fanatical people will give you fox-fire, and the awful ultimation, if you do not take heed, will prove hell-fire.

But the "Tongue Fanaticism" is far the most insid-

SANCTIFICATION. 59

ious, magnitudinous and detrimental thus far incident to the movement. This arises from its *sub vosa* and inservitable character, wrapped in mystery to the speakers and the auditors. If God were giving the tongues, we certainly would be able to find some genuine cases by this time, but having spent three months in the hot-bed of the movement, and in the fear of God, and the honesty of my heart, I having done my best, signally failed to find a solitary case.

Meanwhile, the fact is that the Mormons, the Spiritualists and the Devil-worshippers among the heathens have the same phenomena and make the same professions, and we are assured in God's Word that the air is thronged with evil spirits. (Eph. 2:2, Rev. 12.) It certainly gives us a broad margin for the entertainment of reasonable fears that the manifestations are demonical, hypnotic, *et cetra*. We must take heed, as we are positively commanded to try the spirits (1 John 4).

The Holy Spirit is the Author of every word in the Bible. Therefore it is an easy matter for us to take His infallible Word and settle the question as to the genuineness of everything we meet under the cognomen of religion.

When I traveled around the world, constantly preaching to heathens and Mohammedans, I found them much more religious than Christians. We can hardly get our Christians to pray morning and evening. The devout Moslems all pray five times a day, and are never too busy nor too much environed with company to perform their periodical *genuflections*. The heathens, instead of receiving baptism once in life, take it indefinitely. Doubtless many a devout Pagan in his life, immerses forty thousand times in the Holy Ganges, or Jumna, or the holy tanks in regions far away from the sacred rivers.

When religious people are utterly out of harmony with the plain Word of God, we know they are actuated by evil spirits, adroitly playing the Holy Ghost and deceiving them. These demons, which throng the air by millions, are older than Adam would be if he were now living, and have been acquainted with the nations and know their language from the beginning. Besides they are full of gibberish, i. e., words not identified with any intelligent language. The "Tongues People" seem to be anything and everything in order to captivate the rabble, and especially the helter-skelter element of so-called holiness people.

Therefore, while they deny the charge of preaching the third blessing in salvation; yet, they do preach it more persistently and heroically than any of their predecessors. They so minify sanctification and then rob it of the major part of the Scripture, which has always been used for its support, as to leave it like Samson, "shorn of his locks,"—an easy prey to the Philistines; thus making so little of it, that everybody who has even a superstitious experience of justification, boldly profess it. Thus they claim the holiness horse, and profess to use him to pull the salvation wagon; but at the same time, give him so little provender that he is bound to starve to death; even denying that the Holy Ghost has anything to do with sanctification, therefore, of all the heresies which Satan has brought against the movement, this is really the withering sirocco which has swept its pestilential gales over the Pacific Coast, and is dropping down in blighting tornadoes throughout the continent.

SANCTIFICATION.

The "Gift of Tongues" is all right, and we all ought to have it, as well as the other eight constituting the Christian's shining panoply, but let us not so magnify the armor as to lose sight of the armor-bearer. The Holy Ghost is the custodian of His own gifts, and if we are true He is always ready to supply us with the one we need every moment. 1 Corinthians 12:11: *"All these (gifts) worketh in you one and the same Spirit, dispersing unto each one as He willeth."*

These "Tongues People" not only magnify the gifts above the Giver, but they exalt the gift of tongues infinitely above the other eight, which is positively contrary to the Bible, which specifies the superiority of the other gifts; (and especially that of prophecy, which is the gift of preaching, and consequently the most important, because in this way, God has appointed, that the world shall be saved.) See the definition, (1 Corinthians 14:3.) *"He that prophesieth speaketh to the people edification, exhortation, and comfort,"* therefore we should all consecrate our vocal organs to God and only use them to preach the Gospel publicly and privately in our daily lives; we should always be speaking to edification, exhortation or benefit, and thus verifying God's definition—"A Gospel preacher." No wonder Paul pronounces it greater than speaking with tongues and says, *"I would that you may all prophecy."*

Language is the vehicle which conveys the truth to the people. It is exceedingly important, yet the truth, itself, infinitely more so.

The hand that brings you bread, is to you of great value; but the bread infinitely more so.

s. Regeneration for sinners, and sanctification for

Christians are the only graces essential to salvation. The former gives you life, and the latter gives you health. They are both revealed in decrees positive and irrevocable in St. John 3, *"Ye must be born from above."* This is for all sinners, and without it, damnation is inevitable. *"Without the sanctification, no man shall see the Lord."* (Heb. 12:14.) This is for all Christians. Those who do not heed and verify it, all grieve away the Holy Spirit, whom God gives to sanctify them. (1 Thess. 4:8.) apostasize and make their bed in the lake of fire. (Rev. 20:15.) Therefore when we exalt a non-essential above the essentials, we grieve the Holy Spirit and ruin souls.

The best holiness people I have ever known, have told me that they had thoroughly investigated the Tongue Movement, and there is no edification in their meetings. That is positively contradictory to God's command. 1 Cor. 14:26: *"Let all things be done to edification."*

The Holy Ghost (in whose dispensation we are living) alone has a right to control a Gospel meeting. When He is disobeyed, He retreats away, and evil spirits, actuated by carnal policy, run the meetings.

Before the Lord sanctified me in 1868, I was chaplain in Free Masonry and Odd Fellowship. Those lodges do not claim to be religious institutions, yet in their lodges I have often realized the presence of the Holy Spirit more obviously than in many religious meetings I have attended—meetings where I was raised, the water-god worshipped, and the Holy Ghost discarded and ridiculed; (yet, those people boasted in the claim that they were the only true Christians in the world, at the same time preaching not a word of Gospel truth), yet I doubt not but some of them are saved in

SANCTIFICATION. 63

spite of their false doctrine, and in spite of the devil, too; for certainly they have them both against them, if they would make their way to Heaven.

Many religious meetings exalt church rites and non-essentials above those vital truths without which no one can be saved, yet God saves the sincere people among them who, despite false doctrines and unsaved preachers, yield to the Holy Ghost, forsake all, and finally cast themselves on the mercy of God in Christ.

The problem of religion and salvation is quite another. The world is full of religion. When Satan ruined man, robbing him of spiritual life, he made no assault on his religion, but simply turned it into a greased plank over which to slide him into Hell. While Satan is creeping into all the churches like a vampire, and sucking their life's blood away while they sleep, and at the same time fanning his victims, to lull him into a deeper slumber, lest he wake before he dies, we have the blessed consolation of some true hearts, especially in the Holiness Movement, who have not bowed the knee to Baal.

But we must recognize the fact that Satan is bringing into availability all the artillery of the pandemonium, and marshalling all his hosts (human and diabolical) in battle array against the holiness people.

When Israel fled from Egyptian bondage, a great nation of three millions (in our day not many, but then a great host), a vast multitude of all nationalities, Egyptians, Copts, Ethiopians, Nubians, Arabs, etc., followed them, but as the days went by they melted away, evanesced, were seen no more; no one of them even entered the land of Canaan.

These heresies especially magnify the camp-followers of the Movement.

In California, the "Burning Bush" people were absorbed by the Tongues Movement, scarcely one surviving. They were a fanatical departure that really made a tremendous effort to capture the holiness people.

Dr. Dowey made a tremendous effort, sending his literature gratuitously to all the holiness people, stirring the continent from ocean to ocean. That great movement, which sought to capture us all, is now evanescing faster than it developed.

Reader, be sure that you have reached the stability of Paul, when he said, *"None of these things move me."* Jesus solves the problem in St. John 5:43: *"If any one may come in his own name, you will follow him."*

It is no trouble now for anybody to get a following, if he make the effort. There was a time when people were so scarce in this world that they were estimated above gold and silver, herds and flocks. In the days of Abraham and Job, land was so plentiful it was not worth appropriating, and only the most fertile spots were cultivated. Now it is all appropriated and used, and the price is rapidly rising. Meanwhile the world is thronged with an over-population, sixteen hundred millions crowding each other into the sea. The result is that there is nothing in the world now so plentiful as human beings, and nothing so cheap. The superfluity and depreciation of men, women and children throws open the wide door for all who aspire to leadership to have a following. It is not because they love the people and want to do them good, but the Holy Ghost tells the secret. Romans 16: 17, 18: *"Mark those that cause divisions and stumblings*

SANCTIFICATION.

contrary to the teaching which you have learned; and depart from them. For such men are not serving our Lord Christ, but their own stomach; and by their beautiful speeches and eulogies are deceiving the hearts of the innocent." The truth of the matter is, they want you to serve them. Speaking of the same class in Phil. 3: 18, 19 He says, *"They are enemies of the Cross of Christ: their end destruction, their stomach their God, and their glory in their shame, who are seeking after earthly things."*

Oh, how important that our people understand their Bibles, so they will have wisdom and grace to recognize and resist these ambitious leaders, who are coming in on us from every point of the compass. The end in view, is to appropriate influentially and financially, that they may not only get employment, but a living.

The reason I travel round the world is that I may do my utmost by speech and pen to keep the holiness people on the Bible line, assured that they are the hope of the world. The churches are going deeper into worldliness, and becoming more carnal as the days go by and the Lord draws nigh. The best we can hope in these last days of unprecedented trials and temptations is to preserve a remnant of Israel, who will be found faithful when the Lord appears.

We see in His own testimony (Luke 18: 8) that faith will be so scarce on the earth, when He shall appear, that He propounds the startling question, *"When the Son of Man shall come, shall He find faith on the earth?"* implying a negative answer and invoking the conclusion that it will certainly be a very scarce article.

N. B. The attributes of the Holiness Movement

recognizes no leader but Jesus; no guide but the Holy Ghost; and no authority but God's Word (especially the New Testament, as we are not under the Old Dispensation).

T. An undue emphasis on anything, however true, which is not essential to salvation, is calculated to sidetrack and ruin souls, deflecting the eye from Jesus, and, consequently, like Peter, when he got his eye on the water, he at once began to sink, thus setting up a new departure in spiritual life, conducting a downward trend, which means hell in the end. Therefore, spiritual progression beyond entire sanctification is a cunning device of Satan.

"Do you mean to teach that sanctification is the ultimatum of all progress?" By no means; but the very opposite. Sanctification, which means "emptied of sin, and filled with the Holy Ghost," is matriculation into the heavenly curriculum, where we sit down at the feet of Jesus to be taught by the Holy Ghost the deep things of God and the wonderful things of the kingdom; not only through this life, but all eternity.

Though in sanctification we receive the Holy Ghost, you must not think we exhaust Him; for He is none other than very and eternal God.

You reach the Mississippi River with a burning thirst, and drink all you can; yet the river is still there, moving in his royal majesty to the ocean. The Holy Ghost is infinitely greater than all the rivers that roll their swelling billows from their mountain sources, and disembogue into the sea. You do not need a third blessing of power, fire, tongues, or anything else. These are all right in their places; but you have them in the Holy Ghost, who

SANCTIFICATION. 67

Himself is the power, and all the power you need, or ever will need. He is the fire (Heb. 12:18) that burns up depravity, folly, vanity, lodgery, churchisms, all sorts of trivialities, frivolities, levities and empty nonsense and everything else that you cannot take to Heaven with you. In the school of Christ, with the Bible as our text-book, and the Holy Ghost, its author, our teacher, and the infinite diversity of teachers with whom He so copiously supplies you through the instrumentality of His saints, both by speech and pen, you will be delighted to learn more and more with ever-increasing appreciation, erudition, ratiocination and proficiency illimitable, not only through time, but all eternity; receiving a glorious impetus when you exchange earth for Heaven, as there you will have so much better teachers—angels, archangels and glorified saints, patriarchs, prophets, apostles and martyrs forever. As the people seeking a third experience almost invariably either backslide or go into fanaticism, in the "Tongues Movement" it is a well-known fact that this is no exception to the general rule. They get the eye off of Jesus, grieve the Holy Spirit and backslide, *e. g.*, great meetings, packed audiences, thrilling interest, altars crowded with people seeking the gift of tongues, and not one seeking sanctification or conversion.

Paul, in the inspiration of the Holy Ghost, faithfully warns us. 1 Corinthians 13:1: *"Though I speak with the tongues of men and of angels, and have not divine love, I have become as sounding brass, and a tinkling cymbal;" i. e.,* something utterly worthless. He has just been warning them and forbidding that any one should speak in an unknown tongue, unless it be interpreted.

In these meetings, the leaders encourage downright

disobedience to that commandment. Here you see that if we had not only the gift of all human tongues, but in addition, could speak the language of the angels, and had not perfect love,—which he here calls, *"The more excellent way,"* i. e., better than the gifts of the Spirit,—*"We are as sounding brass and a tinkling cymbal,"* i. e., we have the noise, but no power; because the Holy Ghost, who has been neglected and grieved away, is the power.

When, responsive to invitation, I went and preached in the tongues meetings, I pled with them, as now you read in these pages, not to make this sad mistake, and seek the gift rather than the Giver, and all do their best to get the crowds of sinners converted and Christians sanctified, as this is the only work we have to do in a Gospel meeting; not that we neglect anything that is revealed in the Bible.

Doubtless you have read my book, "Spiritual Gifts and Graces," which I wrote many years ago, and God has wonderfully used. Though I have expounded those gifts faithfully, through all these years and exhorted the people to receive them and use them for the glory of God, I always did such work in my meeting appointed especially on the teaching line; whereas in my evangelistic meetings, I always devoted my time preaching "Jesus" with all my might, the Savior of the sinner and the Sanctifier of the Christians, through His omnipotent agent, the blessed Holy Ghost, whose presence in the audience we always recognized, fully turning over the meetings to Him, to conduct them in His own way.

These great meetings, conducted on side issues which are not essential to salvation, are utterly out of harmony with the Holiness Movement, and their admission and

SANCTIFICATION.

recognition are a gross perversion of our commission to preach the Gospel to the world, which has but one definition, and that is, *"The power of God unto salvation"* (Romans 1:16.)

We are saved from actual sin in regeneration, and inbred sin in sanctification. Therefore, when we are going for anything else, we are no longer conducting salvation meetings. Therefore, meetings conducted on other lines are unevangelical, and should take rank simply as a Bible school, which is all right in its place and of transcendent importance, and in them the Holy Ghost is our only teacher, while edification is infinitely important; yet salvation is more important than anything else. If we do not get people regenerated and sanctified, and keep them there, they are sure of hell. In that case all their boasted education and profound Biblical culture will only augment their damnation, giving them a vastly more awful hell than if they had lived and died ignorant Hottentots.

I used to attend great meetings with thronging multitudes and see nobody saved, yet many immersed in water for the remission of their sins, thus worshipping the water-god and at the same time, actually from the pulpit, blaspheming the Holy Ghost. Shocking idolatry! Can we not keep at least a remnant of the holiness people on this glorious Bible line of sky-blue regeneration for sinners, and Pentecostal sanctification for Christians? Amen.

CHAPTER VII.

CHRISTIAN BAPTISM.

Among the sectarian perversions of God's Word, Christian Baptism has suffered egregiously; being applied only to the symbolic ordinance, which is but a shadow of the blessed reality. Such has been the perversion of the institution that false definitions have actually become bones of contention, over which many hard battles have been fought; the two tallest champions selected by their representatives crossing swords and heroically contending day after day, the one for immersion, and the other affusion; whereas the Word never had such definitions. The Bible is not only perfect in truth, but in wisdom. It is its own dictionary. All truly faithful people are willing to receive its definitions. Only those who have been sidetracked by Satan into humanisms are unwilling to abide the *ipse dixit* of God's precious Word.

St. John 3:25 defines baptism to be a purification. St. Luke 11:37-40 gives us the record of our Savior's acceptance of an invitation to dine with the Pharisee and sitting down at the table without washing His hands, to the astonishment of his host, who was so particular about handwashing every time he ate; as his sanctification, which he boldly professed, was external—keeping the Mosaic law appertaining to clean and unclean,—meanwhile experimentally ignorant relative to the great truth

CHRISTIAN BAPTISM.

of a clean heart. Jesus responded to the astonished inquiry why He ate without washing: *"You Pharisees make clean the outside of the cup and the plate; while the interior is filled with extortion and pollution."* In this passage, the word translated "wash," is *ebaptisthee*, the regular term constantly used in the New Testament revelatory of baptism. Jesus here defines it by *katharizoo*, which has the solitary definition, "to purify."

The reason why baptism does not occur in the Old Testament is not because they did not have it—because they had the symbolic ordinances a hundred times that of our dispensation;—but because it is not a Hebrew word, but Greek. Therefore it occurs constantly in the Greek Testament. It is defined uniformly in the Bible, "a purification," and really has no other definition. It is not a modal word at all; the manner of its administration being incidentally revealed in both Testaments as an unequivocal affusion.

Christian is an adjective from the noun Christ, and simply means in its connection with baptism, "That which Christ gives." John the Baptist (St. Matthew 3:11) tells us: *"Christ will baptize you with the Holy Ghost and fire."* Peter (Acts 2:17) tells us how He did it: *"I will pour out of My Spirit on all fi ,h."* It says: *"The Holy Ghost and fire fell on them;"* therefore it is a matter of indispensable revelation that the mode was affusion from the above Scriptures; that the baptism which Jesus gives is identical with sanctification, which simply means, "a purification."

The Bible would be a very monotonous book if the blessed Holy Spirit did not accommodate our sensibilities with diversified phraseology. Therefore we find' quite a variety of words revealing the very same gracious state. As God tells us (Eph. 4:5) there is but *"one baptism,"* it follows as a legitimate sequence that the symbolic ordinance with water is nothing in the gracious economy but a sign of something infinitely precious, and transcendently glorious. No tongue can tell the value, beauty and glory of the baptism which Jesus gives. It has been so befogged with water-logged heresies, unsaved preachers wresting from their moorings the beautiful Scriptures revealing them, and applying them to the symbolic ordinance, thus recklessly robbing Jesus of the crown He purchased with His blood freely shed on Calvary, and turning it over to the water-god, that the Church has in the main lost sight of this beautiful and glorious work of Christ in the redemption of the world.

It is pertinent that we give attention to these Scriptures by way of candid elucidation for the benefit of Christians, who have not gone hopelessly into hydrolatry (water-worship, sad to say, the most prevalent form of idolatry in the American Church), as to be unable to see the beautiful light which radiates from the precious Word of God, when the mask of diabolical and human mystification has been torn off.

The first twenty years of my life the most preaching I heard was by men who, I am satisfied, were utterly unacquainted with the Savior. They ridiculed Holy Ghost religion, pronouncing it fanaticism; constantly preaching immersion in order to have remission of sins so boldly and emphatically as to lead the people into idolatry.

u. *"He that believeth and is baptized shall be saved."* (St. Mark 16:16.) During my boyhood, I heard this text used more than any other to enforce the great popular dogma of the leading church in the community, *i. e.*, baptismal regeneration. Let us spend a minute in an honest, fair, grammatical and logical exegesis of this Gibraltar of hydrology, and you will see how people with water on the brain see rivers and lakes where there is not a drop.

Here we have but one subject, and that is a noun, understood, to which these pronouns refer. Now the question to be settled in reference to the character of the baptism is the determination of the subject, whether it is the soul or the body. You see the same thing that believes, is baptized and saved. Now after a moment's analysis of the predicates we determine the materiority or spirituality of the subject. Now what does the believing. You know it is the soul; as the body is as incompetent to exercise faith as the chair you occupy. Therefore we know it is not body faith, which is an impossibility. Then what is the subject of salvation? You know it is not the body, since the body of the saint dies just like that of the sinner. Then it cannot be body baptism, because the same thing that believes is baptized and saved. To an absolute certainty, as all intelligent minds recognize and admit, that thing is the soul. Therefore, grammar, logic, truth and common sense all agree to the simple conclusion as revealed in this passage—the soul believes, the soul is baptized, and the soul is saved. Your soul does the believing; Jesus baptizes you and saves you. Shame on a water-logged clergy that will so grossly pervert the Word of God in order to sustain a sectarian cause.

1 Pet. 3: 19-21: *"In which He also having gone*

proclaimed to the spirits in prison; who were at one time disobedient, when the longsuffering of God waited in the days of Noah, while the ark was being prepared, in which few, that is, eight souls were saved through water. Which antitype, baptism, doth now save us (not the removal of the filth of the flesh, but the seeking of a good conscience toward God)." I have often heard them use this with burning emphasis, enforcing the statement that Noah and his family were saved by water, and that in a similar manner water now saves us, at the same time towering, vociferating and ejaculating their favorite dogma, baptismal remission. This is another Scripture they have wrested from the hands of Jesus and turned over to their idol, the water-god.

Water, in reference to Noah and his family, is not here the instrumental dative, but the genitive of transition and is governed by the preposition *dia*, which simply means that they were miraculously saved through the water pouring down and deluging the ark, which was floating in it and lashed by the billows on all sides. Hence they went up through the water. Then follows the statement that the *"antitype, baptism doth save us (not the putting away of the filth of depravity, but the seeking of a good conscience toward God)."* This ceremonial expiation of impurity had existed from the days of Moses in the office of water baptism, and is yet. Peter says that is not the baptism he is talking about.

Everybody who knows anything about the Bible knows that water is a type of the Holy Spirit, and has so been in all ages. Here Peter positively affirms that the antitype, baptism, saves us, and not the typical. Therefore there can be no mistake about it by anybody

CHRISTIAN BAPTISM. 75

who is free from that dangerous and fatal disease, hydrocephalous, *i. e.,* water on the brain, which bluffs the whole medical world, so they pronounce it incurable. Yet it is no trouble for Jesus to cure it, for He cured me, as I once had it, and forced the Methodist preacher to put me in over my head, in order to drown old Adam, but found him amphibious, like the serpent, his prototype, and competent to live in the water as well as on dry land. Then, having duly tested the water-god, I found him weak as water, bade him adieu world without end; left the water line, and began flying to Mount Zion, with no guide, because I never heard a sermon on sanctification, nor even heard a person witness to it; yet I toiled on nineteen years, climbing great, old Mount Zion; often finding my way intercepted by craggy steeps, frightful precipices and yawning chasms till necessitated to retrace my steps and try another route. Thus wandering round and round, often crossing my own track, after the roll of nineteen years in the howling wilderness, though preaching the best I could, finally, in the good providence of God, I fortitudinously reached the Pentecostal summit in the midst of a great revival in my own pastoral charge, in which I was doing all the preaching; then, to my infinite joy, the fire fell and the victory came to stay.

v. 1 Cor. 12:13: *"For by one Spirit we are all baptized into one body, whether Jews or Greeks, whether bond or free; and have all been made to drink in one Spirit."* Children are always born before they are baptized, therefore the baptism of the Holy Ghost and fire, which Jesus gives, is an unanswerable proof of the two distinct works of grace in the plan of salvation. We have a right to baptize no children but our own. God never baptized the devil's children, but His own. The Zinzendorfian heresy would have the people all born and baptized at the same time, which is an absurdity, because they are always born first and baptized afterwards. When regeneration brings you into the kingdom of God, you know we are not born adults, but babes, and so remain till the second work of grace, which is our majority, marking the transition out of infancy into manhood. Little children often have controversies and quarrels among themselves, frequently fighting each other over their toys. All of this is discontinued by those who have reached majority.

I was a Free Mason, an Odd Fellow, a Methodist preacher, and a college president, when the Lord baptized me with the Holy Ghost and fire, burning all of these carnal personalities, and leaving me nothing but Jesus. Though chaplain in those lodges, I never went back after that notable epoch in my biography in 1868, before the Holiness Movement began her march to reach the Millennial glory. I never had heard anything against lodgery, but had been led thither by the example of Methodist preachers. Why did I never go back? When we reach manhood, we never again ride stick horses, chase June bugs and butterflies; infancy has evanesced and the stern realities of manhood have supervened. Oh, the beautiful simplicity, glory and victory which brightens the sanctified life! Divested of earth's miscellaneous entanglements, no longer encumbered by lodgery, sectarianism, nor any other complications, secular and ecclesiastical, but free from carnal bewilderments and perplexities, hand in hand with Jesus, we walk life's journey, with Heaven in view and glory flooding the soul.

CHRISTIAN BAPTISM. 77

You see from the above Scripture that the baptism which Jesus gives with the Holy Ghost and fire (which is but another name for entire sanctification, simply revealed and elucidated from another standpoint, and its normal result) is to unify all the children of God. If the Methodist Church all had it, there are not bishops enough in the world to keep the North and South from uniting. In this wonderful baptism, the fires of the Holy Ghost heats us so hot that we spontaneously run together, and, like Solomon's temple in its paradoxical construction, are welded without the sound of a hammer.

The great trouble with the denominations is the fact that their creeds are formulated on the regeneration plane, keeping their members in perpetual babyhood. Therefore they cannot agree, but must all have separate houses, as if they would be separate in Heaven, and each vieing with the other in vanity and display; thus gratuitously pouring out the Lord's money, which is so much needed to save the lost millions of pagandom. If the denominations had all received the baptism which Jesus gives we would have a million of missionaries in the heathen field. Oh, the vanity and foolishness which fills the church down on the carnal plain! They even hold great debates and have perplexing controversies over water baptism, as if it ever did have anything to do with saving a soul. Meanwhile, Jesus is ready to baptize all, and in that case they would be really baptized, *i. e.*, sanctified wholly. Whereas they may receive the symbolic baptism of every church in the world, and go headlong into hell, lost through all eternity.

There are more than four hundred millions of nominal Christians in the world; to the rank and file of whom this wonderful baptism which Jesus gives with the Holy Ghost and fire is an utter stranger. "Is there no balm in Gilead? Is there not a physician there? Then why is not the health of the daughter of my people recovered?" Yes, there is balm in Gilead, and a Physician there. Jesus is the Physician and His blood, the balm. Why will not all come and get saved and healed?

w. In Romans 6:1-6 we see a man crucified. In our day it would mean a man hung for murder, responsive to the mandate of criminal law. The government always buries the man they execute, never leaving him to occupy a pauper's grave. Here we see Old Adam executed for crime, pursuant to the *ipse dixit* of the violated law and responsive to the proclamation, *"The soul that sinneth, it shall die"* (Ezek. 18:4, 20.) In this judicial transaction, we see it is all done by baptism, the personified executive; by metonymy the transaction substituted for the Omnipotent Agent, our wondrous Lord. As you read it, you see it is all done by baptism; the man of sin crucified, the body destroyed and buried into the death of Christ, *i. e.*, the atonement.

"The fountain filled with blood
 Drawn from Immanuel's veins;
And sinners, plunged beneath that flood,
 Lose all their guilty stains.

"The dying thief rejoiced to see
 That fountain in his day;
And there may I, though vile as he,
 Wash all my sins away.

"Thou dying Lamb! Thy precious blood
 Shall never lose its power,
Till all the ransomed Church of God
 Are saved, to sin no more.

CHRISTIAN BAPTISM. 79

"E'er since, by faith, I saw the stream
Thy flowing wounds supply,
Redeeming love has been my theme,
And shall be till I die.

"Then in a nobler, sweeter song,
I'll sing Thy power to save,
When this poor lisping, stammering tongue
Lies silent in the grave."

How astounding to think intelligent preachers can apply this to the immersion of the body in water. It does not say that baptism is a burial, but that the "Old Man,"—*i. e.*, devil-nature, called "Old Man," because he is as old as the devil,—when crucified in us, is buried by baptism; *i. e.*, the baptism is the agent by which the old man is crucified and buried.

You know, the immersion of the physical body in water has no more power to do that work than to give you wings to fly to the stars. I tried it, and found it an utter failure. After it, I tried Jesus, and to my infinite joy found the old man crucified, dead and buried into the death of Christ as here specified, and not with water.

In immersion, the same thing is buried and immediately raised up. Do you not see that flatly contradicted in the Word of God relative to His great transaction? The old man is buried and left under the blood forever. The "new man" is resurrected, to *"walk in newness of life."* If the old man is raised up, *"the last state of a man is worse than the first."* This beautiful truth, so copiously and irrefutably revealing the mighty work of entire sanctification through the baptism which Jesus gives and by which our old man is crucified and the body of sin destroyed and buried so deep into the atonement, that Satan can never resurrect it, if we only keep our eye on Jesus, is also by the same Author beautifully revealed in Col. 2:6: *"As you received Christ Jesus the Lord, so walk ye in Him."* You received Him by faith, and by faith alone; therefore, we are to walk in Him by faith alone. Paul terribly castigated the Galatians, who had been awfully stumbled and almost ruined by legalistic preachers, who had come among them and preached the sensuality of ordinances, as the Campbellites and Mormons do now. Amid these castigations, he says: *"I wish only to learn this from you, Did you receive the Spirit by works of law, or the hearing of faith? Are you so foolish? having begun in the Spirit, are you now made perfect by the flesh?"* (Gal. 3:2, 3.) The Holy Spirit in conviction and regeneration begins every work of grace. Here Paul denounces the idea that we are to submit to ordinances to finish it, as so many do; but exhorts them to go on and let the Holy Spirit finish the work of entire sanctification.

Col. 2:8: *"Beware lest any one shall be leading you astray through philosophy and vain delusion, according to the tradition of men, according to the learning of the world, and not according to Christ."* Immersion is a human tradition, unknown in the Bible, and never practiced till long after every Apostle had gone to Heaven, when it was doubtless brought in by the pagans.

Col. 2:9: *"Because in Him dwelleth all the fullness of the Godhead bodily."* Here you see the contemptuous superfluity of adding anything to the work of Christ, because in His glorified body dwelleth all the fullness of the Godhead; therefore, when you receive Christ, you have all the resources of Heaven—Father, Son and the

Holy Ghost—in our wonderful risen and glorified incarnate Christ. *"You are complete in Him, who is the Head of all government and authority."* (Col. 2:10.) Therefore, if you are complete in Him, you will treat Him with contempt, if you go after something else, *e. g.*, water baptism or churchisms of any kind, in order to make you complete. The very fact that you are going after these things demonstrates the deficiency of your faith in Him. At that point, so many dishonor Christ and grieve the Holy Spirit by going off after the water-god or some other idol.

Col. 2:11: *"In whom you are circumcised with the circumcision made without hands, in putting off the body of the sin of carnality by the circumcision of Christ."* As the physical birth typifies the spiritual, so the circumcision typifies the sanctification. Circumcision was administered about eight days after the physical birth, illustrating the pertinency of sanctification quickly following regeneration, before backsliding has set in. Here he says it is *"the circumcision made without hands,"* which is but another name for sanctification. (Deut. 30:6.)

That triple compound noun, *apekduusi*, in putting off the body of the sin of carnality, *i. e.,* "Old Adam" (Rom. 6:6), is exceeding significant and powerful, from *duooo*, "to put on," *da,* from *apo,* "away from;" therefore, the meaning is thrillingly potent, signifying a taking off of "Old Adam" like an old filthy garment and shipping it to the first station beyond the North Pole, so it can never get back. Oh, how wonderfully and significantly does the precious Word of God reveal the stupendous truth confirmatory of this great and wonderful salvation we have vouchsafed to us in the Prince of Glory, who came, suffered and died to redeem us all from sin, death and hell!

Here it is specified that this is all done by baptism, which is in apposition with circumcision both grammatically and logically, showing that it means the same thing. Out of this burial in baptism, it says, *"we are raised by the faith of the operation of God by which He raised up Christ from the dead."* Hence we see the resurrection is by the same power that raised Christ from the dead, and is received through faith. Therefore, it is utterly impossible to apply it to the immersion of the body in water, because in that transaction the resurrection is not by faith, but by the physical power of the administrator.

In these two epistles, Romans and Colossians, water is not mentioned; meanwhile all the phraseology vividly describes a miracle of grace, which cannot possibly be imparted to water baptism; but if we let it stay where God has put it, and as it does indubiably and irreparably describe the baptism which Jesus gives with Holy Ghost and fire, then it is all play-easy and perfectly consistent with the uniform teaching of the Scriptures. How surprising that they apply this to water baptism in order to symbolize it to the death, burial and resurrection of our Lord,—a conclusion utterly alien to revelation and untenable, as water baptism never does typify our Lord's death, burial and resurrection; but throughout the Bible water is the constant symbol of the Holy Ghost; while our Lord's death, burial and resurrection are all typified by the eucharist, the surviving monument of the paschal lamb, which annually for fifteen hundred years bled at

Christian Baptism.

the Passover, typifying the great anti-type destined to bleed on Calvary.

These and many other Scriptures have been torn from the place the Holy Ghost put them, revealing the baptism Jesus gives, when He pours on us the Holy Ghost and fire, and simply turn it over to the water-god.

Baptism has but one signification in the Bible, and that is "purification," *i. e.*, "sanctification." Oh, how copiously fruitful do we find that glorious truth revealed in the Bible, and how lamentable to see it grossly perverted by so many preachers, who thereby illustrate the sad conclusion that they are not experimentally acquainted with our wonderful Christ, but only know Him historically, like men of the world.

CHAPTER VIII.

The Pentecostal Experience.

The Pentecostal experience, through Christ, was always in the world from the beginning, shining on every human soul that ever existed or ever will.

St. John 1:9: *"Here is the true Light, which lighteth every man that cometh into the world."* The Greek here is *anthropos,* which means a woman as much as a man. *Aner* always means a man; *gunee,* a woman; but *anthropos* simply means "a human being," and may be either a man or woman. This is a word uniformly used in the Bible illustrating the fact that "woman is man's equal in the kingdom of God." You see from this Scripture that our wonderful Christ has always been in the world and was effectually a *"Lamb slain from the foundation of the world."* His atonement was as efficient before His incarnation as afterward; simply postponed these four thousand years in order that the earth might be populated and literature developed, so that history could apprehend it and transmit it to all coming generations; whereas if it had taken place in the early ages it would have been obliterated amid the fogs and myths of the pre-historic centuries, mixed up with the legendary stories of heathen divinities, obscured and lost sight of forever.

John the Baptist (St. John 1:23) and Paul (1 Cor-

The Pentecostal Experience.

inthians 10:4) certify that He was identically the Jehovah of the Old Testament, the former proving it by Isaiah, and the latter by Moses. Therefore, He was in the world from the beginning, mighty to save and strong to deliver.

x. Analogously to the terrestial history of the Son excarnate, before His birth in Bethlehem, and incarnate subsequently, we may pertinently observe that the Holy Ghost, who was present in creation, as we read in the first chapter of Genesis, moving upon the face of the waters, but excarnate till Pentecost, when His wonderful incarnation took place, because on that notable occasion, He came into human bodies, thus incarnating Himself to abide. Antecedently to the Pentecostal incarnation, He operated on the people extrinsically, though frequently exceedingly potently; *e. g.*, catching up the prophet and carrying him away on a lonely mountain as Elijah, or in the great dreary valley, as in the case of Ezekiel, who found himself in a totally strange place and everywhere surrounded by the dead, dry bones, to whom God called him to preach. In the Pentecostal experience He incarnated Himself in the people, operating intrinsically, in contradistinction to His extrinsical operation antecedently.

St. John 7:37, 38: *"On the last great day of the feast, Jesus stood and continued to cry out, If any one thirst, let him come unto Me and drink. For whosoever believeth on Me, as the Scripture said, out of his heart shall flow rivers of living waters."* This Jesus spoke concerning the Spirit, who those believers on Him were about to receive; for the Spirit was not yet given, because Jesus was not yet glorified. When man sinned, a chasm deep as hell, high as heaven and broad as creation opened between God and man, thus forever alienating them from each other. The Son, responsive to the gift of the loving Father, volunteered to espouse the lost cause, and redeem the whole human race from sin, death and hell; thus becoming the bridge over which they could pass across that awful chasm, thus treading on His crucified body and make their escape from Satan's awful torment back to the bosom of the loving Father, whence sin had hurled them down to the brink of irretrievable woe. The son of God saw our ruin and volunteered for the rescue.

> "Down from the heights above,
> In joyful haste He fled,
> Entered the tomb in mortal flesh,
> And dwelt among the dead."

This was absolutely necessary in order to bridge that yawning chasm between man and God.

Gal. 3:13, 14, 16: *"Christ hath redeemed us from the curse of the law, being made a curse for us; because it is written, Cursed is he that hangeth on a tree; in order that the blessing of Abraham in Christ Jesus might come upon the Gentiles; that we might receive the promise of the Spirit through faith. For the promises were to Abraham and his seed. Not with seeds, as of many; but to his seed, which is Christ."* Thus you see the identity of the Abrahamic with the Messianic covenant, which God had made with Christ to redeem the whole world from sin, death and hell, and He simply reiterated it with Abraham, promoting him to the honored paternity of all saints.

THE PENTECOSTAL EXPERIENCE. 87

Peter, on the Day of Pentecost, in that wonderful sermon, certifies Acts 2: 32, 33, *"This Jesus hath God raised up, whose witnesses we are all now. Therefore being exalted at the right hand of God, and having received from the Father the promise of the Holy Spirit, He has poured out this, which you see and hear."* You see from this, and parallel passages, that the gift of the Holy Ghost was the great salient point at which all the promises focalized; that glorious culmination of the whole redemptive scheme, and really the climax of the sanctified experience. For this the plan of salvation was inaugurated in Heaven and launched upon the earth. Conservatively of this most glorious enterprise in the history of the universe, so far as revelation has transmitted to us, the Son of God vacated the throne of His glory, came into the world, suffered and died, that He might clear all the difficulties out of the way, satisfy, honor, and magnify the violated law, and thus clear the way for the reunion and eternal reconciliation of offended man and offended God.

Hence you see that the sanctification of humanity is the grand ultimatum of everything revealed in the Bible, because this book, with its wonderful contents, is simply the history of sin and its remedy. If sin had never come into the world, it would never have been needed. The great redemptive work of Christ, from Alpha to Omega, all culminates in the gift of the Holy Ghost, who is none other than the very eternal God, returned from Heaven to take up His abode in the human spirit, actually incarnating Himself in our bodies, and dwelling with us in these tenements of clay, as we occupy them.

N. B. The Holy Ghost is the Spirit of God and

identical with Him. He is also the Spirit of the Son, and identical with him (Acts 5:3, 4; 16:6, 7); therefore, when Jesus had finished His redemption of the whole world on Calvary; risen triumphantly over sin, death and hell; ascended up to the Father; reported His stupendous work, and the Father, perfectly satisfied, accepted it forever, He then gave Jesus the Holy Ghost, His own Spirit, very and eternal God, whom Jesus poured out on the people on the Day of Pentecost, and He entered into the waiting disciples, demonstrated by the sweeping tornado and flaming tongues of fire, His visible and audible symbols, the one of power and the other sanctification. This was really the return of God to man after the alienation of four thousand years. Meanwhile, He had operated on Him extrinsically and potently; but now He enters into the human spirit and body, thus incarnating Himself to abide forever.

Pentecostal means "fifty," because it was instituted and observed in commemoration of the wonderful epoch which dates the inauguration of the Mosaic dispensation at Sinai, when the great Jehovah descended in flaming fire, forked lightnings, waving thunder—peals and frightful earth-quakes, all demonstrating His righteous indignation against the transgressor of His law, and the terrible retribution, certifying the fulfillment of the awful denunciation, *"The soul that sinneth, it shall die."* (Ezek. 18:4, 20.)

The flagrant heresy now propagated by the so-called "Tongues People,' denying that there was any sanctification at the Pentecostal revival, is patent, when we contemplate the very signification of that time-honored festival, which originated from the wonderful Divine intervention on Sinai, in its annual celebrations, keeping vivid in the popular mind the awful doom of the transgressor. Therefore, in all the brilliancy of its institutional significance, it proclaims to the world the enforcement of the violated law, which thundered from Sinai's melting summits, and had already been repeated fifteen hundred times in order that the guilty conscience should never grow oblivious of the impending retribution, which, though of tardy pace, delayed so long by the longsuffering of God, is nevertheless absolutely certain to overtake the criminal with the glittering sword of irretrievable vengeance, only whetted the sharper by the retardation of its velocity. Hence the very institutional significance of that great holiness camp-meeting in the Hebrew calendar was the execution of Old Adam, the transgressor in every human heart; therefore the lexical definition, "Pentecost," is "The crucifixion of the Old Man," which is a current Scriptural phrase, denotation of entire sanctification.

Oh, what a novelty the heretical hypothesis is in comparison with the sanctification at Pentecost. Each murderous dealing with the precious Word smacks of the very audacity of Diabolus. Verily the crucifixion of Old Adam is the climacteric signification of the Pentecostal experience, as on that occasion God, in the person of the Holy Ghost, returns to man, reincarnating Himself in human souls and bodies. It follows as an irresistible sequence from the uniform teaching of the Bible, that the Man of Sin was executed, and forever ejected from the human organism as is certain, God will not abide with him. On the contrary, He always executes the penalty of the violated law against the transgressor and usurper, crucifying the Old Man and destroying the body of sin (Rom. 6:6) before he returns to the temple, which He created to occupy forever, but from which He has been alienated by sin. Responsive to the glorious vicarious substitutionary atonement which Jesus made, by His expiatory blood for the sins of the whole world, thus forever satisfying the violated law, when having perfected His work on Calvary, broken the fetters of death and even triumphed over all hell, having ascended up to Heaven and taken His seat, sceptered and crowned on the mediatorial throne and received this great promise of the Father, *i. e.*, the restoration of the Holy Spirit to humanity. (Acts 2:3, 4.) Peter, preaching to the multitudes, certifies that He has sent Him down, amid the miraculous demonstrations of the roaring cyclone, symbolizing His power, and the tongues of fire, typifying purity; the alienated Jehovah returns to man, whom He had created for companionship, fellowship and eternal co-operation in the glorious economy of the celestial universe. After a four thousand years' war, the Son of His redeeming love, having pushed the battle to the glorious victory of Mt. Calvary, and so signally and triumphantly defeated all the powers of darkness and even proclaimed His victory to Satan and all his myrmidons, when He descended into hell, while His crucified body hung on the cross and lay in the sepulchre, and having led up the multiplied millions of Old Testament saints (Eph. 4:8-10) from the intermediate paradise, Abraham's bosom (St. Luke 16:22) to augment the splendor of His victory by their thrilling testimonies electrifying the countless millions of unfallen angels, filling Heaven with their jubilant shouts, congratulating the glorious Conqueror of Mt. Calvary on His triumphant return from the battle-fields of earth to the effulgent throne of His mediatorial grace.

z. As the Lord returned in the person of the Holy Ghost on that memorial day of Pentecost, and reincarnated Himself in the disciples, to abide in their hearts and radiate into the world in their lives, sending them all out veritable ministers of His own definition, *"A flame of fire"* (Heb. 1:7), the brilliant Gospel symbol of cloven tongues having fallen on them, one to preach hell-fire to sinners, in order to convict them and to keep them out of hell, and the other heavenly fire to Christians, to sanctify them for Heaven; therefore the great salient truth proclaimed by Peter (Acts 2:38), *"Ye shall receive the gift of the Holy Ghost,"* (God's gift in the person of the Holy Ghost) confirmatory to His glorious return to His long-vacated temple, to re-occupy it, and abide forever, all conspire in the enforcement of the great truth, that those people then and there were sanctified wholly, the man of sin crucified and forever buried into the atonement, so recently perfected on Calvary.

To this Peter positively witnesses (Acts 15:9), certifying that God not only at Jerusalem in the Jewish Pentecost, but at Cæsarea in the Gentile Pentecost, in both of which he was the leading preachers, *"Purified their hearts by faith."*

All Bible readers recognize the synonymy of "purification" and "sanctification." Eph. 5:25, 26: *"Husbands, love your wives with Divine love, as Christ loved the Church, and gave Himself for her; that He might sanctify her, purifying her by the washing of water through the Word."*

Here you see these two verbs, "sanctifying" and

"purifying," used synonymously. Oh, how wild the fanaticism that attempts to take sanctification out of Pentecost, and how significant of the great importance that we hold fast to the precious Word, by which we are saved, sanctified, fed, edified, panoplied and by which we will be judged in the Great Day. While experiences are uniform and identical in all ages, regeneration, which is the creation of Divine life in the dead soul, and sanctification, which is the extermination of sin out of the heart, preparatory for the indwelling of the Holy Spirit, are unchangeable as God, who alone can execute them; the environments and phenomena are infinitely diversified and variant.

In this respect, there has never been a literal repetition of Sinai, or Pentecost. In the latter, the roar of the tornado, the visible fiery tongues, the instantaneous gift of languages which they knew not, and the miracle of hearing each one in the language in which he was born, and reared, have never been literally repeated, I trow, in the history of the world. God is the same yesterday, to-day and forever. We are living in an age of awful fanaticism.

I heard the "Tongues People" certifying that all the miracles performed in the apostolic time actually had taken place there in Los Angeles. They contend stoutly for the literal repetition of Pentecost, and claim to have it, reminding me of a drunken man on the steam-boat, who certified that he owned all the crafts running on the Ohio River. The reason why they got so many down to the altar, seeking the gift of tongues, they say it is the infallible concomitant of the baptism of the Holy Ghost; while that statement is not sustained by the inspired record; *e. g.*, when under the ministry of Peter and John at Samaria they received the Holy Ghost, there is no mention of them speaking with tongues. If they invalidate experiences, because they do not speak in a foreign language, why not require the visible sign of fire falling on them and the miracle of hearing in the language other than enunciated by the speaker? On that occasion, Peter and doubtless all others preached in Greek; but the people heard the Word, each one on his vernacular tongue. The miracle of ears was there quite as obvious as that of the tongues; therefore, if the fanatics demand identical repetition, why so particular about the tongues, and leave out the ears?

The Bible is a spiritual Book throughout; *physical phenomena being only incidental, and in no way essential.* Keep this truth in view, *i. e.*, the clear spirituality of Bible truth and the Gospel salvation throughout, and you will have the victory over the fanaticism which evil spirits are manipulating everywhere.

A. Do not forget the commandment (1 John 4:1), *"Try the spirits,"* as the Holy Spirit is the Author of every word in the Bible, He can never contradict it.

Twenty-five years ago, a lot of holiness people in this city (Cincinnati) went into fanaticism, so wild that they discarded the Bible, alleging they did not need it, as they had passed beyond it, having received the Guide, they no longer needed the Guide-book. Of course they went into spiritual wreckage. You see how this attitude is self-contradiction; as the Guide normally prosecutes His office in the use of the Guide-book. Of course God is not tied to the Book, or anything else, but as He is Immutable it is certain that He will never contradict, or antagonize anything that He has recorded in His Word. Therefore, there is no reason why any of us should go into error; because the way of holiness is so plain *"that way-faring men, though fools, shall not err therein."* (Isa. 35:8.)

The normal Pentecostal experience is the crucifixion of "Old Adam," as the institution commemorating the giving of the Law on Sinai determines without the possible evasion from the simple fact that God's law is immutable and indefrageable. Therefore the edict, *"The soul that sinneth, it shall die,"* must absolutely be verified; in every case Adam the First must die. Therefore as Pentecost was instituted to commemorate the giving of the law; it follows a logical sequence that if you have the Pentecostal experience, the Old Man of sin has been crucified and exterminated. When this is a glorious verity, the Holy Spirit always comes in and fills the vacuum; really He, the Executive of the Divine government, crucifies the Old Man. So if you have the Pentecostal experience, the Old Man is dead, your heart is clean, the Holy Ghost has come in, taken up His abode, and incarnated Himself in your spirit which fills your body and, consequently, He fills you soul and body, and reigns in your heart and life without a rival.

CHAPTER IX.

THE DIVINE "AGAPE" AND SPIRITUAL GRACES.

Two words in the New Testament are constantly translated "love." *Agape* "Divine love," and *philia,* "human love." They differ so widely in signification that they should be differentiated in the translation. I am astonished that this has never been done in any translation, so far as I know (except my own).

While *agape,* "Divine love," is the very essence of salvation, because it is really the definition of God, (1 John 4:8, 16) *"God is love."* This *agape* is poured out (not shed abroad, as English Version has it,) in the heart, by the Holy Ghost given unto us. (Rom. 5:5.)

The Latin Bible was the only one in use during the long roll of the Dark Ages, a thousand years; meanwhile not one man in a thousand could read it or anything else; the Greek original being almost unknown to the world. Consequently, the translators, in 1611 A. D., used the Latin much more readily than the Greek, of which their knowledge was very imperfect, consequently, this error got into the English Version from the Latin, which in some way had suffered the change from *effusa,* to *diffusa.* Therefore, "shed abroad," should be "poured out."

As the Divine love is native only in the heart of God, constituting the essence of His moral and spiritual being, and, consequently, always exotic in the human heart, that word means a foreigner, whose native land is Heaven. When the sinner thoroughly repents of all his sins with a broken and a contrite heart, which restores all of the ill-gotten gains willingly and gladly, as you see in the case of Zacchæus, who had long enjoyed a revenue office in the Roman government, and become wealthy; but when he genuinely repented of all his sins and cast himself on the mercy of God in Christ, the Holy Spirit poured out into his heart the Divine "agape," which quickly demonstrated its presence by certifying to Jesus, *"The half of all my goods I give to the poor; and if I have defrauded any one, (and he implies that he had), I will restore fourfold;"* thus climaxing the Mosaic law, under which he had spent his life, whose penalty for theft is simply restitution: for a sheep, two; for an ox, three, and for a horse or a camel, fourfold restitution. Therefore, he begins by cutting his fortune in two in the middle and giving half of it to the poor; then restoring fourfold to all whom he had defrauded. Thus immediately becoming a poor man, he is in good fix to leave all, follow Jesus, and preach the Gospel.

B. The *agape* poured out in the heart by the Holy Ghost is real regeneration, making you a new creature; old things having passed away. As this *agape* is an exotic from Heaven, it makes you a stranger and pilgrim on the earth, and henceforth a citizen of Heaven. Phil. 3: 20.)

But this heavenly exotic finds enemies, though subjugated, still resident in the heart and ever plotting against the new administration. The result is civil war, constant vigilance and awful battles frequently necessary to hold these enemies in subjection. There is eternal warfare between *agape* and carnality, till the latter is washed away by the crimson blood and all the debris consumed by the fires of the Holy Ghost; then the love is perfect, fills the heart and reigns without a rival.

The *philia,* "human love," is indigenous in the fallen spirit. While it is good and all right in its place, it is utterly destitute of salvation. The wicked people all have it; they love their wives, husbands, children, comrades and friends; but there is no salvation in it; no, not a scintilla of redeeming grace.

The rich man in Hell loved his brethren so that he wanted Abraham to send them a preacher to keep them out of there. You see there was no salvation in his love, because it was carnal; not the *agape,* but the *philia.*

As to this carnal love, which all sinners have, it is equally peculiar to the animal kingdom. When a boy, attending to my father's sheep, I soon observed that the yelp of a dog would stampede the whole flock; whereas, in the case of a young lamb, the mother seeing an innocent cur passing by, dashes at him, butts him down, and before he can get away, downs him again, repeating it the third time; till he runs away, howling for his life, lest the sheep's head break all of his ribs.

When Livingstone was traveling in Africa, looking from a mountain summit, he saw a lion rushing out of his jungle, seize a calf in his ferocious mouth, to make its breakfast on it. With lightning velocity the mother darts to the relief of her panic-stricken loved one, with terrible impetuosity; and plunging her sharp horn through the ribs of the voracious monster, tears his heart to pieces before he has had time to hurt the calf, which leaps out of his mouth, and gambols by the mother's side; meanwhile the monarch of the mountain roars his life away.

c. Then, how can I know whether I have the *agape,* "Divine love," which is salvation; or only the *philia,* "carnal love," which is common to sinners and animals? *"By their fruits you shall know them."*

Early in the Holiness Movement in Kentucky the Lord sent a great revival, thronging the premises with people and crowding the altar with seekers. One night an especial landslide drops down from Heaven and it takes half the house to accommodate the mourners. A union of fervent ejaculatory prayers brings waves of salvation rolling like ocean billows over the altar; meanwhile souls are passing triumphantly out of death into life; out of the wilderness into Canaan. Amid the shouts of victory and the cries of penitence, a hoarse voice is heard on the left, "O Charlie B——, where are you?" And a juvenile cry from the right, "Uncle Tom, where are you?" They press their way through the packed crowd, and meet in front of the altar, and mutually embrace. About that time, an old woman, contemplating the scene, falls and seems to swoon away. The tide rolls, on, souls sweeping into victory; when the old woman having convalesced, stands up and tells the people why she fainted; observing, "This young man is my son; he shot at that old man several times with a revolver. The old man shot at him a number of times, actually shooting a hole through his hat." Meanwhile the fact is developed that they came to meeting with their revolvers to kill each other, but when the Holy Ghost poured the love of God into their hearts, each one thinks of his enemy first of all, and rushes to him with confessions of guilt and pleading for pardon. I mention this as illustrative of Divine love, which is the same in the heart of man as in God, who loves all people with perfect love, even the vilest of the vile, His bitterest enemies, and has abundantly demonstrated it by coming all the way from Heaven to die for them.

When a circuit rider, I went to a place in my pastorate, pursuant to announcement, to hold a protracted meeting. On arrival, my members notify me that we will have to give it up for the present, as two prominent brethren had fallen out and were carrying revolvers to kill each other on sight. Consequently, they said it would not do to hold a protracted meeting, because those men would break it up. I respond: "You mistake; this is the very time we need a revival; so, we will go on with the meeting, and you turn over those brethren to me. and I will go the security that they will give us no trouble."

I went at once, called on one of them and asked him to come to the meetings unarmed. He refused to do so, alleging that the other one would kill him. I told him that I would stand security for the other man, that he would come unarmed. Then he consented. I called on the other one, and told him that his enemy would come to meeting, if he would, and he acquiesced. Consequently, I had them both in the meetings, quite a multitude turning out, and holding basket meetings (as it was in the country), all day and night services in a village nearby. The Lord gave us a wonderful revival, and those two, under the effulgent light of the Holy Spirit, which was flooding the audiences and crowding the altar, among others, hitherto irreconcilable enemies, received an inundation of God's wonderful regenerating, reclaiming and adopting love. The result was electrifying, when all embrace, mutually forgive, forever dropping the curtain over the dark by-gones, whose lubricous tale of woes each one had persistently endeavored to tell me; but I utterly refused audience.

During the greatest camp-meeting in the world, in Waco, Texas, founded somewhat through our humble instrumentality, where we had four thousand tenters and twenty thousand auditors, the power of the Lord was present in wonderful conviction, prostrating stalwart people on all sides. Amid the multitudinous altar services, having labored hard personally in prayer and exhortation face to face with a stalwart man of about thirty years, suddenly wheeling round, he fled away; impressing me with the conclusion that I had pressed him too hard, and he had fled from the fire. Then I proceeded to labor with others; a half an hour has flown, and I recognized his face returning, radiant with celestial glory, and a man in his arms, utterly contorted with thunder-polt conviction, so he could not walk, but crying aloud for mercy. Down in the straw they fall, and oh, such praying! Eventually they rise with shouts of victory, and in due time tell their experience. They were inveterate enemies, either seeking the life of the other, and came thither armed with revolvers for the mutual work of death. When number one wheeled round and fled from the altar, and I thought he had run from the fire, it was because the lightning of regeneration struck him, and instantaneously he thought of his worst enemy and ran, shouting to all he saw, "Have you seen Tom J——?"

Ere long he finds him, and rushing on him with flowing tears, impleads, "Oh, Tom, do forgive me; I have been so mean to you; I deserve all the punishment you have ever tried to give me, and much more; I could not have blamed you if you had killed me." Tom is appalled and hesitates to believe his own senses, responding, "Why, Bill T——, is that you? Surely I am mistaken—the man who has been after me to kill me?" "Yes, Tom, it is I, and I have come to tell you how I love you." He retorts, "What in all the world has come over you?" "Why, they got me down in the straw at the mourners' bench, and God has given me another heart, and I love you so, I want to die for you." By this time, the lightning of conviction has riddled Tom from head to heel, and he is begging Bill to take him to the altar.

D. "If this wonderful Divine *agape* of regeneration performs such miracles, surely there is nothing left for you to do." In this you are widely mistaken. Sanctification, after all this, has a wonderful work to do. This love is poured out (Rom. 5:5) into a depraved heart. This follows as a legitimate sequence, as we have no other kind of a heart in which to receive it. Now the expedition of this fallen heart from all the contaminating debris of devil-nature is a work of stupendous magnitude.

I once read a book on horticulture, written by a London millionaire, after he had made a princely fortune by gardening. He migrated into the garden regions of London, and as he was unable to buy land at the current price, one thousand dollars an acre, he took a lease on a hundred acres, at the same time adroitly leading the proprietor into an obligation never to take it out of his hands without paying him for his crops. By the time he got all of his horticulture machinery, economy and enterprises in operation, the time supervened, when the crop was worth more than the land, even at the enormous estimate of a thousand dollars per acre. Consequently the proprietor was as unable to pay him for his crop, as he was to pay for the land. Thus he caught him in a financial trap, where he held him tight, and walked in all his own wisdom, improving the land and deliberately fixing it up for permanent occupancy, as if it belonged to him. The result was that in due time, as the years rolled by, he made the money and paid the hundred thousand dollars for the land. Then moving on the even tenor of his way, he accumulated and became a millionaire. In his book he states that he kept that rich land, naturally so prolific of filth, so clean that there never was a time you could have gathered a bushel-basket of weeds on the whole hundred acres, thus beautifully illustrating the purity side of the sanctified experience, which is the utter elimination of inbred sin. He also states that at the beginning, he proceeded to purchase unlimited qualities of manures from the city scavengers, and had vast processions of carts running all the time, carrying it out and dumping it on his lands; thus making them rich as the garden of the Lord.

E. When Satan succeeded in the massacre of humanity, the guardian angels snatched up the tree of life from withered and blighted Eden, carried it away to the Elysian fields beyond the stars. In regeneration, this lovely evergreen is brought back and transplanted in the filthy soul soil of fallen humanity. This is a necessity, as we have no other ground to receive it. If we do not protect it, the spontaneous crop of obnoxious weeds, brambles, thorns, and thistles quickly and utterly choke it out, the last hope taking her everlasting flight. Therefore, the first thing to do, is to utterly expiate the soul soil, by unrooting and exterminating heterogenous filth, Spanish needles, cockleburs, Canada thistles, deadly nightshade, the pestilential upas and the narcotic strychnos; thus thoroughly purifying the soil. Having thus finished the negative side of the experience, by the utter eradication and destruction of everything obnoxious and hateful in the sight of God; then we proceed to the inimitable enterprise of reaching the soul-soil. The Holy Ghost comes in, incarnates Himself to abide forever with spiritual enlargement. We shall eternally continue to be recipient of this paradoxical superabounding enrichment of our soul soil, eternally approximating the glorious Divinity, sinking deeper into God, broadening into vaster spiritual attitudes, moving forward into more glorious longitudes, and climbing to loftier altitudes, and achieving more and more glorious similitudes, thus eternally approximating the ineffable glory, as we shall forever continue to receive a nearer proximity to the heavenly hierarchies.

The negative side of the sanctified experience is definite and complete, when the Old Man is crucified and the body of sin destroyed and buried in the Atonement forever. When God says a thing is dead, it is dead sure enough. Dead means "destitute of life." If the Man of Sin is utterly destitute of life, he is as dead as he can be. When God says you are free from sin, it is veritably and indisputably true. Not so with the positive side.

The susceptibility of increasing fertilization is illimitable. The soil of the Nile Valley is in many places forty feet deep; yet it is getting deeper, as its inundations deposit additional strata. This is a transcendantly consolatory fact to contemplate, *i. e.*, our eternal susceptibility of spiritual as well as intellectual enlargement, rising to loftier heights, and diving to deeper depths, exploring to the vaster widths and moving on to more illimitable proficiency, while the cycles of eternity move.

In Gal. 5:22, 23 you find catalogued the nine graces of the Holy Spirit, *i. e.*, "*Love, joy, peace, longsuffering, kindness, goodness, meekness, faith, holiness.*" This catalogue is captioned, as you see, "Fruit of the Spirit." You recognize here the singular number. Therefore the logical sequence legitimately follows that love is generis, embracing the other eight in their specific relation to the great genus. Consequently we find them all resolvable into the Divine *agape*.

"Joy" is love exultant, *i. e.*, leaping and shouting are swooned away in the unutterable rhapsody.

"Peace" is love resting in the arms of Jesus; placidly, like the infant, reposing on the bosom of its mother, bereft of every care.

"Longsuffering" is love at the lion's mouth or burning stake, delighted to seal her faith with her blood, like the martyrs during the first three centuries preceding the conversion of the Emperor Constantine, while they use them to fatten their lions, bears, leopards, and hyenas and enrich the imperial coffers with the bushels of gold and silver, constantly poured in by the hundred thousand spectators who thronged the Colloseum night and day, to witness these bloody tragedies. They called the north gate "The gate of life," because they brought them in through it alive, and the south gate "The gate of death," because through it they carried out their bones, after the wild beasts had devoured their flesh.

"Kindness" (English Version, "Gentleness,") is love flooded with sympathy, pity and tenderness for everything that has feeling.

"Goodness" is love in the capacity of the Good Samaritan, going about doing good.

"Meekness" is love sitting low down on the bottom, in the valley of humiliation; secure because she can never fall, as there is no place to fall to, thus solving the problem of final perseverance.

"Faith" is love on the battle-field, pressing the war to the gate of the enemy; seeking the thickest of the fight and the hottest of the battle. It is the measure of your efficiency for God." *"As your faith is, so be it unto you."*

"Holiness" (English Version, "Temperance,") too weak to convey the idea of the Greek—*egkratia,* from *ego,* "I," and *kratos,* "government." Therefore, this significant compound word means that beautiful "self-government" which puts us in perfect harmony with the law of God, so we delight to do His will on earth, as the angels do it in Heaven. It is not holiness in the sense of sanctification, which means "taking the world out of you." 1 John 2:16: *"All this is the world, the lust of the flesh, the the lust of the eye, and the pride of life;* "*i. e.,* the unholy trinity. These all go out when you receive a clean heart.

You see these eight graces of the Spirit are all resolvable into love, corroborating that beautiful affirmation (Rom. 13:10), *"Love is the fulfilling of the law."* Therefore this Divine love really climaxes all law by fulfilling it. *"Man looks on the outside, but God looks on the heart."* God is not poor, nor weak, that He needs our obedience. He says, *"If I were hungry, I would not tell you, for the cattle upon a thousand hills are mine."* At His bidding, countless millions of angels are ready to rally and fight His battle.

These nine graces are all essential and indispensable to salvation, in vivid contradistinction to the gifts of the Spirit, which are not essential to salvation, but only to our efficient panoply, for the salvation of others.

Paul, after elucidating the gifts of the Spirit in 1 Corinthians 12, and exhorting us to covet them earnestly and diligently appreciate them, clearly certifies, *"Yet I show unto you a more excellent way."*

Despite the erroneous translation of this chapter in the English Version we have the unmistakable revelation, confirmatory of the conclusion, that it is "perfect love." The reason why the translators of 1611 A. D. put it down "charity" instead of "Divine love," is because "charity" is a work, *i. e.,* something we do in behalf of he needy, with an eye single to the glory of God. We all need thunderbolts of conviction, stirring us up to be charitable to the poor, responsive to the uniform teaching of God's Word. Charity is not a definition for *agape,* but "Divine love," which is really the summary of all the graces, as we have seen.

With this translation, we are in harmony with the uniform teaching of the Bible, *"By grace you are saved through faith: that not of yourselves: it is the gift of God: not of works, lest any one should boast."*

Three hundred years ago, when the English Version was translated, the world was just emerging out of the Dark Ages; a long and dismal night of a thousand years; the Church having, with the world, passed through this awful barbarous age, and consequently, teaching salvation by works, a dangerous heresy.

Now, if you drop your eye down to the eighth verse of this chapter, you find four superlative complements, qualifying *agape,* the subject of the chapter. *"Love beareth all things, endureth all things, believeth all things, and hopeth all things."* (1 Cor. 13:7.) So you see it means love in the superlative degree, *i. e.,* none other than perfect love. You see how clearly the Holy Ghost in these Scriptures uses Paul to climax perfect love, certifying *"Though I speak with the tongues of men and of angels, and have not Divine love, it profiteth me nothing."*

Here you see how he pronounces a gift of tongues in the very highest sense, including not only the languages of men but of the angels, utterly worthless without the love of God in the heart. Oh, what a rebuke to the wild fanaticism now distracting the Holiness Movement relative to the gift of tongues. *"Though I have all wisdom, and all knowledge, and faith so as to remove mountains, and have not Divine love, it profiteth me nothing."* Here he specifies three most important gifts and assures us that without the love of God, they will do us no good. Baalim, the false prophet, and even the donkey he rode, had the gift of prophecy; so did Caiaphas, the ungodly high-priest, who assigned the death warrant of Jesus, and received the gift of prophecy and exercised it. Here Paul scans over the catalogue of spiritual gifts and not only pronounces them far inferior to the love of God in the heart, but utterly unprofitable to us without it. Paul exalts the gift of prophecy far above that of tongues. Baalim, the false prophet had it in a very pre-eminent sense. We read no grander eloquence, no more fervent pathos, brighter beauty, nor more exalted sublimity in the Bible, than those thrilling, transporting prophecies of Baalim; yet, while they do us good, they were utterly unprofitable to him, because he did not have the love of God poured out in his heart given unto him. In the exercise of these prophecies, while overlooking the goodly tents of Jacob, hear him shout, *"Let me die the death of the righteous, and my last end be like his."* We have no evidence that this fervent ejaculatory prayer was ever answered, because we have the gloomy record that he was killed in the Moabitish war, fighting against Israel, and the legitimate conclusion is that he lost his soul. Paul exalts prophecy far above the gift of tongues; yet here is a man who had it, in the superlative degree, and lost his soul, because he did not seek and find *"the more excellent way."*

It has been the climactive policy of Satan in all ages to magnify all non-essentials, lifting them between us and Christ, till we get our eyes on them, and lose sight of Jesus. Then we always begin to sink, whether, like Peter, we get our eyes on the water, or a third blessing, or spiritual gifts, or anything else not essential to salvation. I have often known people to backslide while building a wonderful church edifice; because in their enthusiasm for the fine house, they lost sight of Jesus, grieved the Holy Ghost and drifted away into a very seductive form of idolatry, *i. e.*, ecclesiolatry.

F. The great trouble with Israel was, not that they did not worship Jehovah, the God of Abraham, Isaac and Jacob; but that they would worship other gods in addition.

King Hezekiah, the greatest holiness leader in his day, in his iconoclastic enthusiasm, even utterly destroyed the brazen serpent, a very precious souvenir of a great deliverance, *i. e.*, because the people would burn incense to it. That is the reason why George Fox, the bright light of his age, repudiated the ordinances altogether, because he saw that the people would look to them for salvation; thus running into idolatry, living and dying without hope and without God.

Though the Babylonian captivity saved the Jews from the paganistic idolatry, into which they always, hitherto, would run headlong, despite the constant warnings of the prophets and the terrible judgments of God; though the effect of the captivity and its concomitant chastisement to effectually save them from the idolatry of the heathens, so that after their emancipation and restablishment in their own land, they nevermore went off after the paganistic idols; yet such was their predilection for idolatry, that after their emancipation and restablishment in Palestine, they actually idolized the Mosaic ordinances, and went deeper into idolatry, and became more abominable in the sight of God than ever before, so Jesus pronounced them hypocrites, "whited sepulchres," externally fair; as their professions were very bold and demonstrative, but internally filled with dead men's bones, and the blackest pollutions.

Satan is not particular what form of idolatry you go into; all he wants is to get your eye off of Jesus, and your feet side-tracked, and your bark stranded.

The ancient poets described two awful whirl-pools—the Scylla on the Italian shore, and the Carybdis on the Sicilian coast. The ancient mariners, without the power of the steam engine, to resist the suction of the gyratory waters, or the mariner's compass to guide them through fogs and storms, trembled with awe when they had to sail between these two whirl-pools, as they were in so much danger of abduction to the one or the other.

This illustration is exceedingly pertinent to the Holiness Movement, the most hopeful ship that plows the spiritual seas this day. We have dead churchisms, with the carnibinal allurements and seductions of the world, bringing into availability all power of money, style fashion, pomp, pageantry, influence and popularity, and at the same time, so winking at not only the popular sins, and seductive sins, but even the darker vices, that they come in like a tornado, throwing their seductive lassos through the air, thick as hail, to drop around the neck, hand or foot, or the whole body, and drag you away captive at Satan's victorious chariot wheels.

On the other side, we have multitudes of people marching under the broad and liberal banners of the

Holiness Movement, making the loudest professions and aspiring to the leadership, who are utterly out of harmony of the Word of God, and thereby demonstrating to all luminous people that they are the votaries of wild fanaticism, already side-tracked, derailed and wrecked, and in many cases, actually turned all the way around, and running on the Black Valley Railroad, on down to Hell.

The definition of a fanatic is, "A person who is led away by an evil spirit, passing himself for the Holy Ghost." We have many now cognomened "Holiness," who clearly demonstrate the incontestable fact that they have gone into fanaticism, led away by Satan, or more probably, through some of his myrmidons.

G. We are nowhere commanded to follow the Holy Ghost, but all the time exhorted to follow the Lord, assured that in so doing, that the Holy Ghost is our Leader, *i e.*, our Guide and Escort, giving us all needed help in following Jesus. He does not call his own name but the name of Jesus. Therefore, beware of the spirit who says, "I am the Holy Ghost, so follow me." Look out, lest you get captured by a lying demon. The Holy Ghost always reveals Jesus, and gives you all the help you need to follow Him.

If we try to follow the Holy Ghost in his spiritual capacity, Satan and his myrmidons will walk right in, and say, "I am the Holy Ghost," deceive, side-track, and ruin you. But while Satan and the demons can play the Holy Ghost or the angel because they have no incarnation, they cannot play Jesus, because he has a human body, was born and lived and died on the earth and left His biography, Matthew, Mark, Luke and John, thus given as you have it in my translation in parallel columns, so you can read and thoroughly study this quadruple history; and in connection with it, you need, "Life of Jesus and His Apostles," and "Foot-prints of Jesus in the Holy Land."

You have most ample facilities to qualify you to follow Jesus securely and triumphantly defiant of all of Satan's side-tracking, derailing and ditching and stranding devices. So you are actually left without excuse.

Jesus tells us in St. John 5:43: *"I came in the name of My Father, and you will not follow Me: if another may come in his own name, you will follow him."* How alarmingly is this prophecy of our Infallible Savior now receiving its verification! People are constantly doing their best to get you to follow them, instead of following Jesus; while if you do, you will be lost forever.

How wonderfully God has perfectly provided for our security, if you follow Jesus only, neither devil nor demon can side track you, because none of them can play Jesus; from the simple fact, that they have no incarnation. But these evil spirits in cooperation with false prophets on all sides, whom they occupy and through whose vocal organs they speak, preaching your sermons so beautiful and seductive, and at the same time, bragging on you (Rom. 16:18), that if you do not watch and pray, and keep your eyes steadfastly on Jesus, they are going to deceive you, deflect you, step by step from the narrow way.

The Holy Ghost, both through human instrumentality, using the people in whom He abides, and His control of the vocal organs, and *per se* (through Himself) He has commanded us (2 Tim. 2:15), *"Study to show thy-*

self approved of God, rightly dividing the Word of truth, a workman not to be ashamed." The holiness people are constantly invaded by interlopers, actuated by carnal motives (Rom. 16: 18), *"not serving the Lord Christ, but their own stomachs," "whose end is destruction, whose God is their stomach, and whose glory is in their shame; they are after earthly things."* (Phil 3: 19.)

When you examine the plain Word of God, you find them out of harmony with it, proving demonstratively that they are led away by demons who played the Holy Ghost on them, inflated them with vanity and egotism, so that they have actually gone into fanaticism.

Jesus and the Apostles in their clear and unmistakable latter day prophecies, faithfully warn us against these seducing spirits, *"who pervert the Word of God into lasciviousness, professing freedom,"* but at the same time, being the slaves of corruption, bringing upon themselves swift destruction.

God, in His great mercy, amid these awful perils, has fortified us by perfect security, so that we are left without excuse. The only safe attitude is to follow Jesus, being led by the Holy Ghost, not only *per se,* but especially through His Word, which diligently studied, honestly and heroically appreciated, actually affords us infallible guidance; Jesus, the only Leader; the Holy Ghost, the only Guide, and God's Word, our only Authority. When out of this beautiful triple leadership, look out! because there is danger in darkness.

The inspired prophet says, *"The entrance of Thy Word giveth light."* The great trouble is, demonized leaders, actuated by carnal motives of filthy lucre or self-aggrandizement, *"if possible, will deceive the very elect." "Therefore, watch and pray, lest ye enter into temptation."*

H. N. B. Grace finds every human being a spiritual corpse, without a solitary scintilla of spiritual vitality. Therefore, the Omnipotent resurrection power, as a matter of absolute necessity, must supervene first of all. The Holy Ghost (the Executive of the Trinity, who is none other than the very and eternal God, the Creator of all things), must intervene, conquer the grim monster, who holds the soul in his black grip, monarch of all he surveys, and having conquered death and wrested from him his own scepter, thus clearing the way with the tread of a Conqueror, fully master of the situation, He executes the stupendous work of the new creation, as literally and really as when He created a world.

This conclusion is irrefutably sustained by the plain and unequivocal phraseology of God's Word, *humas epoyesse ontas nekrous tois paraptoomasin kai hamaritiais humon, "You hath He quickened, who were dead in your trespasses and sins."* Here God positively certifies that all sinners are spiritually dead; whereas the word used for "quicken" is that strong Greek compound *zoollpoyesc,* from *zooll,* "life," and *poyes,* "to create." Now this life is created in the spiritual corpse, which must afterward be divested of the grave-clothes and all the habitude of the dead. (St. John 11:43, 44.) When Jesus raised Lazarus from the dead He commanded them to, *"loose him and let him go."* This was absolutely indispensable. With his whole body wrapped in the winding sheet and the napkin bound on His face, so that He could not open his mouth, he would have been utterly incompetent to go and preach, as he actually did leave the city with

Jesus and preached the balance of his life. The reason why the churches are full of dummies and inefficient members is because, though raised from the dead, and brought into the Kingdom, they have not received the second work of grace, which is indispensable, to loose them, let them go, shine and shout and press the battle for God and souls.

1. While regeneration brings down the Tree of Life from Celestial Gardens, plants it in the soul-soil, it must receive inundation and perpetual attention, stirring the soil with the Gospel plow, digging out all of Satan's thorns with the Gospel mattock, diligently using the hoe and spade in the destruction of every obnoxious weed, insiduous bramble, cockle burr, Spanish needle, Canada thistle, deadly upas, narcotic strycknos, scrub pine, black jack, *et cetra*, whose seed is still lingering in the soul-soil, where Satan has sown it, and ready to spring up and dispute the prerogative of the new-comer to the sole occupancy of the land. Not only must you thus diligently expurgate the soul-soil, but irrigate, especially in times of drought, not neglecting to fertilize, and the more copiously the better, and the more prolific your crop and superabounding your harvest.

"But will not Satan sow more seed in your fields and gardens after you have actually destroyed every obnoxious weed and bramble, so that you will have to be always repeating your expurgatory labors?" Glory to God! grace is stronger than sin; the Holy Ghost is more than a match for the devil. You throw wide open the door and invite Him to come in, expel and destroy your enemy, and take complete possession and abide forever. In that case, He is sure to do it, giving you an everlasting victory over the world, the flesh and the devil. Verily Satan comes daily with his great bag of Spanish needles, cockle burrs, Canada thistles, deadly upas and narcotic strychnos, sowing these pestilential seeds with his *huncalun anus in* copious quantities from his gigantic hands, literally filling the atmosphere, determined to verify that Scripture, *"He that sows bountifully, shall reap bountifully."* But not a solitary seed lights on my soil. Why? Because the fires of the Holy Ghost are sweeping in Heavenly conflagration over my soul, consuming all the need the devil, *"the prince of the power of the air"* (Eph. 2:2), can ever sow.

N. B. These two great works of grace, regeneration and sanctification, constitute the pair of oars, by which we row the life boat across time's stormy sea and reach a safe landing on the bright golden shore, where we sing and shout, our troubles o'er, where the wicked cease from troubling, and the weary are forever at rest. Be sure you make the landing safe. Many a storm you must stem; many a tornado you must weather; many a hurricane you must meet; many a cyclone you must outride.

I launched my bark in 1849 A. D. These sixty-two years God has given me headway o'er this stormy sea. I now have a constant view of the heavenly highways; see bright angels on the wing, and many loved ones waving palms of victory, as they tread the radiant heights. Meanwhile I already snuff the heavenly breezes, laden with the delicious fragrance of never-fading flowers, and never-failing fruits, while the melodies of celestial psalms and golden harps, mingled with angelic anthems and redemption's triumphant song, vocalized by the sacramental host, so electrifying my soul, as already to drop the oblivious curtain over bygone troubles, broils, sorrows and disappointments, and even superinduce regret, that I have not been permitted to suffer and endure more for Him, who bled and died for me.

"I've found a Friend in Jesus; He's everything to me;
   The fairest of ten thousand to my soul,
The Lily of the Valley, in Him, alone, I see,
   All I need to cleanse and make me fully whole.
In sorrow He's my comfort, in trouble He's my Stay;
   He tells me every care on Him to roll.
He's the Lily of the Valley; the Bright and Morning Star,
   He's the fairest of ten thousand to my soul.

He all my grief has taken, and all my sorrows borne;
   In temptation He's my strong and mighty tower;
I've all for Him forsaken, and all my idols torn
   From my heart, and now He keeps me by His power.
Though all the world forsake me, and Satan tempts me sore,
   Through Jesus I shall safely reach the goal;
He's the Lily of the Valley; the Bright and Morning Star;
   He's the fairest of ten thousand to my soul!

He'll never, never leave me, nor yet forsake me here,
   While I live by faith and do His blessed will,
A wall of fire about me, I've nothing now to fear,
   With His manna He my hungry soul shall fill.
When crowned at last in glory, I'll see His blessed face,
   Where rivers of delight shall ever roll,
He's the Lily of the Valley; the Bright and Morning Star,
   He's the fairest of ten thousand to my soul."

J. This *agape is the Divine nature.* (1 John 4:8, 16.) "*God is (agape) Divine love,*" when poured out into the heart of the poor, despondent penitent, who dares to reach forth the withered hand of faith and receive God's pardoning mercy in Christ; actually brings the resurrection power into the dead soul, the Holy Ghost creating a new world in the heart, and making the dead sinner a new creature in Christ, so that he leaps for joy, shouts day and night, and fondly dreams that he will never sin again. He goes to bed happy, and wakes up in the morning as blue as indigo; looks into his heart, and finds it enveloped in a black cloud; exclaims in his horror: "Is it possible, I have slept my religion away, and am again a miserable sinner?"

Such was the experience of Bud Robinson, after a joyous conversion, followed many days with shouts of victory. It has been the experience of thousands. What is the solution? Inbred sin in an old log in the deep interior of the spiritual organism, surrounded by dark jungles, generating miasmata, whose pestilential vapors rise in clouds, and anon prove too much for the heavenly breezes to blow away and the effulgent rays of the Son of righteousness to dissipate in the normal grace of regeneration. Consequently, the life is an alternation of light and darkness.

John Fletcher, expounding this beautiful and wonderful problem about Christian perfection, tells us about a community in England, where malarial fevers and chills so prevailed that people sickened and died on all sides; many actually migrating away to heathful regions. Physicians with one voice imputed the malaria to a great bogg in their midst, whose stagnant waters generated the miasmata. In time of the raging fevers, deep distress and general alarm, the magistrate calls a mass-meeting to consider the enterprise of removing the boggy drainage. To this they unanimously consent, and resolve to begin with the next rising sun. Consequently, they are all on hand the ensuing morning with their wagons and teams (as they had no machinery then, as we do now), to haul away the water and tilt it over a contiguous hill, thus draining the bogg. They work hard all day, and sink it down considerably, so they are much encouraged. But next morning, when they return to resume their labors, they are dumbfounded to find the water just as high as the preceding morning when they began their drainage. This puzzles them out of their wits, and superinduces the cry, "What shall we do?" When a philosopher, rising up, brings a sun burst to the relief of the prevailing despondency, observing: "Gentlemen, this brings us light and joyous hope. There is in the bottom of this bogg is a never-failing spring. Consequently we never can get rid of it by dipping out the water. We will go to work, tunnel the hill, and let the water all run out." All agree and proceed at once. Soon the bog is gone forever, and the beautiful spring of nice, limpid water, is the joy of the community. Meanwhile, the lands relieved of the bogg, which had occupied them from creation's morn, and made them rich as the Garden of the Lord, became the most valuable in the entire community, marvelous in fertility and productiveness, and actually worth a thousand dollars an acre.

You will find this literally true, if you will drain away the old boggs which have infected the atmosphere of this lost world with the malaria of hereditary depravity ever since the days of Eden. The drainage of that bogg not only relieves the community of the pestilence, but turns it into an earthly paradise, augmenting the value of the profits a hundred per cent.

If all the world had told me I would be a book-writer while I lived on the regeneration plane, those nineteen years, from 1849 A. D. to 1868 A. D., I would not have believed it. Yet, it is a fact, to myself paradoxical, when I tell you you are now reading the fiftieth book dictated by your humble servant. Before I got rid of the old bogg, it was harder work to prepare two sermons a week for Sunday than since that day to preach twenty-five a week. Now, in the fifty-fourth year of my ministry, and seventy-fourth of my age, I preach day and night all the week and three to six times on Sunday.

Sanctification actually made me a preaching-machine. If I had not received it, my conference would have superannuated me ere this, not because I am seventy-four years old, but for the obvious reason that they superannuate all of their old men, after their service, their physical power, the voice, becoming weak and cracked; therefore they superannuate them, because they can get no appointment where the people are willing to receive them, as they correctly recognize power as a *sine qua non* of ministerial efficiency.

K. Oh, how Satan fools the preachers, telling them that if they get sanctified they will have no place to preach, as nobody will want them. One thing we must admit, and that is the devil is the biggest liar in the world; demonstrated in this very instance, as the facts overwhelmingly confirm the very opposite. Instead of having no place to preach, we are bewildered with more open doors than we can possibly enter; *e. g.,* myself this day have openings enough for a thousand preachers,

THE DIVINE AGAPE. 121

actually calling me from the rising of the sun to the going down of the same. I have them in the old world, as clamorously for my humble service, as I traveled around, that I actually promised them, D. V., to come back after three years and help them in their arduous labors to save the lost millions from ages immemorial, sitting low down in the valley and shadow of death; the insatiate cry of the soul for the Bread of Heaven, and the Water of Life, only mocked by the senseless mutter of pagan priests and Moslem prophets. We cannot censure the people for demanding power and availability on the part of their preachers. When we get old, of course, we all realize an abatement of physical power. Consequently the unsanctified preachers all have to superannuate. But do you not know that spiritual power is infinitely better than physical? This, if you are sanctified, will never evanesce, but accumulate grander impetus and momentum, not only till we lay the armor down and arise to the Mount of Victory; but triumphant over all the gloomy shadows with which the grim monster beclouds and eclipses the last hope of this world, our evacuation of this tenement will be like that of the chrysalis, that bursts his cumbrous shell and soars on butterfly wings in the golden sunlight. The fact is, unsanctified, you are utterly ignorant of your own availability. Therefore, even appertaining to this life, you clip your own pinions by neglecting sanctification, thus consigning yourself to mediocrity; while God wants you to shine—a star of the first magnitude, in the constellation, in which His Infallible Providence has placed you.

It is your glorious privilege to succeed and excel in your day and generation, if you will drain the bogg, get rid of the malarial fevers, and chills, and cultivate the rich virgin soil of Emmanuel's lands, lying at the bottom, forever obscured and vitiated by the superincumbant stagnant waters, fit for nothing but to generate miasmata and disseminate malaria, hastening millions to premature graves.

L. As God is a trinity, so is man, consisting of spirit, soul and body. While God is a Trinity in three personalities, accommatory to the wonderful scheme of redemption, yet He is a unit, an omniscient, omnipotent, omnipresent Spirit, a perfect sphere, without beginning or end; so man is a unit, an immortal spirit, whom God created in His own immortality. While the human spirit consists of the conscience, the will and the affections, the soul consists of the intellect, the memory, the sensibilities, and the physical life—the spirit which is the man himself, in the providences of God, the proprietor of the soul and body, alone is totally depraved, *i. e.,* utterly destitute of vitality.

When God said, *"Thou shalt surely die,"* He did not say, "Your mind shall die," as in that case he would have become utterly idiotic when he sinned; neither did He say, "Your body shall die," as in that event, he would have dropped a corpse; but he did say, *"Thou shalt surely die,"* consequently, he then and there forfeited the Divine life out of his spirit. This life was not essential to his existence, as a mental and physical being, which he certainly was antecedently to the impartation of his human spirit, when God breathed it into him. While total depravity is literally true, it is purely spiritual in its significance, because man neither forfeited life, mental nor physical by the the fall, but only entailed on the former an awful distressing paralysis, obviously contrasting with the wonderful brilliancy and intellectual power, which qualified Adam by simple diagnosis to look through every animal and apprehend its real character, which was abundantly evinced by the name he gave them all in the powerful and simple Hebrew, relatory of their true character.

The effect of the fall on his physical being was simply the forfeiture of immortality, and a verification of the decree, *"Dust thou art, and down to dust shalt thou return."*

The reason why the preachers stagger so over the doctrine of total depravity, which is so positively and copiously revealed in the Bible, as to leave no room for cavil or controversy, is because the antagonistical phenomena so abound that walking in the light of their intellect, they intuitively acquiesce in it; failing to discriminate between mentalities and spiritualities.

N. B. All religion is spirituality. Here is the lamentable deficiency of the popular pulpits, which has been side-tracked by Satan down from the heights of spirituality to the lower plane of mentalities, conserving human learning as a vain and empty substitute for the Holy Ghost.

M. The human spirit, which is the man proper, is made perfect in the glorious restitutionary of entire sanctification. Subsequently to the reception of this experience, we are more or less encumbered with infirmities, which are mental and physical, and not spiritual; though unilluminated people are prone to think they are, and consequently, discount our testimony.

Sin is manifest in three distinct departments—actual, original and inadvertent (through ignorance.)

Actual sins, with all their condemnation, are eliminated in conversion, which consists of justification, removing condemnation, and regeneration, raising the dead spirit into life, and making you a member of God's family, and a citizen of His Kingdom.

Original sin, which though conquered in regeneration, and grace given to keep it from breaking out into actual transgressions, still survives regeneration, warring against the Holy Spirit (Gal. 5:17), giving us terrible trouble ever and anon, and constantly exposing to the liability of defeat in spiritual combat; is utterly expurgated away by the cleansing blood and its contaminatory debris, thus consummating the glorious experience of Christian perfection, as taught in the Bible.

N. As the human spirit, or heart, which is the man proper, is made perfect in the glorious work of entire sanctification, therefore this experience brings its happy recipients up above the regeneration plain, where they have grace to tread the Heights of Holiness, till called from labor to rest, having been delivered from all sin, actual and original.

This glorious experience, however, is incident to a vast amount of popular criticism, even incurring the condemnation of many honest, sincere people, because they see them do things, which they regard incompatible with the profession which they make. Therefore, stumbling over the lives of its votaries, many, to their own serious detriment, reject the doctrine, and decline to seek the experience of Christian perfection. This arises from the fact that sanctification only takes away inbred sin, and does not save us from sins of ignorance, which are neither condemnatory nor contaminatory; but innocent inadvertencies, under which we do wrong, aiming to do right.

These infirmities, *i. e.*, *sins* of ignorance, though compatible with Christian perfection, are utterly out of harmony with the angelic perfection, which we must all receive before we enter Heaven.

This angelic perfection is not for this life, but Heaven. We see it revealed in St. Luke 20: 35, 36 in the response of our Savior to the insidious question of the Pharisees, relative to the woman who had successively been the wife of seven brothers, beginning with the first, who died, leaving her to his younger brother, and continuing to the last; she finally surviving all. Jesus said, *"In that day, they neither marry, or are given in marriage: but are like the angels of God; the sons of the resurrection."*

Here the word is *isoiangeloi,* from *isos,* "equal" and *angelos,* "angel;" therefore, it means "equal to the angels, or like the angels." The angels have knowledge so perfect, within their sphere, as to be free from mistakes, being a higher order of being than we are, till this mortal shall put on immortality.

The Holy Ghost, the omnipotent executive of the Trinity, administers three great works of grace in the stupendous redemption of humanity from the fall; regeneration for the sinner, creating in him spiritual life; sanctification for the Christian, eliminating out of him all the debris of spiritual death, and filling him with the Holy Spirit; and finally glorification, in the hour of physical dissolution, which delivers us from sins of ignorance, which are the infirmities resultant from the fall, and investing us with angelic perfection.

Much opposition to sanctification originates from a mistake at this point, confounding it with glorification, and thus discarding it as inattainable in this life, and incompatible with it, acquiescing in the conclusion, that we should content ourselves to do without it till we die, trusting God to sanctify us in the article of death. This is not only false, but fraught with imminent peril, superinducing the lethean slumber of carnal security; till it is too late and like Dives, looking out for Heaven, found himself in hell.

This deplorable mistake illustrates the importance of true Bible teaching, which relieves the unhappy misapprehension, which is so eminently fraught with danger of losing our souls.

God has decreed, *"Without sanctification no one shall see the Lord."* (Heb. 12:14.) Therefore we should beware of Satan's siren song, constantly ringing in unsanctified ears, to lull them to sleep in carnal security, till the golden moments all have fled and the last grain of sand dropped from the dial of time and the soul, seized by cruel demons, hurried away into hell-fire.

The mistake they make is that of confounding sanctification with glorification, for which we have to wait till we reach the end of this life, and this mortal shall put on immortality. This is the work that would sweep away all our infirmities, so after we get to Heaven, we will never make any more mistakes.

While sanctification gives us spiritual perfection, it does not make our memories, judgment, apprehension, and reasoning perfect, as these do not belong to the realm of spirituality, but mentality.

The blessed Holy Spirit in the great consummating work of the transfiguration, in case we live till His glorious appearing, and glorification, if He tarrieth, till our work is done, and sends an angel for us, as in the case of Lazarus; when He will forever sweep away all our infirmities, conferring on us angelic perfection, which will give us perfect intellect, memory, judgment, and sensibilities, and flood us with ecstacy and rhapsody of unmingled joy, which will last through all eternity.

In the disembodied state, we will have neither brain to be crazed, nor nerves to be paralized, as we will no longer need them. We will be free from all infirmities, which are the normal effects of the fall, but amply provided for in the blessed and wonderful atonement. The infirmities of temporal affliction and age, will be a matter of the eternal past. We will never get old, but bloom in immortal youth, through all eternity.

We frankly admit our real identity in the glorious beyond. Those who have been honored to live long and die old, will still be themselves, but free from all of the infirmities of age.

o. While sanctification is the indispensable *sine qua non* of Christian experience, as God in His precious and infallible Word positively reveals in Heb. 12:14, *"The sanctification, without which no one shall see the Lord;"* He does not say this about any other grace, evidently because sanctification is the climax, everything else subsidiary and conservatory, and without which, soon or late, justification, regeneration, adoption, reconciliation, yea the entire constellation of those beautiful graces which constitute the great work of initial salvation will, e'er long, go into eclipse, amid the fogs exhaled from the dismal miasmatic swamps of inbred sin; their glory wane; their beauty evanesce; their feet slide, and the once hopeful pilgrims, expectant of glory and immortality, retrogress, and finally land in a backslider's hell; the blessed Holy Spirit, their keeper, having been grieved away, because by diabolical unbelief, they rejected his sanctifying office, and power.

While the corner-stone of the beautiful holiness temple is a clean heart, without which, like every other house built on the sand without a foundation, it will, soon or late, topple and fall; we must all admit that perfect love, which is none other than Divine nature, unmixed and utterly alien from carnality, which is Satanic; constitutes the superstructure.

The fondest device of Satan is to manipulate the leakage of love, which he brings about in many ways; *e. g.,* unwatchfulness, trivialities, frivolities, follies, hilarities, levities and everything trashy and valueless. The fond device of Satan is clandestinary, to drop his gall into the honey of perfect love. Heb. 2: 1: *"Therefore it behooveth us to give the more earnest heed to the things which we have heard, lest at some time we may leak out."* Here the blessed Holy Spirit solemnly warns us against the leakage of love.

If a water-barrel begins to leak, it will never stop till every drop is gone; because the staves above the water exposed to solar heat shrink up all the time, extending that shrinkage a little below the water surface, thus perpetuating the leakage incessantly *ad infinitum*, till every drop is gone, and the barrel falls to staves.

The Divine Agape. 129

Now what is the effectual preventive of this calamitous result? Rest assured, there is but one, and that is to keep the barrel full of water; therefore its place is under the spout, where, of course, it will run over; but that is all right, because the goslings, ducks, and chickens are entirely dependent on this overflow.

At this point, we discover the missing keystone from multiplied thousands of fallen arches, followed by the ruinous dilapidation of Christian character, which in days gone by did shine with the beauty inspiring all to press their march up the King's Highway. You must have a clean heart and keep it clean, with a conscience void of offense toward God and man; you must be filled and keep full of the sweet, perfect love of God, or you will collapse, soon or late, and drop into a backslider's Hell.

This *"perfect love thinketh no evil."* That does not mean that you never think *about* the evil which is in the world, but no evil thoughts of the carnal mind, and you get to where you truly say,

> "Lord let me die so dead,
> That no desire shall rise,
> To pass for good or great or wise,
> In any but my Savior's eyes."

Jesus prayed earnestly for His enemies, while their hands were red with His innocent blood, and demoniacally they were revelling in the work of death; not only killing Him, but mocking and insulting Him at the same time. Yet He used His dying breath praying for them, *"Father, forgive them; for they know not what they are doing."* He is our only Exampler and Leader. If we do not walk in His footprints, we are undone and our hope evanesced.

p. Here multitudes of holiness people, to their inefficable shame, give themselves away, advertising their hypocrisy to all the world; *e. g.*, the people who followed the "Burning Bush" into the wildest fanaticism, reading and imbibing and feasting their sordid vanity and curiosity on their satirical caricatures, and cruel cartoons.

Perfect love does not discriminate. God loves the vilest sinner as truly as the purest saint. He has already demonstrated His perfect love for the vilest of the vile, by coming down and dying for them. "Must I love the drunkard, thief, debauchee, the murderer, the harlot, with perfect love?" Certainly! In case of these poor souls, wrecked and ruined with which we pursue them for their salvation, even gladly imperil our lives, takes the form of sympathy, pity and kindness, which are so powerful as actually to induce us to lay down our lives to save them.

On the contrary, our love for the beautiful and amiable saintly characters, who light this dark world with the effulgence, radiate from the glorious Son of Righteousness, is characterized and accompanied by appreciation, endorsement, adoration, fraternity and fellowship; yet it is no stronger, nor more intense, heroic and self-sacrificing than our love for the poor victims of Hell's cruelty and Satan's murder, low down in the filthy cesspools, on the bottom of slumdom.

Veritively, perfect love is the angel color-bearer on every battle-field fought by Immanuel's host against the armies of Hell, in order to conquer the world for our King, who has redeemed it with His precious blood.

THE DIVINE AGAPE. 131

Therefore we must always keep it prominent, not only before our own eyes, but all the people to whom we minister the Word of Life. It is the testing phrase of the sanctified experience; whose deficiency demonstrates the problem, discriminating between the genuine and Satan's counterfeit.

Does your heart run out in real love, sympathy and kindness for every human being; yea, the animal creation too?

Q. No wonder Satan by his counterfeits—third works of grace, and so magnifying non-essentials as to cunningly manipulate to get the eye off of Christ and the heart turned to something that has nothing to do with salvation; seeking after power, the baptism of fire; getting immersed in water; seeking the gift of tongues, all of which are proper in their places; but when unduly magnified, become mountains between you and Christ, and as a normal sequence, utilized by Satan to subterfuge us into Hell.

The truly sanctified experience, saved from all human following, and walking in the foot-prints of Jesus alone, with no guide but the Holy Ghost, and no authority but His Word, actually taking Jesus for everything—your Prophet, Priest, Atoning Savior, Glorious Lord and Coming King—emptied of sin and filled with the Holy Ghost; deaf to every human voice, which does not simply reiterate the Word of God; actually demanding a *"thus saith the Lord"* for everything; accepting nothing for authority but the *ipse dixit* of the Almighty; ever wakeful and appreciative of the battle tocsin, your sword unsheathed and the scabbard thrown away; ready, responsive to the drum beat, to rush to the scene of conflict, tip-toe the firing line; always seeking the hottest of the battle and thickest of the fight; ever ready *"to endure hardness as a good soldier."* I care not how plausible the sugar-coated message that even indirectly depreciates the supernatural birth and entire sanctification and the perfect love filling the heart, you may know it is the intrigue of the enemy, *"by fair speeches and eulogies to deceive the hearts of the innocent."* (Rom. 16:18.) Rest assured, all such machinations and maneuvers are from the bottomless pit, freighted with delusion and damnation.

CHAPTER X.

ELECTION OF GRACE AND REPROBATION AND FORE-KNOWLEDGE.

In some theologies, election is so prominent, as actually to become the pillar of the entire superstructure; *e. g.*, the Calvinistic theology expounds the Bible from the standpoint of election and reprobation, hypothecating a certain number elected, and the balance all reprobated.

On the subject of election, we have to recognize the election of grace, as absolutely necessary to salvation; whereas the election of the Messianic progenitorship is in no way essential to salvation.

The election of grace has two phases homogeneous with the two great works of grace—regeneration and sanctification. In the first place, regeneration secures our election to citizenship in the Kingdom; whereas reprobation forever alienates and abnegates that citizenship.

The second election secures our membership in the Bridehood of Christ. This is an irrefutable confirmation of the two works of grace, executive of the redemptive scheme; the one conferring on you citizenship in the Kingdom, and the other membership in the Bridehood.

At this point, the Zinzendorfians run into difficulties absolutely inextricable. Their hypothesis of full salvation by a single work of grace, inevitably charges our Lord with going to Satan for a wife; which is utterly untrue and revoltingly incompatible with His Word, which positively forbids us to do such a thing.

Rest assured, Jesus always practises what He preaches. The reason why it would not do for Isaac to wed a daughter of Canaan, was because they were idolators, Therefore Eleazar had to go far away to Chaldea and bring Rebecca from the house of his kindred, who were worshippers of Jehovah.

But the subject of election is beautiful, charming and copious throughout the Bible. The word is *eclestos,* from the Greek *lego,* "to choose," and *kaleo,* and *ec,* "from."

Now the popular idea prevails that the foreknowledge of God is determined by the election of the righteous and the reprobation of the wicked. Rom. 8:30: *"Whom He did predestinate, them He also called: and whom He called, them He also justified: and them He justified, them He also glorified."*

The people get tangled upon the subject of election when they undertake to harmonize it with the illimitable foreknowledge of God; drifting to the conclusion that His foreknowledge determines all human destiny, whether for weal or woe. That is impossible for us to controvene our own destiny and deflect it from the annunciated decrees of God.

If you will investigate an item in the biography of David, during those memorable seven years, while Saul was on his track with his army to kill him, and he was a fugitive for his life (read 1 Samuel 23:1-15), you will find he, with his six hundred men, went down to the city of Keilah, which had been seriously troubled with

Philistine invasions, making raids into the country, robbing their threshing floors and spoliating their herds and flocks. When David and his men fought and defeated them and drove them out of the country, the people of Keilah showed their highest appreciation of the priceless benefactors, which David and his men had conferred on them, thus delivering them from the distressing and protracted annoyances of their enemies.

Ere long, David gets word that Saul is on his track with a great army. The normal conclusion would have assured him of security there among the people who had manifested the greatest appreciation of the kind service and glorious victory he had achieved for them over their enemies. But, blest as he was with the spirit of prophecy, he suspected unfaithfulness on their part, despite their great indebtedness to him for the priceless deliverance he had conferred on them. Thus suspicious that in a case of emergency, if Saul should come, they would purchase royal favor with his head, he takes the ephod from Abiathar, the surviving priest of Nob, whose sacerdotal comrades, eighty-one in number, had all been slain by Doeg, the cruel Edomite, responsive to the mandate of Saul, because they had protected and fed David and his men, while flying from Saul. This ephod had those precious stones Urim and Thummim, whose colors by their strange mutations gave responses revelatory of the Divine Word. So, David taking the ephod, inquires of the Lord, *"Will Saul come down to Keilah?"* The answer follows, *"He will come down." "Will the men of Keilah deliver me up?"* The answer comes, *"They will deliver thee."* Then David arises at once, blows the bugle, marshalls his men, and bids them: "Off without a moment's delay; forward march; double quick out of Keilah with all possible expedition, as Saul is hot on our track, coming with a great army, and though the Keilites have been making all the world of us, they are going to play treason, and purchase royal favor with our heads." Consequently, they all stir, put out at once and make their escape. Meanwhile, Saul, who had his scouts constantly reconnoitering David's movements, having heard that he had gone away from Keilah, did not come to it; but changed his course, bearing eastwardly, in order to intercept David in his flight.

Thus after God had said, *"Saul will come down to Keilah, and they will deliver thee up,"* you see neither of these apparent decrees took place. The Bible is the most sensible Book in the world. David was acquainted with God and understood His speech, knowing that he was free, and if he did not take warning in making his escape, Saul would come down and the Keilites would deliver him up. If David had been superstitious enough to believe that "what is to be will be," and that "human agency could not contravene the 'shalls and wills' in the Bible," he would have put his face between his hands, sat down and wept over his impending doom. But when the answer of God came, *"Saul will come down; and they will deliver thee up;"* this was David's warning to make his escape in order to save his life.

R. We must recognize two great cardinal facts, *i. e.*, God's providence, and man's free agency. They are both true; yet we cannot always harmonize them. It is a mistake to try. *We are saved by faith* and not by knowledge; therefore, the thing for us to do is to believe and obey.

ELECTION OF GRACE. 137

"Can events transpire, which God does not foreknow?" We answer it in the negative, as God is omniscient; He knows the future, as well as the present and the past. "Then, does not that foreknowledge predestinate it?" We respond in the negative from the simple fact that knowing that a thing will come to pass does not necessitate the verification of the thing known. You see your son drinking and debauching his life away, filling his body with poisons, so he cannot live. You know he is killing himself, body and soul, yet your knowledge does not make it; on the contrary, you would give your life to prevent it.

N. B. Knowledge is not causative, and consequently, does not cause anything. Jeremiah foreknew that the Chaldeans would take Jerusalem, and carry the Jews captive to Babylon, yet his knowledge did not cause those terrible calamities. The rulers of the city arrested him, and would have killed him for high-treason, if God had not delivered him. Hence you see the foreknowledge of a thing does not cause that thing to take place. People are still free, and if they change, then the events predicted will be changed.

Jonah prophesied, *"Yet forty days and Nineveh shall be destroyed."* The Ninevites believed his message, and repented before God, in sackcloth and ashes; God had mercy, and spared them. Two hundred years rolled away before the terrible doom of destruction came on the city. There can be no doubt, but Jerusalem would have been captured and the Jews carried into captivity by Sennacherib, in the days of King Hezekiah, if the people, lead by the sanctified King, and the prophet Isaiah had not cried mightily to God, so that He heard their mournful wails and saw their tears and sent an angel at midnight to destroy Sennacherib's army, actually slaying 185,000 men, thus bringing deliverance to the people, and postponing the awful destruction coming upon Jerusalem, for her wicked idolatry, till that generation had passed away.

The Bible repeatedly says that God's mercy endureth forever. Therefore the thing for us all to do, is to repent of all our sins, seek the Lord with all the heart, and soul, and never desist. Satan's fond device is to run people into despair, so they will not repent, then he will get them. Truly it has been said, that men make their own election. *We elect God and He elects us; it is mutual and reciprocal.* Paul, in Rom. 1:28-32, clearly answers the complicated question on election and reprobation, submitting in beautiful candor and simplicity the mournful history of the world's apostasy from God, first into intellectualism; then into idolatry, and finally into brutality, where the description is horrific beyond all conception. *"And as they did not approve to have God in their knowledge, God gave them up to a reprobate mind, to do the things which are abominable; being filled with all unrighteousness, wickedness, coveteousness, vice; full of envy, murder, strife, hypocrisy, evil affections; eavedroppers, calumniators, haters of God, insulters, proud, arrogant, covenant breakers, without natural affections, unmerciful; who knowing the righteousness of God, who knowing that those doing such things are worthy of death, not only do the same things, but indeed take delight in those who do them."* This description is black and appalling as Hell can be, it is spiritually a Hell on earth; the poor brutalized people, actually, not only living like animals, but infinitely worse, like brutalized demons, such is the awful condition of the heathens this day. Oh! what an inspiration to run to their relief.

You see, as Paul here certifies, "the people reprobated God and then God reprobated them." God never interferes with our free agency, as in so doing, He would dehumanize us.

A great holiness evangelist recently wrote in a leading holiness paper, an article stating that God sometimes saves people against their will. He made a great mistake. Let us profit by it, and steer as clear from error as possible, as it is to be dreaded like the rocks by the sailors.

s. The logical error in this matter is confounding things which are dissimilar, *i. e.*, making the heterogenous homogeneous. Arminians in order to escape the dilemma sometimes limit the foreknowledge of God, which is a great mistake, as with Omniscience all things are present in one eternal now. Meanwhile, Calvinists drift to the other horn of the dilemma, and acquiesce, in the dogma of unconditional election, and absolute predestination. These dogmata are true appertaining to the Messianic progenitorship, which is not essential to salvation, while the mysterious problems, so far as they appertain to personal salvation, are in perfect harmony with the freedom of the will. (Rom. 8: 29.) *"Because whom He did foreknow, them He did also predestinate to be conformed to the image of His Son."* Here you see the foreknowledge is precedent to the predestination, *i. e.*, God foreknows what we are going to choose, and makes our appointment accordingly. Meanwhile, He lays no restriction in the freedom of our will, from the simple fact that knowledge and influence are not identical, nor even homegeneous, but dissimiliar and heterogeneous.

An old pilot, who has spent his life on the Atlantic Ocean, and knows every track through the briny deep, stands on the wharf at New York, and sees his ship sail. He knows she will be wrecked, because insuperable obstructions lie in that route; yet his knowledge, being in its very nature uncausative, has actually nothing to do with the wreckage.

All illustrations elucidatory of these mysteries, are only partial in their efficiency, because all human knowledge is imperfect, but they do perfectly illustrate the fact that knowledge is not influence.

Thus we see in the above Scripture, which is the Calvinistic Gibraltar, that the foreknowledge preceeds the predestination, and is not identical with it, that the perfect Divine wisdom simply makes the appointment, according to the character of the appointee. Meanwhile, every one is the maker of his own character, freely doing what he will: yet Omniscience seeing just what he is going to do of his own free-will and accord, makes His appointment accordingly.

Then you see, it could not be otherwise. This conclusion, you see, refuted in the case of David at Keilah; when he asked the Lord: *"Will Saul come to Keilah,"* and received the answer, *"He will come."* Then propounding the question, *"Will the Keilites deliver me up;"* the answer comes, *"They will deliver thee up."* (1 Samuel 23.) David, understanding the ways of God, better than the predestinarians of our day, immediately fled away with his army. Then, Saul hearing that he was gone did not come down. Therefore the Divine decrees and predestinations are perfectly compatible with our freedom, so that so far as salvation is concerned, it has been truly said that we make our own decrees.

Sam Jones pertinently said: "The elect is the man that will, and the none-elect, the man that will not."

What about Pharaoh? (Rom. 9: 17.) *"For the Scripture says in reference to Pharaoh, For this very thing I have raised thee up, in order that I may show forth my power in thee, and my Name may be proclaimed in all the earth."* This Pharaoh, Rameses II. was, as history identifies, Sesostris, the first man to conquer the world (which was quite small at that time), and stand at the front. Consequently, he had at his command all the men and money of all the nations, and was the very man to preach the Gospel to all the world. God never mocks anybody. He dealt candidly and justly with Pharaoh, sending him His two best preachers to proclaim to him the true God, then worshipped by his Hebrew slaves. It was His purpose that Pharaoh should receive the Gospel at the hands of Moses and Aaron, and become a convert to the great Jehovah, then only known to one, here and there, except those Hebrew slaves. The mistake of Pharaoh's life was his rejection of the Gospel, preached by Moses and Aaron, and this proved his ruin. Oh! what a grand opportunity he had! Monarch of the world, with all the resources of the earth to carry the Gospel throughout the world, thus proclaiming the Name and salvation of the true God in every nation. Pharaoh, like all sinners who reject the Gospel. and make their bed in Hell, was freely the arbiter of his own destiny.

T. V. 21-23. "*Hath not the potter power over the clay, of the same lump to make one vessel unto honor, and another unto dishonor? If God, wishing to manifest His wrath, and make His power known, endured with much longsuffering the vessels of wrath having been perfected for destruction: that He might make known the riches of His glory in the vessels of mercy, which He prepared for His glory.*" The word "honor" here means, "financial remuneration," *i. e.,* the vessels which brought good money to the potter be called "honorable;" while he designated those, on which he lost money "dishonorable."

You know, every mechanic simply works for remuneration, therefore, when the potter proceeds to make his diversified ware, he invariably contemplates financial remuneration in case of every one. Then, as he never aimed to make a dishonorable vessel, how does it happen that he gets them on hand? While he is going with the *modus operandi,* doing his best to make a vessel that will command the money all right, and remunerate him for his labor and material, behold, the clay mars in his hands, and the vessel is cracked and spoiled, till it is utterly worthless, and fit only for the ditch. Therefore, he has the expense of hauling these spoiled vessels away and casting them into the washes. If the potter were omnipotent, he would never make a vessel unto dishonor; he does it inadvertently, because he cannot help it. Then how does this apply to the omnipotent potter? You see, from the analogy, as the potter always aims to make an honorable vessel, which will remunerate him, it follows that God always aims to make a good man, who will

ELECTION OF GRACE.

glorify Him in time and eternity. Then, why does it turn out that He ever makes a bad one? The potter never aims to make a spoiled vessel, but the clay mars in his hands, while on the lathe, and the job turns out a failure, despite all he can do. Then, how could this apply to an omnipotent potter? God has created us with a free-will, consequently we are optionary to reciprocate or antagonize. When we do the latter, we actually mar God's glorious and merciful work, and spoil it forever, ultimately landing in Hell, the only receptical of the ruined vessels.

Here we have the word, *kateertismena,* the perfect passive participle from *katartizoo,* which means "to make perfect;" this strong perfect participle is followed by *eisapooleian,* "unto destruction."

This is God's revelation of the awful destiny, incident to the wicked. Just as the potter's vessel, in the midst of his best efforts, to make it all right, despite all he can do, breaks in his hands, and is fit for nothing but the ditch as it is a well-known fact, that he cannot use the spoiled vessels in any way, hence he is under necessity of dumping them into the deep washes, and leaving them forever. So God does His best to make a good man every time, and would certainly succeed if the human will were perfectly acquiescent in the Divine, but here the trouble comes in; all do not say constantly and perseveringly, from the depth of the heart, "Thy will be done." Consequently, our non-cooperation with God, and frequently, actual antagonism, utterly defeats the Divine mercy and grace brought into availability for our success, and happiness in time, and eternity.

u. Just as every soul must receive a perfect work of grace, in order to eternal salvation, you see from the above Scripture that every one that makes his bed in Hell, will have Satan's work of damnation perfected in him, rendering him absolutely hopeless and irretrievable before he goes into the awful bottomless abyss, where he will never rise and have another chance, because the material was spoiled before God ever gave him up, *i. e.,* the last hope taken her flight. This perfection unto destruction is the antithesis of the Christian's perfection unto salvation. Therefore, this probationary life settles the destiny of every one for all eternity.

The reason why the omnipotence of the potter does not prevent the clay from marring in his hands, is because this property of the clay, which caused it to mar in the hands of the potter, so as to utterly defeat all of his efforts to succeed in makng a success which will remunerate him financially, symbolizes the same property in the human heart, which actually defeats all the efforts of the omnipotent Potter. This property is none other than the freedom of the human will, which, in its very nature, confers on us the option to reciprocate, or antagonize God's work in our hearts, minds, and lives. This non-reciprocation continued indefinitely, culminates in our perfection, for eternal destruction, thus Satan believes in sanctification, and as you see from this Scripture, he always confers it on his votaries, before they drop into Hell. Therefore, the doctrine of Hell redemption, preached by heretical professors of Christianity. flatly contradicts the Word of God.

PART II.

TRUTHS BEAUTIFUL, CHARMING AND DELECTABLE FOR EDIFICATION, BUT NOT ESSENTIAL TO SALVATION.

Here we continue the preceding chapter elucidatory of the Election of Grace and expound the Election of the *Messianic Progenitorship.*

While this election was the most glorious honor ever participated by mortal man, *i. e.*, consanquineous with the Lord, actually his earthly fathers and mothers, yet it had nothing to do with personal salvation. The failure to apprehend the discrimination between this and the election of grace has erroneously given prominence to the dogma of absolute predestination, determinative of Heaven or Hell.

Rom. 9:11: (*"For the children not yet having been born, nor having done anything good or evil, in order that the purpose of God according to election might stand, not of works, but of Him that calleth."*) This has reference to Jacob and Esau, and simply contemplates the Messianic progenitorship, which God gave to Jacob, and from which he reprobated Esau. Yet salvation was free for Esau, and for Jacob.

Heb. 12:17: *"For you know that indeed afterward, wishing to inherit the blessing, he was reprobated: for he found no place for repentance, even though having earnestly sought it with tears."* The conclusion generally obtains that Esau lost his soul, because of his failure to receive repentance. This is because they do not apprehend the fact that he was not seeking a repentance in his own heart for his sins, but in the heart of his father. Repentence means, "the change of mind." Esau at the time to which this Scripture refers, having arrived in the presence of his father to receive his patriarchal blessing, but a few minutes after the departure of Jacob, who had disguised himself, and in the darkness deceived his father, passing himself for Esau, and in that way received the patriarchal blessing and gone away. Esau, when he found out the stratagem, and the fraud, broke out in a loud, bitter cry, with gushing tears, pleading with his father to revoke the blessing from Jacob, and confer it on himself. In this he signally failed, because his father could not do it, from the simple fact, that God was in it, as you see He predestinated Jacob to it, before he was born. (Rom. 9:11.) Of course, God had nothing to do with the wicked stratagem played off by Jacob and his mother, in order to deceive Isaac and defraud Esau. If they had done nothing, Jacob would have received it, because God had already conferred it on him, even before he was born.

Consequently, Isaac could not change it. Therefore, Esau sought the repentance of his father, *i. e.*, the change of his mind, which would revoke the blessing from Jacob and confer it on him; he found it not.

When Jacob spent that memorable night on the banks of the Jabbok, twenty-two years, subsequently, in which he got sanctified, *i. e.*, saw the face of God, and called the place Peniel, *peni,* "face," and *el*, "God," in contradistinction to his Bethel experience, twenty-two years antecedently, which was his conversion; *beth* means, "house," and *el*, "God," so there he, by the supernatural birth, became a member of God's family, and crossing the river, walking on, limping, because God having wrestled with him all night, to get him to the point of perfect abandonment, finally found it necessary to knock his thigh out of joint, which is the symbol of power, and hence, its dislocation, symbolizes the crucifixion of Old Adam. Then, meeting his brother, from whom he had fled for his life, at the time of the fraud, for which he had resolved to kill him, and had an army of four hundred men, to execute what he considered righteous retribution against his fraudulent brother, who had taken advantage of him, robbed him of his birth-right, and afterward cheated him out of his blessing. On sight, he runs to meet him, embraces and kisses him, shouting, "*Oh, my brother, I see you, as the face of an angel,*" after an absence of twenty-two years; and the two brothers mutually embrace, and thank God for His preserving mercy.

This involves the legitimate conclusion that Esau, as well as Jacob, had spent the preceding night with God. But you say, Jacob had bribed him with the ten-thousand-dollar present of the valuable live stock he had already sent to him, and thus won him. This conclusion breaks down when we consider his refusal to take it, observing, that he had enough of his own—as God had wonderfully prospered him, as well as Jacob. But when Jacob plead with him to receive it as a souvenir of his love, then he accepted it. From that very hour, from which Jacob renewed perfect love, and, doubtless Esau, first love, the two brothers became firm friends, and so continued to the end of life, both uniting in the burial of their father.

In reference to the Messianic progenitorship. Abraham was elected, and all the balance of the world reprobated; the same is true of Isaac and Jacob, yet Christ died for all the world, as really, as those who enjoy the exalted honor of a place in his progenitorship. It does not necessarily follow that all of his progenitorship were saved, as that was a matter involving personal repentance, faith, loyalty and obedience. Meanwhile, salvation was always free for all the world, who would receive it. A recognition of this unconditional election of the progenitorship, which had nothing to do with personal salvation, is indispensably necessary to fortify us against the erroneous conclusions of unconditional election in the realm of grace, which is as free to every soul, as the air we breathe.

As a rule, we find the truth midway between two errors. The Christian world, from ages immemorial, has exhibited two great theological hemispheres, *i. e.*, the Calvinistic, giving a special prominence to the Divine sovereignty, and the Arminian, giving a special prominence to free grace. They are both true, and have their errors only, when people pursue them beyond the realm of truth; *i. e.*, Calvinism to the *ulltimathule* of unconditional election and reprobation, which is only true in reference to the Messianic progenitorship, while the Arminian heresy goes to the extreme of denying the illimitable foreknowledge of God, and even laying embargoes on the Divine sovereignty.

If high Arminianism, and low Calvinism, would actually come together, and unite on the great truth of the Bible, as the only Creed of Christendom, recognizing, not only the futility of all human creeds, but frankly confess the mistake made by the Nicene Council, and the Emperor Constantine, when they formulated the first human creed ever made by the Apostolic Church; if they had simply recognized the New Testament as the only Authority of faith and practice, worlds of blessing would have followed. The organization of denominations was a great mistake, but if they had never formulated creeds those denominations would never have gotten half so far apart as they have, to the serious detriment of the Christian union, which is so essential to our efficiency in the salvation of earth's lost millions.

CHAPTER XI.

SPIRITUAL GIFTS.

As we clearly see in Paul's presentation of these gifts (1 Cor. 12 and 14), he parenthesizes Chapter 13, evidently to fortify the reader against the natural mistake of thinking those gifts essential to salvation, contrastively certifying, *"Yet I show unto you a more excellent way."* That "way," he proceeds lucidly to reveal, and it is none other than perfect love, without which, he assures us, all the gifts are worthless, and shall profit us nothing. *"By grace ye are saved,"* is the battle-cry of the Bible, *"not of works, lest any man shall boast."*

There is but one utility of the gifts, and that is, that we may be efficient in the good works, by which we save the lost. Therefore, while none of the gifts are essential to our salvation, they are all essential to our usefulness in the salvation of others. Consequently, we cannot appreciate them too highly in their place, while we should guard against the trick of the enemy, who would have us exalt them above the graces, by which our own souls are saved. For this Paul labored with all his might. At this point the "Tongues People" are so egregiously erratic, and actually calculated to do immense detriment to Christian experience wherever they go, thus marking their track with spiritual desolation.

You find gifts in the Pauline catalogue. (1 Cor.

12:8.) "Wisdom" heads the column. This is the right use of knowledge.

When Kentucky was an unbroken primeval forest, an Irish family, migrating thither, built their log-cabin in the wild woods. E'er long, the beautiful little baby closes its eyes in death. Those utterly illiterate, superstitious Roman Catholics are plunged into the deepest grief, especially because they think its soul is in purgatory, from the fact that no priest was on hand to baptize it. Consequently, they ransack the country, clamoring to every "squatter," "Where can we find a priest to get the baby out of purgatory?" They are utterly unable to hear of any, as they have not yet reached the wild West. They find a woodman, who responds: "There is no priest in all this country, but there is a man, called a circuit-rider, coming round once a month, who may be a priest, for aught I know." As they are utterly ignorant, and never heard of a circuit-rider, the forlorn hope, ready to catch at a straw, leaps to the conclusion, "Perhaps this man may turn out to be a priest?" Therefore they tell the woodsman to give him word at once.

It so happens that he is in this part of his monthly round, and soon the woodsman finds him, and tells him about the deep distress now filling the Irish cabin with unutterable sorrow, and directs him to it.

Thus, James Hawe, the first Methodist preacher in Kentucky, having been sent by Bishop Asbury, from the Baltimore Conference, and with the whole State for his circuit, traveling around on horse-back, now reaches the Irish cabin.

Dismounting, he knocks at the door, and says, "I am that circuit-rider you sent for." They respond, "Oh, we are hunting a priest, are you one?" Here note the gift of wisdom enjoyed by this uncultured pioneer preacher If he answer in the negative, then and there he would have lost his job, so, he responded frankly, in the affirmative; true, because he was a priest of the Most High God, in the succession of Melchizedec. Then in order to be sure they put the question stronger: "Are you a Roman Catholic priest?" Of course, he could not answer that in the affirmative, but mark the gift of wisdom, when he responds: "Not exactly, but I can do anything that a Roman Catholic priest can do." That settles the question, because none of them can read, and they are full of superstitions and priestcraft. Therefore, they, at once turn over the case to him, to get the baby out of purgatory, in reference to which he responds: "Having heard the case from your neighbor, I have already had it before God, and am happy to say, the baby is not in purgatory, but in Heaven, and the angels are perfectly delighted with it, and it has never cried a whimper since it got there, and they all want it in their arms at the same time; neither will it ever cry again."

This pleases them so, that they almost die of joy; for they are so ignorant and superstitious that they verily believe everything that a priest tells them.

Now they plead with him, "Holy Father, do come and see us, just as often as you can." Here you again note the gift of wisdom. He had no preaching places, except the cabin of the squatters, and the green trees. So he at once takes the Irish cabin for one of his monthly appointments, saying to them, "Look for me, one month from this day."

Spiritual Gifts. 153

In his peregrinations, he everywhere publishes his appointment in the Irish cabin. So on the appointed day the house overflows with the red-hot Methodists, as there were no other sort in that day, because Satan had not yet invented the Mehodist ice-factory, which is now, sad to say, doing a land office business.

Those fire-baptized Methodists throw their mouths open like alligators, and roar like lions. Responsive to their cyclone prayers and Pentecostal songs, the power descends, and the fire falls. It seems that the very clap-boards will fly from the roof, and lodge among the stars and the puncheons of the floor break through. The whole family fall to the floor, under a thunder-bolt of conviction, all get converted, and turn preachers, and I am one of them, for that was my family 175 years ago.

The glorious achievement of the gift of wisdom, was enjoyed by Bishop Asbury's blood-washed, and fire-baptized circuit-rider. *"He that winneth souls is wise."*

Would you be a soul-saver? You must have this gift; the Holy Ghost will give it to you, if you will sink into the Divinity, and use it for the glory of God.

While a sanctified circuit-rider, and God was actually rolling a Pentecost over my circuit, my good members notified me that a man had migrated thither and settled in my territory, and was going to build a meeting-house on the land which he had purchased, and they said he would take my material to build up a church of his own denomination, and their idea was to hedge him up and defeat his enterprise.

I said to them, "No, God has sent that good man to

help me run the devil out of this country, and we must all help him."

I went to see him; introduced myself, ate at his table, and slept in his bed, and he and myself became like David and Jonathan on the battle-field. As I had a revival moving at race-horse speed all the time, he put in his bid for my service, notifying me to be ready as soon as the house was done, to hold the first meeting in it. So I preached a solid month, first of all in a new house, and witnessed to one hundred bright conversions, and some sanctified, though the movement had not yet reached that country, but I was in the experience. During the glorious revival this preacher crossed over Jordan. Holiness Churches at that time had not been born. All the converts joined the denominational churches.

At the close of this wonderful revival, I opened the doors of the church and had Brother P——, the owner of the house, stand and receive the members, while all sang the grand old recruiting song:

"Am I a soldier of the cross,
A follower of the Lamb."

I appointed a clerk to receive their names and their statement of membership. Ninety out of the hundred took membership in "Brother Godbey's" pastoral charge; then the preacher, leaping aloft, with a big shout, exclaimed, "Yes, and I go too," then the other ten walloped over in a minute. So a new star was added to my constellation, the accession of the new house, a hundred members, and their pastor—all because the Lord gave me the gift of wisdom.

He will give it to you, as He has commanded us to be *"Wise as serpents, and harmless as doves."*

Since the Lord sanctified me in 1868 A. D., my life has been crowded with incidents similar to the preceding, confirmatory of His wonderful goodness, conferring this gift on unworthy me.

"Knowledge" is the gift number two. The Greek word is *gnosis*. It means, "Insight into Divine truth." It is the key to the blessed Bible. It does not supercede our own efforts, as God has commanded us to study. (2 Tim. 2:15.) *"Study to show thyself approved of God, a workman not to be ashamed, rightly dividing the Word of truth."*

When I graduated in college I proceeded to ransack all the world for books, thinking I needed them to study the Bible, so I could preach it to others. Nine years rolled away, and the Lord gloriously sanctified me, and to my astonishment, began to reveal to me the wonderful gifts of the Holy Spirit. The true complete consecration gives up all of our plans, then the fire falls, and burns up all of our air castles. Meanwhile, the Free Mason, the Odd Fellow, the College President, (for I was one,) the Methodist preacher, the candidate for the Episcopacy, all went into ashes, leaving me nothing but Jesus. My Napoleonic ambition to be a big preacher, having meanwhile gone down in the conflagration, till I was willing to be anything or nothing for Jesus' sake. About that time, the Holy Ghost wonderfully revealed the Bible to me, and I soon found myself in the great meetings, surrounded by the luminous people of God, using my humble instrumentality as a Bible exponent.

v. *"The gift of faith,"* is Number Three, in the

catalogue. N. B. Do not confound the gift with the grace of faith. We are saved by the latter; we save others by the former. Therefore, the grace of faith is infinitely more important to us, than the gift, because our personal salvation must be first, and we cannot afford, under any circumstances, to take any risk on it.

Besides, the normal place of the gifts is with the sanctified, though not always so, as you see Baalim, the false prophet and Caiaphas, who signed the death-warrant of Jesus had, for a short time, the gift of prophecy, and even the donkey Baalim rode.

Our Savior's promise (St. Matt. 9:29), *"As your faith is, so be it unto you,"* is as true of the gifts as of the graces.

Dr. Finney, in his lectures, tells about an old blacksmith, who lived in a very ungodly town, and having become so burdened with the lost souls all around him, he shut himself up in his shop, and spent a week in prayer, the people coming, knocking at the door, and receiving no answer, then going to his house and failing to find him, giving up and going some where else for their work. Finally, when Sunday came, he went to meeting and asked his pastor to give out a seekers' meeting in his church the next week. Astounded, he said, "Why, there is not a seeker in twenty miles of this place, and has not been in many years," and so he found himself utterly unable to persuade him to announce the mourners' meeting. Then he asked him to announce it at his house. He responded: "Of course you have a right to appoint any meeting you please at your own house, but nobody will be there." "Why, will you not come?" "Oh, yes," says he, "I will come for your sake, but you and I will be all." So he gave it out for the afternoon the ensuing week. Before the arrival of the hour, the house was full, and by the time appointed, the yard was full, and some of the worst and most desperate men in the town and community, actually broke down crying, and said, "If there is anybody here, who can pray, I want you to pray for me, for I am in an awful fix." Thus, one of the greatest revivals ever known, broke out, responsive to the gift of faith, on the part of that illiterate stammerer.

Within the last year, I have attended a Bible School, and a Holiness College, where they told me, a revival had broken out in that way without any especial effort.

These two instances are demonstrative of the wonderful potency of the gift of faith. In both instances, they said it broke out, suddenly, and unexpectedly, except to the few faithful ones, who had prayed through to God, and laid hold of the omnipotent arm.

A sanctified woman in Indiana, whose husband was a hard, wicked, steam-boat captain, running from Cairo to New Orleans, holding on to God in prayer for him, at midnight received the gift of faith, and the answer for his salvation. The next morning she receives a telegram, stating that her husband's boat is burnt, and he is lost. Having read it, she rolls it up, hands it to the boy, saying, "My husband is alive, and coming home to get religion and go to Heaven with me."

The boy returns to the office, and reports what she said, and they all pronounce her crazy, her mind dethroned by the awful news. In three days her husband comes home; she meets him at the door, and tells him about her prevailing prayer at midnight, and the telegram the ensuing morning, and her answer to it.

Though, hitherto, she never could move him, he now falls on the floor, and cries for mercy. She sends away her children to call her godly neighbors. They pray for him all day, and the ensuing night; with the dawn of the morning, the glorious daybreak of Heaven floods his soul. Soon he crosses into Beulah land, and takes his place beside his good wife at the front of a holiness army.

You actually must learn to utilize this invaluable gift.

We now reach Number Four, *"Bodily healing."* It is really indispensable that you have this gift, not only for the sake of your own health, but that you may be useful in the ministry of healing everywhere you go.

Heathen jugglers and enchanters in all ages have professed to heal diseases, though they are utterly unacquainted with our Savior. Christian Scientists, who are so heretical that they may be catalogued with practical infidels, also claim to heal diseases. All of these utilize a principle, well known in metaphysics, *i. e.,* the superiority of the mind over the body, and consequently, frequently the latter is cured, through the medium of the former. The abstraction of the mind from the disease, very frequently relieves it on the principle that the greater subordinates the lesser. Yet the people, who are so fortunate as to have access to the great Physician, can have diseases healed through His wonderful administrations, when the whole medical world, with all the enchantment, sorcery and legerdemain, have signally failed. As the world abounds in poor sufferers on all sides, we should all so commit ourselves to the Great Physician, as to become His humble servants, in the despensation of this infinitely valuable gift of bodily healing.

w. In this connection, I corroborate the encouraging truth of bodily healing by the Great Physician, and encourage the reader by the submission of my humble testimony.

Thirty-five years ago, I was abandoned by the physicians, and given up to die of serious lung trouble. We had almost no light on Divine healing, but the Lord, in His mercy to us, used my dear wife to call saints around my bed, and pray the Great Physician to descend and heal me. Our family physician, and another, whom he invited, were present to witness to them the novel scene of Divine healing.

It came suddenly, and I spoke out and told them all that I was healed. The doctors proceeded to examine me, and pronounced it true; our family physician, at the same time, falling on his knees, and calling on the saints, who had prayed me through, to confer the same favor on him, and pray for the healing of his soul.

In three days, I mounted my horse, and put out preaching, and have been at it ever since, and as I opine, I preached more, perhaps, than any other man in the world, since that time, and never had a sympton of the old trouble.

Twenty-three years ago, while preaching in Texas, I was stricken down by an awful attack of sciatic rheumatism, the most difficult to cure; at once losing my power to walk without a crutch. The Lord wonderfully healed me, so it has been many a day since I had any rheumatic trouble, and am exceedingly active and really a paradoxical walker, for a man of my age.

About ten years ago, a troublesome sore under my apparel, which I had frequently endeavored to bandage, so as to protect it from the friction of my clothing, as it was utterly denuded, upon medical examination, was pronounced a cancer, and a letter written, turning me over to the surgeons of Cincinnati for its amputation, exhorting me to come at once, for treatment.

I had many engagements for the Coast and Interior, which I regretted to disappoint. Taking the letter, which had been written by an able physician, who had been educated in Cincinnati, introducing me, and turning me over to them for the important surgical operation, instead of going, I went to the Great Physician, and turned it over to Him, lifting up my heart in prayer; "Now Jesus, this troublesome sore has at last been pronounced a cancer; I know cancers do their work quickly, therefore, if You have more work for me to do, You will have to talk to this cancer; I know it is bound to obey Your voice, if you tell it to go, it is certain to depart." Then I held on, without a quaver, till in utter abandonment, I reached believing ground, and got to where I was enabled to say, "I believe You heal this cancer." Yea, I heard the benedictory voice, "Cancer get away." The physician, a cousin of mine, had put a bandage on it, using no medicine whatever, but simply by the intervention of raw cotton, protecting it from the friction of my clothing, illustrating the fact that we need physicians diagnostically, *i. e.*, to tell us what the disease is, mechanically, *i. e.*, to perform operations for which we are incompetent, and hygienically to tell us how to live in harmony with the laws of health. Yet, the best physicians as I have consulted them extensively on both Continents,

SPIRITUAL GIFTS. 161

utterly disclaim all power to heal diseases, simply claiming to help nature.

While I was praying for the healing of the cancer, I realized the mitigation of the pain, but made no investigation till that bandage wore off, then to my infinite gratitude, I looked in vain for the cancer, and saw but the souvenir, a big scar, which will abide till the transfiguration glory abliterates every memento, which the Adamic transgressions has left on my person.

We not only need this gift, *per se, i. e.*, for its own sake, as these bodies are indispensable to the completion of the work God has given us to do, but as a powerful auxiliary to soul-saving. The body and soul are so intimately related, that the healing of one is sure to confer a blessing on the other. I have seen this manifested in my own history, on innumerable occasions.

Responsive to an evangelistic call, I went to South Georgia, to hold a protracted meeting in a Methodist Church. When I began boldly preaching sanctification by the second work of grace, I found myself seriously obstructed by the antagonizing pastor, who had called me to his work, as it was early in the Movement, and sanctification but little known. When he arose in the congregation, contradicted and antagonized me, I knew my work was done, unless the Lord interposed. Consequently inwardly and inaudibly, lifting up heart and voice, I said, "Oh, Lord, you will have to put your hand on this preacher, if you have work for me to do." I heard from Heaven, and rested easy. I soon miss him out of the meetings, and hear that he is on his bed, and burnt by that prevalent malarial fever peculiar to that country. I go on with the meeting. The next day, immediately after dinner, I go to the parsonage, to see him, find him burning, as if he was in a furnace; tell him Jesus is ready to heal him; explain it to him, and give him the precious promises; fall on my knees and pray. With my hands on his body, I feel the abatement of the burning fever. He feels it too; gets up, and proceeds to dress himself for meeting. I run away, as the hour is at hand to begin the meeting. While conducting the introductory, Brother S—— walks in at the door, a happy surprise to the congregation. He takes the meeting out of my hands, and proceeds to tell the wonderful news, how he is healed; the fever gone, and the perspiration on his body, which is the well-known phenomenon of convalescence. Divine healing was an utter novelty in the community, therefore, the people were astounded, and electrified by his testimony. While all eyes are centered on him, and all ears listening spellbound, suddenly he changes his theme, and rushes to the altar, shouting, as he went, "Now, Brother Godbey, I want that other thing you have been talking about." His example and testimony moved the people like magic, so they rushed pell-mell and filled the altar, and a glorious revival broke out and no more opposition to sanctification. That preacher actually came to the front of the Holiness Movement in that country.

x. Arriving in New York City, responsive to a call to preach in a Suburban Church, and going to the parsonage, the pastor's wife meets me with the news that he is very sick; after the manner of old King Publius on the island of Melita. (Acts 28.) He was not favorable to healing by Christ, so I was straitened for a time, but rushing into his room, falling down, I put my hands

SPIRITUAL GIFTS. 163

on him, and proceeded to pray for his healing; holding on until I realized audience from Above. Claiming healing for him, and exhorting him how to receive it by simple faith, utterly regardless of the symptoms, I held on until he actually took hold by faith and arose from his bed.

That night he astonished the congregation by his presence, as they had heard of his sickness, and, still more, by his testimony. As he proceeded deliberately to tell them all about it, stating that he was really surprised as I came rushing into his room, as he had never seen me, and so enthusiastically taking hold for his healing, falling down by him, and putting my hands on him, crying out to the Great Physician, meanwhile the unbelief, and repellancy in his own mind rising, so that at first he found quite an inward conflict, but he said, as I moved on praying so importunately to the Holy Ghost to inspire a perfect abandonment pertinent to putting him on believing ground, to receive healing by faith, a soliloquy sprang up in his mind, as follows: "As I am certainly in a bad fix, surely I need just what this preacher is praying for." Then his heart spontaneously drifts over to my side, and joins me in the prayer for the consecration, putting him on believing ground, and the inspiration of his faith to receive Jesus in the capacity of bodily Healer, so he goes on with me in my protracted prayer, till he actually does utterly abandon and exercise faith for his healing, till his heart responds, "Yes, Jesus, I believe You do heal me." The result followed, that he was gloriously healed of both these ailments and they left him, and he convalesced with cheering rapidity.

When our Savior sent out the twelve, two by two,

He commanded them to heal the sick, wherever they went. He also gave the same commandment to the seventy, when He sent them out. It is a great pity, that Christians do not all understand their glorious privilege in Christ, to have their bodily ailments cured.

The consecration, which puts us on believing ground for healing, is the simple recognition, that this body, the mysterious harp of a thousand strings, *i. e.*, a thousand nerves and five hundred muscles are not ours to be used for selfish enterprises and gratifications, but God's, to be used with an eye single to His glory. Therefore, it will be to the interest of His Kingdom to heal them, so we can do His work. When we thus commit to Him, unreservedly and eternally to be used to His glory, then we are in position to receive healing by simple faith.

When I was preaching in the Free Methodist Camp, in Emporia, Kansas, the wife of a preacher, who had been dumb thirty months, was healed and her voice restored all right, to utter astonishment to all. They requested me to devote a meeting to the subject of bodily healing, which I did, expounding the beautiful truth from the precious Word, and inviting seekers to the altar. While we prayed and instructed, they arose, one by one, and a number with triumphant shouts, testified to healing.

Still a lonely sister remains, while I exhort her, "Believe that He doeth it." The Presiding Elder, approaches me in an undertone, "That is our dumb sister; I have never heard her voice." Then I perceive how Jesus cast out dumb demons, and healed the dumb everywhere He went, so they spoke fluently. While exhorting her, "Believe that Jesus heals your dumbness, loosing your tongue and gives you your speech," she became much excited, falling over on the carpet, her face turned Heavenward, her lips moving in her fervent prayer. I saw a radiance gather around her countenance, flashing over her face, which became really luminous when, suddenly, leaping to her feet, she shouted aloud, and running up and down the aisle almost at race-horse speed, continuing to shout. Meanwhile, it seems that every person in the house shouts with her. Fifteen minutes roll away, the house resounding with incessant roar. When they somewhat tranquillized, a fine-looking gentleman stands up and asks permission to speak, which is granted. He at once proceeds to tell us that he was that woman's physician, and with his comrades of the healing art, everything possible had been done by man to remove that dumbness, and he carried her away to the cities and had her treated by specialists, and he wanted to witness that it was really a miracle of the Lord. She went to preaching, and had the good use of her voice. That was six or seven years ago, I still hear from her, that her voice is all right. We certainly have a wonderful Healer and should all keep our bodily organs, all so fully consecrated to Him, that we will constantly abide on believing ground for healing.

In my late tour around the world, traveling thirty to forty thousand miles, I had no sea-sickness, whereas, at times, amid rough weather it seemed that almost all on board were sick. In my three tours in the old world, I have had no trouble with sea-sickness. When going to sea, I always take the Lord to prevent the sea-sickness.

While laboring with people in the ministry of healing, do not make the mistake, which is very common, exhorting the patient, "Believe it is done." To believe it is done, when it is not, does not make it done, but upsets your faith, and thus keeps you from receiving it.

Others tell you, "Believe He will," which is not faith at all, but hope, whereas faith is the hand by which we receive everything from God. Then what is the true attitude of the patient, seeking bodily healing?

John Wesley believed it, taught it, and received it. He tells us we are to BELIEVE HE DOETH IT, and keep our faith in the present tense, till we know it is done.

N. B. Faith in lively exercise in the present tense, receives it. John Wesley states in his diary: "I was riding along, my head aching, as if it would burst, and my horse limping, as if he would fall. I lift up my heart and voice to God, and say, 'Oh, God, Thou hast created me, and my horse; I know thou canst heal us both; I now believe Thou dost deal my aching head and limping horse.'" That moment his head ceased to ache and his horse to limp, brisking up and nimbly pacing away. Meanwhile he raises a loud shout of victory. He visited John Fletcher, when in the last stage of consumption. Falling on his knees, by his bed, lifting up his voice, he cries, "Oh, God, I cannot do without this man; Thou must heal him." Leaping to his feet, he shouted, "He will not die but live to declare the mighty works of God." He did get well, lived eight years longer and wrote those wonderful books on "Christian Perfection," that have been shaking the world ever since.

v. The key to this great and important gift of the Spirit, you find in Rom. 8:11, *"But if the Spirit of Him that raised up Jesus from the dead dwelleth in you, the One having raised up Christ Jesus from the dead will*

SPIRITUAL GIFTS.

indeed quicken your mortal bodies by His Spirit dwelling in you."

This is the effectual guarantee against that fanaticism, which preaches universal healing homogenius with universal salvation, i. e., that it is the privilege of all to be healed indefinitely, and under all circumstances. In the great and prevailing fanaticism, at the present appertaining to the gift of tongues, I have found the same people equally erratic on Divine healing. In their enthusiasm, they tell every patient he can be healed, if he will only consecrate and believe for it. This is true, as the wonderful promise, *"As your faith is, so be it unto you,"* (St. Matt. 9:29,) and so current in our Savior's preaching, as to become axiomatic, that when he is not healed, they tell him his faith is deficient, which is true, because if he had faith for it, he would receive it, as the Lord's Word never fails. But their great mistake is their own failure to discriminate between the gift of faith, by which the body is healed and the grace of faith, by which the soul is saved, consequently, their enthusiastic efforts to get the man to believe for healing, when he cannot, simply because the Holy Spirit does not impart the gift, culminates in the abatement of his faith for salvation, and, perhaps, drives him into despondency and ultimates in permanent detriment to his Christian experience.

This illustrates the importance of solid Bible teaching everywhere. At this point, we all have great encouragement in the current trend of the Holiness Movement throughout the world to organize Bible Schools for the faithful and assiduous study of the precious Word, by which we are saved, sanctified, edified, fortified and have constant victory over the world, the flesh, and Satan.

Regeneration and sanctification, the essentials of salvation are for everybody who will have them, as the old maxim, *semper et ubique,* "Always and everywhere recognizes, there being but one exception, and that is the contempt of the Holy Ghost" (St. Matt. 12:31, 32), their only Dispenser. But not so with bodily healing, which is not by the grace of the Spirit, but the gift, which, like the entire nine, is conferred by the sovereign discriminating grace of God. We may always assure the patient that God will give him either health or Heaven.

The normal place of Divine healing is with the sanctified, who have the Holy Ghost dwelling in them. He is the only Healer in the world, both of the saint and the sinner. If any one doubts the healing of sinners, read the history of the ten lepers in St. Luke, and you will find they were all healed, but only the one who turned back with a shout of gratitude was saved. If God did not heal sinners, they would quickly all be dead, as all mortals are full of diseases hereditary from the fall.

In the ministry of healing, we should always give preeminence to the soul and see that the patient is saved and sanctified before we proceed to the ministry of healing. N. B. That is the point-guard against the fanaticism, that would withhold the ministry of healing, till you see evidence of salvation. Simply, and briefly give the Word, and if the patient shows a willing mind, repents and believes with manifest candor and earnestness, proceed at once to the ministry of healing, lest he might die.

If the patient be stubborn in his wickedness, manifesting no penitence, pray earnestly for the conviction, and salvation, and subsequent healing, but do not anoint him,

SPIRITUAL GIFTS.

before he is saved; as *the oil* is the symbol of the Holy Ghost in physical healing, just as the water of baptism in salvation. While it is always proper to anoint, as in so doing you honor the Holy Spirit by recognizing Him as the Healer, and the oil will prove a quickener of the patient's faith, and in that way auxiliary in his healing.

N. B. Beware of the heresy that teaches that healing is for everybody and at all times, like salvation. I have been healed of the worst diseases, *i. e.*, lung trouble, thirty-five years ago; cancer, ten years ago; rheumatism, twenty-three years ago; and cholera, in Burmah, in 1906. The Lord healed me of all these serious troubles so quickly that I have never been confined to my bed a day at a time since I was a child. I am now seventy-four, bodily organs fast wearing out, consequently, I keep them all before the Lord for repairs, responsive to His infallible, merciful diagnosis, He wonderfully keeps me at constant labor; though some times the morning finds me in such a condition, physically, that I could not leave my room, if He did not heal me; yet He does, and I go along to my appointments, making no mention of physical ailments. From a human standpoint, I may say, He heals me, because I have faith in Him to do it. Therefore, so long as I have faith for healing, He will heal me, because His Word cannot fail. Yet, if He tarrieth, this frail body will soon fail, and I will not be healed any more, till the glorious resurrection, the perfection of bodily healing, whereas, all we will see antecedently, is but a patching up, till we can finish our work.

As I have passed through those terrible diseases, why did I not die? Because I had faith in Jesus to heal me.

I am looking for Him constantly to come and translate me, in which case this body will receive the perfection of healing for ever, and never die. If He tarrieth, very soon this body will die, because when my work is done, then I will have no faith for healing any more. Oh, that will be the glorious victory, which brightens before my spirit, amid all the toils and sufferings of this frail body! Therefore, when your patient has no faith for healing, instead of discouraging him, you ought to shout with him; because the very fact that he has not is *prima facie* evidence that God is going to give him Heaven, instead of health, as He often gave him before, simply that he might have time to finish his work.

That wonderful Scripture at the head of this prolix paragraph, recognizes the Holy Ghost, dwelling with the pilgrim in this tenement of clay; the house gets out of repair, and He gives it the needed attention, whether the breach is in the roof, the wall, the floor, or the flue, He kindly repairs it, and still is with you in the home.

During my long life, the house has been repaired, perhaps a hundred times. When I am at home, I live in a house, which was built by the grandfather of my dear wife, who occupied it till up in the eighties; her father succeeding him, till also an octogenarian. She is now on the sunny side of seventy. The house is still all right, because the inmates have diligently and faithfully repaired it; yet it will not stand for ever. If we would cease to repair it, our neighbors recognizing its delapidations, would all conclude that it was no longer worth repairing, and that we would soon vacate it for another. Thus the blessed Holy Ghost, dwelling with me in this mortal mansion, wonderfully repairs it, over and over,

Spiritual Gifts. 171

and frequently anticipates coming ailments, and heads them off altogether, as in my recent tour round the world, responsive to my faith, to keep off sea-sickness, I had it not a single moment, while my comrades all around went down.

Oh, the unutterable goodness of God, not only to live with me in this house of clay, but to keep it in repair until my work is done, when He will bid me evacuate it, and come away to a, *"House, not made with hands, eternal in the heavens."*

> "Christ went a Building to prepare,
>   Not made with hands;
> All decked with jewels, rich and rare,
>   Not made with hands.
>
> "I know, I know, I have another Building,
>   Not made with hands.
>
> "Some morning fair, I'm going away;
>   Not made with hands,
> And will not get back, till Millenial Day,
>   Not made with hands.
>
> "Then, come along children, and get your crown,
>   Not made with hands;
> When you shall lay the armor down,
>   Not made with hands."

2. *"The workings of dynamite,"* ranks Number Five in the catalogue of these wonderful spiritual gifts. In the English Version, this gift is called, *"Working miracles,"* and has led people into fanaticism, as we observe now in the "Tongues Movement," some claiming to work miracles.

Regeneration and sanctification are the stupendous miracles executive of the gracious economy. In the above Scripture definition of this gift of the Spirit the word translated "miracles" in the English Version is "dynamites."

When men of science recently made the wonderful discovery of the greatest mechanical power the world has ever known, they ransacked the vocabulary of the English language, with its hundred and fifty thousand words to find one strong enough to define the transcent possibilities involved. Consequently, they went to the grand old Greek, and selected the very word, which is God's only definition of the Gospel. Rom. 1:16: *"The Gospel is the dynamite of God unto salvation to every one that believeth."* Consequently, in this way "dynamite" became an English word, as we have only twenty-three thousand original words in our language, the other one hundred and twenty-seven thousand having come in from foreign languages. You know, dynamite is the greatest explosive in the known world. Oh, how thrillingly significant of the Gospel, whose province it is to blow out of the human spirit, mind and body, soon or late, not only every devil, but everything Satan has ever put into us.

We find four Gospels in the gracious economy, and five, if you count Divine healing, which is certainly correct, though the body is not the man, but simply the house he lives in. God's preacher takes his stand on Mount Sinai, hurls the thunder-bolts and earthquakes and lightning-shafts, as the Holy Ghost supplies him, till a nightmare conviction settles down on everybody, which will never let up till Satan's chains are all broken. Then he changes to Mt. Calvary, and to the broken-hearted penitent preaches the dying love of Jesus, till he sweeps triumphantly out of death into life. (1 John 3:14.)

Then he takes his stand on Mt. Zion and preaches to the regenerated people, the great work of entire sanctification, thundering against inbred sin, like a messenger from Heaven, till the tornado comes, and the fire falls. Finally he climbs great Mt. Olivet to the summit, where our Lord's hallowed feet bade the earth adieu, and in His transfiguration glory, He ascended in a white cloud.

This wonderful gift of the Spirit makes you a regular dynamiter.

When I was Professor in College, and delivering lectures on electricity, I would in my experiment put a student on the insulator (a stool with glass legs, so electricity could not pass into the earth), and having put his finger on a charged galvanic battery, till it would fill him up with electricity, his hair standing straight on his head, and if a student would touch him, immediately preceding the contact the fire leaps out and burns him. That is what this spiritual gift will do for you. It will fill you up with dynamite till you will shock and burn wherever you go. I have often seen it manifest in wonderful demonstration, knocking people down and unqualifying them to rise and walk, or use their bodily members. I have actually held meetings, which were like Heaven, as the poet says:

> "Congregations never break up,
> And the Sabbaths have no end."

During the morning session, people fall and get unable to go away, and have to remain on the spot, till the afternoon service. Then still more following and losing their power to travel, remain till night, when many are stricken down, and are unable to get away and stay all night. Consequently, there is no adjourning of the meeting, but we had to divide up the workers and keep some on the ground all the time, laboring with the seekers, who were physically incompetent to go away.

This state of things obtained at Waco and other camps in Texas in the early years of the Movement. I saw it in a very prominent manifestation in a protracted meeting I held at Soule Chapple, Pulaski County, Kentucky, the church of my father, and grandfather. Doubtless you have read about the wonderful phenomena of falling and jerking, floundering and leaping, characteristic of Caneridge Camp-meeting, Bourbon County, Kentucky. In 1800, and also the next year, which electrified the great wild West, at that time reaching from the Alleghenies to the Mississippi River—a vast territory thinly populated with pioneers and squatters; the Methodists, Presbyterians, perhaps some Baptists and Universalists, united in the enterprise preparing an auditorium in the woods, where they all pitched their tents. They all united their hearts and hand in an earnest effort to pray God down from Heaven in saving mercy to visit the people. Toward the close of the stipulated two weeks a wonderful unprecedented and unheard-of spiritual power fell on them, reaching everybody on the ground. Consequently, they held the meeting on till the Winter disqualified them to continue in their tents.

Meanwhile the paradoxical news, flying on the wings of the wind in all direction brought on the people in vast crowds. It was currently reported that everybody coming thither got knocked down and took the jerks.

I will now, from memory, give you an illustrative case, which you will find in the biography of Rev. J. B.

Finley. He lived in central Ohio, and aspired to the championship of bullyhood. When the people returned with these wonderful reports, and testified that they got knocked down; were seized with jerks, etc., he boasted that they could not knock him down, and in order to show the world the validity of his claims to athletic championship, he resolves to go, and test the matter. On arrival, he sees a vast multitude spread over the earth, under the green trees, and recognizes a man standing in a wagon and preaching with all his might, manifesting power and excitement, such as he had never seen in the pulpit. As he moves about, and diagnoses the situation, he finds preachers everywhere, till he counts twenty, at the same time, preaching with all their might, *i. e.*, with the Holy Ghost sent down from Heaven. (1 Peter 1:12.) Meanwhile, the people are falling, jerking, leaping, crying, shouting, and all sorts of demonstrations, such as he had never seen before. Soon a strange weakness begins to come on him, and increases, till his knees knock together, and he finds himself just about to fall. Then resuming the stalwart and remembering the boast he had made to his neighbors, and his bold defiance of the camp-meeting, and audacious claims to the championship, making his escape with difficulty, feeling so weak, he could scarcely walk, goes away to his horse, and stays a little while, and somewhat recovers his strength, and does his best to recuperate his flagging energies, just mustering all of his resolutions to meet the thing face to face, and have the victory over it, he goes back into the camp. He is surprised to find the tide much higher, and rising like a flooded river; meanwhile, his attention is attracted by a crowd of about five hundred people, who look like they had but recently arrived. He watches them to see what effect it will have on them, when suddenly, they *en masse,* fall to the ground, as if a battery of a thousand cannons had been turned on them, and such screaming, mourning, crying, and wailing, jerking and leaping, no tongue can describe. Again, that strange weakness comes on him despite all his effort to keep it down, and stave it off, and he finds himself tottering to fall, and gets away with all possible expedition back to his horse again. Determined not to give it up, and forego the humiliation of defeat, after all his boasting, he now goes away a mile to a tavern, and gets some brandy to settle his nerves, and feels that he certainly can resist the influence and stand the tide and go home shouting over his bullyhood. So he goes back again, and finds the tide higher than ever. People all around stretched out on the ground, utterly unable to stand on their feet, others jerking, as if they will break to pieces, the long, disheveled hair of the women, cracking like whip-lashes, and many shouting aloud the victory won.

Now that strange tremor comes back on him, despite the effect of the brandy, and all his heroism. This time it comes on him like a tornado, and with all of his antelope fleetness, and alligator hardihood, with great difficulty he reaches his horse, in utter despair of his boasted enterprise of beating the camp-meeting, but now only thinking of making his escape. So active that he could leap over his horse flat-footed, now he has to get him to a big log and with great difficulty succeeds in mounting him and had to hold to the horn of the saddle to keep from falling off, not daring to ride out of a walk, he creeps along about ten miles, when he can hold on no longer, but actually falls off in the road, (I have often seen the spot.) The people in the little settlement are afraid to go near him, lest he may have some dangerous disease, but it so happens that an old Dutchman lived there, who had been to the camp-meeting, got knocked down and wonderfully saved. He comes to him, and tells the people not to be afraid, that it is nothing but the effect of that wonderful camp-meeting on him, and that he has no epidemic, but has been to the camp-meeting, and the hand of God is on him. Then they carry him into the Dutchman's house, and he prays for him, and talks to him, in his broken English, all night, and with the morning dawn the glorious Heavenly day flooded his soul. So he mounts his horse and goes home, shouting all over the community, no longer the boasting bully, and egotistical prize-fighter, but a flaming preacher of the Gospel, who, in the providence of God, came to the front and led the pioneer Church to victory in the great wild West, as it was then.

A. *"Prophesy,"* is gift Number Six, in this wonderful constellation, shining like diamonds in the firmament of the Gospel kingdom.

Satan builds a heresy, antithetical to all of God's gifts and graces, in order to deceive the people by his counterfeit, in that way so side-tracking them that they will never get the genuine, but rest in the transparent hoax, that he plays off on them.

In the current "Tongues" Movement, "prophecy" is very prominent, as they say it is the companion of the "tongues." That is all true, but they have Satan's counterfeit, like they do in reference to the "tongues." The counterfeit, of course, instead of proving that there is no genuine, confirms its reality, as, otherwise, there would be nothing to counterfeit.

In the Old Dispensation, perhaps not one prophet in a thousand was used of the Holy Spirit to reveal the Bible; but they simply verified the definition, which you find in 1 Corinthians 14:3: *"He that prophesieth speaketh to the people edification, exhortation, and comfort."*

God, alone, has a right to define His own institutions, yet Satan is alway meddling with them, in order to foil the people with his counterfeit, and thus defeat the mercy of God in the salvation of every one who will receive it.

We read in the last chapter of the Bible, a statement, that it is finished, and a terrible woe pronounced on those who add anything to it, or take from it. Therefore, the people who claim the gift of prophecy in the sense, in which the inspired Authors had it, *i. e.,* "to reveal saving truth to the world;" are false claimants raised up by Satan to deceive people, *i. e.,* I saw a "Tongues" woman in Denver, who, as I was informed, by most reliable people at Colorado Springs, that while preaching in that city, she had predicted that it would be destroyed by earthquake like San Francisco; but, unfortunately, she had given the date, and it had already passed, and the city is still standing.

You see, from God's definition of "prophecying," that it simply invests us with the illumination and utterance, necessary to our usefulness, elucidating, and preaching the Word, which our prophetical predecessors, from the day of Enoch have revealed to us in both Testaments.

God's Word is the settlement of everything, actually forever putting an end to all controversy. Therefore you see this prophecy is really the preaching gift, therefore Paul prayed that we might all have it.

When we consecrate our minds and voices to God, that means that we are to use them with an eye single to His glory. Jesus preached to the lonely Nicodemus that wonderful sermon on regeneration that has been shaking the world ever since. Again, He preached to a lonely fallen woman at Jacob's well in Samaria; converted her soul, and sent her a flaming preacher through the city. God help us to imitate His example, and preach to everybody we meet, utilizing each fleeting moment in the great work of saving earth's lost millions.

You see from this definition of "prophecying," that whenever you are speaking to "edification," *i. e.*, telling any person the truth of God; exhorting them to appreciate it; to flee the wrath to come; do good and make sure of Heaven, or comforting them with the wonderful promises of God, you are "prophecying," *i. e.*, preaching the Gospel with the blessed assurance that it shall not return void. Therefore, I do not wonder that Paul gave prophecy the preeminence.

B. *"Spiritual Discernment"* is Number Seven, in this wonderful Pauline catalogue. We absolutely cannot afford to be without all of these gifts. Praise the Lord, I have them all, in a measure, and pray night and day, for a more copious endownment.

Without "discernment of spirits," we are exposed to mistake incessantly, and detrimental to the cause, which is nearer to our hearts than life. Without this gift we are in great danger of giving the wrong medicine to the wrong patient, and doing harm instead of good. Oh, how common it is for people to come to the altar, seeking sanctification when they are not converted! How frequently do we find seekers at our altars who are not even convicted; in that case, the thing to do is to pray, preach, and exhort, till God puts conviction on them.

A Presbyterian preacher up in the eighties, died in my home-town a few days ago, in glorious triumph. He and myself, forty years ago, preached together in revival meetings. His experience will illustrate this point.

His father, mother, brother and sisters, were all sinners, and he was rushing headlong to Hell; when standing in the midst of Satan's rabble, during an altar-call, a wicked comrade said to him, "John, I dare you to go to that altar; if you will, I will." He aspired to the bullyhood of the community, and boasted that he would not take a dare, therefore, when the fellow said it, he just said to him, "You are after the wrong fellow; I never take a dare; so, now, come ahead." The result was, they both walked down side by side, and both fell at the altar; the other fellow worked his way out, and ran off, and never came back. John tried to get out, but the red-hot Christians just thronged around him, held him down, prayed for him like lightning, and he soon saw that it was utterly impossible for him to get away from there. God answered prayer, and sent conviction, though he had none when he went. In a half hour he was rent by a cyclone from head to foot, and crying aloud from the depths of a broken heart. Another half hour rolls away, and he is powerfully converted and up shouting. In another half hour he is back in in the midst of that rowdy rabble, and preaching with the Holy Ghost sent down from Heaven. He spent his life heroic and true, and now plays on his golden harp.

Early in the Holiness Movement, I was called to a camp-meeting in East Tennessee. Arriving Saturday evening, I found a precious Holiness evangelist there, preaching with all his might, having arrived at the opening, two or three days antecedently. His theme was "Sanctification," as it had been from the beginning. Having concluded, with an invitation, a few souls came forward, but it was a very hard pull. Then he asked me to speak, when I arose and surveyed the great audience tabernacle, crowded and overflowed. The blessed Holy Spirit in a moment imparted to me the gift of discernment. I proceded to speak, as He gave me utterance, saying to the people, "I'm not going to preach sanctification to you, because you must first have justification, and I see Satan's black grip is on you. Sanctification is for Christians, but I read you like Greek, and see the devil here, big as a rhinoceros." They got awfully mad, and sent me a kuklux notice to leave immediately, or my neck would be stretched. The Methodist pastor also wrote me a letter, ordering me to leave the ground, or he would arrest me, and have my license taken from me. I simply answered him with a kind invitation to attend the meetings, and let us have a good time together, but never afterward heard from him. Though I had no information about the environments, the Holy Spirit revealed the situation to me, as it was afterward corroborated by the testimonies of the people. There were no sanctified people in that country, but the camp was invited by a few who were seeking the experience; a holiness band in Knoxville, eighty miles distant having launched it for the glory of God. Satan had circulated all kinds of evil reports about Holiness people, and the rabble believed them. Meanwhile, all the preachers and all the pastors had stirred up the people to antagonize the meeting, and keep us from doing anything. Consequently, the Methodist pastor ordered me to leave.

The evangelist, who preceded me, left the following Tuesday, leaving me the labor. At night I stood on Mt. Sinai, and preached to the wicked—Hell and damnation, with all my might, God furnishing the thunder-bolts, lightning-shafts, and earthquakes. Meanwhile, I devoted morning and afternoon expounding the precious Word, and helping the Christians into Beulah Land. On the ensuing Sunday, the closing day, according to the schedule, I preached morning and afternoon to vast audiences, mixed messages, both to Christians and sinners, proposing to give them Sinai at night, as hitherto. I was feeling all day that a cyclone had left Heaven and was moving toward us, but just where it would strike us, I could not tell, and I was standing on Mt. Sinai, telling the falling of the Walls of Jericho. Having spent an hour in prayer and testimony, beginning at sunset, I rose to preach, and, perhaps, had announced my text, but do not think I had spoken a sentence, when that cyclone struck us, and it seemed that the whole multitude sprang to their feet, and, without an invitation, many rushed to the altar, crowded and filled it. Meanwhile, others in the aisles from all directions, wending their way to the altar, fell and cried for mercy; a Pentecostal conviction swept the whole congregation; people falling and crying out in audible prayers in all directions, it seemed that a simultaneous baptism of the Holy Ghost and fire came on them all. Of the Holiness band, who had come out from Knoxville to conduct the meeting (about fifteen persons), so receiving the gift of prophecy, they all began to preach like the hundred and twenty in the Day of Pentecost. The scene was absolutely indescribable, there was no order, but that of the Holy Ghost, which is perfect, yet utter disorder from a human standpoint; all the sanctified people scattered about, preaching with all their might, with the Holy Ghost sent down from Heaven. (1 Peter 1:12.) Amid the cry of penitents, soon waves of salvation began to roll over the multitudes, souls tiding over into the kingdom, and fording the Jordan into Beulah Land, with loud shouts of victory. The scene, to all human observation, was a perfect medley. At one place they were preaching powerfully to sinners; at another, praying and exhorting the seekers; at another, shouting with the young converts. Two hours rolled away without a vestige of human order.

Meanwhile, I repeatedly endeavored, in vain, to take the meeting into hand, and conduct it; and had to conduct myself in the simple attitude of a lay-worker, surrounded by people, so filled with the Holy Ghost that their stentorian voices, like the roar of a mighty sea, constrained me to content myself with the privilege of simply conversing with the people, as I moved about amid the roaring multitude.

Early in the scene, my attention was arrested by a stalwart man of middle age, rushing down an isle toward the altar, which was full and overflown; and falling on the straw, prostrate and crying aloud; his stentorian voice, doubtless audible several hundred yards. Feeling especially drawn toward him, I, in vain, attempted to command his attention, hoping, by the grace of God, to serve him, but signally failed to get his attention, as his eyes seemed to be fixed upon something beyond the stars, and uncognizant of anything about him. His vociferous prayers have continued with impotent fervency about forty minutes when an amber haze dawns upon his countenance, developing with increasing brilliancy, till his whole physiognomy is literally illuminated, and his eyes sparkle with preternatural brilliancy. Then, springing to his feet, his shout is like the roar of a lion, commingled with the clapping of his brawny hands, reminding me of thunderpeals. About that time, he recognizes me, snatches me up like an infant (as he was a physical giant), lifting me aloft in his arms, leaping and shouting, he says, "Last Sunday, I cursed you, as the stumbling-block of this meeting, and said that if you had stayed away we might have had a respectable meeting, but you had come and disturbed everything. It is true, you are my stumbling-block, I was rushing at race-horse speed to Hell, you got in my way, and I stumbled over you, and God, in His mercy, has turned me around, and now I am running the other way, Heaven-born, and Heaven-bound, and shall praise God for ever, for sending you to this meeting."

The camp was scheduled to close with that service; but such was the sweep of the Heavenly cyclone, which had caught it in its foils, that it was impossible to stop it, therefore it moved on, and the mighty works of God were manifest in the glorious Pentecostal revival, which descended that memorable hour, with "a rushing mighty wind." The opposition, which had been so bitter and persistent, all evanesced when God came down in His majesty and glory.

SPIRITUAL GIFTS. 185

c. Now we reach the currently agitated "Gift of Tongues." While Paul decisively subordinates it to the "Gift of Prophecy;" while the latter is the special endowment of the Spirit for the preaching of the Gospel, which is, *"The power of God unto salvation to every one that believeth"* (Romans 1:16), the former is simply the vehicle, by which it is transmitted from the preacher to auditor. We readily see, with inspired Paul, the decisive contrast, in favor of the gift of prophecy, as the Bread of Life is certainly more important than the vehicle that brings it. However, this "gift of languages" is certainly transcendently important, and in no way to be depreciated though, doubtless, more susceptible to counterfeit and fraud than any of the other eight, as evil spirits, both incarnate and excarnate, can utilize it, as well as good, thus capriciously playing the Holy Ghost, and deceiving the people.

In case of foreign missionaries, this gift is indispensable to their greatest efficiency. In the providence of God, I have taken three tours into Asia and Africa, in the interest of God's kingdom. If I were young, I certainly would be a missionary.

During my youth, the missionaries in the foreign field were few. There was but little interest in the great work of heathen evangelization, consequently, the best I can do is to travel among them in the capacity of an evangelist, preaching to them through interpreters, as I have a field so vast that I can stop but a few days in one place.

In India, during 1905-1906, I traveled six thousand miles, preaching through interpreters all the time. In that great country there are a hundred nations, speaking so many different languages. As a transient man, with no time to study the language, the blessed Holy Spirit did not impart to me the gift, as He has in the important language of the Holy Scriptures. If I should settle as a missionary, I would at once seek the gift of language spoken by my people, and, of course, do my uttermost to appreciate, corroborate, and utilize the blessed gift bestowed by the Holy Spirit, as God positively commands us in 2 Timothy 2:15: *"Study to show thyself approved of God, a workman not to be ashamed, rightly dividing the Word of truth."*

Surely God sets no premium on laziness, therefore, the thing for every missionary to do, on reaching his field of labor, is to proceed at once to study the language, utilizing every opportunity and every facility, and the same time praying incessantly, to the blessed Holy Spirit, to impart the gift, responsively to the intercession of the Savior, with the Holy Majesty, in behalf of the poor heathen, who long ages have been sitting in darkness and the shadow of death, that He may utilize His ordained economy in their enlightenment, as, *"The entrance of Thy Word giveth light."*

In my recent journey around the world, I was everywhere impressed with the mercy of God in giving the languages. Some of the missionaries assuring me that in the pressures of their labors, having been deprived of the opportunity to study the vernacular, God had given it to them, so they were preaching it constantly.

Brothers Worcester and Johnson, in Africa, notify us that within one year they have received the gifts of the native tongues, in which they are now preaching.

Bishop Taylor gave an instance in which he sent a

missionary to a nation, and came around in three months and found him preaching fluently and powerfully in the native language, many of the people having been convicted, the king getting gloriously saved in his presence during that quarterly meeting.

The present revival of the Gift of Tongues in this country, though awfully infected with fanaticism, should be hailed as the harbinger of our Lord's glorious coming, to arrest Satan, take him out of the world, and bring the sunburst of His Millennial Kingdom on all the nations of the earth. Doubtless some of the Lord's dear people in the homelands are receiving the gift of unknown tongues, now spoken by the Pagan nations. Certainly every case of this kind should be recognized as the call of God to the recipient, to go at once and preach to the people, whose language they have received.

Since the "Tongues" revival has broken out in this country, some having received foreign languages, have gone away to hunt up the nations, to which the Holy Ghost, in this decisive manner called them to preach the everlasting Gospel. I have diligently investigated to my utmost ability, but as yet, found no case of a verification, however it is not yet too late, and I am constantly expecting to hear of real authentications to the Gift of Tongues, to which not a few have claimed, and especially in California.

When our Lord was on earth, He did no imitable work; all of His miracles verifying benefactions, patent to universal diagnosis. He filled the whole country with His works of mercy, healing all the sick whom they brought to Him. He never performed any miracles capriciously *ad captandum vulgus.*

King Herod, while He was on trial, did his best to get Him to work "miracles;" but signally failed. He could not even get Him to speak. He knew the haughty autocrat, who had beheaded His precursor, had no good motive, but simply wanted Him to use His Omnipotence, to gratify his vain curiosity.

D. Where there is much smoke, wild-fire, and fox-fire, there is apt to be some of the true fire. Dr. Clark says the true fire is very apt to be attended by more or less of the counterfeit. Therefore, we sanguinely hope that there is some genuine work of the Holy Ghost, actually conferring the gift of foreign language on the people, who are speaking them in the "Tongues" meetings.

However, we certainly have much to discourage us, and to force on us the suspicion of the counterfeit. I spent three months in the very hot-bed of the Movement, associated with them all the time, as they attended my meetings, and I attended theirs, meanwhile, in the integrity of my heart, walking softly before God, at the same time soliciting the co-operatioon of others, to find genuine cases, but signally failed to find any that were really satisfactory and indubitable.

E. G. A woman in Los Angeles claimed to receive a tongue, and spoke in the meetings in an unknown language, which some French people who were present, identified as their language, and so certified, then the people were encouraged to pronounce it a genuine case, verified to their satisfaction. But the woman comes back to the meeting, and actually confesses that she had played the hoax on them, and though having spoken the

French language, that it was not as she had claimed, a gift, but her native tongue.

California, the hot-bed of the Movement, is the rendevous of many nations, from the ends of the earth attracted thither by the gold. Therefore, in these great meetings, the curious all draw in, and many through capricious and vain motives, some can speak a little Spanish, Indian, German, French, Italian, Russian, Portugese, etc., hence you see, in a great crowd huddled together, there is a wide open door for promiscuous delusion, and all sorts of trickery. Besides that, we remember that the Mormons have always claimed the Gift of Tongues, their ritual consisting in immersion for the remission of sins, and laying on of hands, for the gift of the Holy Ghost, which was confirmed by the unknown tongues.

The Spiritualists, in their seances, have always had more or less of this tongue phenomenon. Also, it is a well-known fact that the Devil-worshippers of India have this gift of tongues.

When we consider the fact that the air is thronged with demons, (Eph. 2:2,) and that when Lucifer fell, and was cast out of Heaven, that his influence drew one-third of the angels, (*i. e.*, the dragon's tail drew one-third of the stars, and cast them down to the earth;) these fallen angels all became demons, and actually got here before Adam was created, and have had ample opportunities to get acquainted with all nations, as they have developed on the earth, and, of course, know their languages. Oh, how easy for a demon to play the Holy Ghost on the seeker after an unknown tongue, to come in and actually use the vocal organs of the deluded soul, as in the case of the girl in Philippi, who told fortunes through the demon dwelling in her, and whose ejectment utterly disqualified her for the further pursuit of her profession, which brought much gain to her masters; just as God's true people preach with the *"Holy Ghost sent down from Heaven,"* (1 Peter 1:12,) thus speaking, *"As He gives them utterance,"* (Acts 2:4,) in a similar manner, Satan's myrmidons are ready to play the Holy Ghost on the deluded human spirit, come in and take possession of the vocal-organs, so that the reciprocant speaks as the demon "gives utterance."

The best holiness people have certified to me that they realized the presence of evil spirits in those meetings. *"All things work together for good to them that love God."* (Romans 8:28.) These wholesale delusions, which characterize the "Tongues" Meetings, I trow, prove a blessing to God's true people, as He says, (1 Corinthians 11:9,) *"Indeed it behooves heresies to be among you, in order that the approved may truly be manifest among you."*

The extraordinary phenomena characteristic of the last days, are now fast coming on us, in the multiplication of heresies: *"Signs and lying wonders, and every delusion of unrighteousness to them that perish, because they did not receive the love of the truth, that they might be saved. And on this account God is sending to them the working of delusion, that they may believe a lie: in order that all who do not believe the truth, but take pleasure in unrighteousness may be condemned."* (2 Thess. 2:9-12.)

Here the Holy Ghost shows that all of this is the work of Satan. These awful heresies, which are rising

Spiritual Gifts.

in tornadoes on all sides and sweeping over the country in the name of the Holiness Movement, rest assured, Satan is stirring all his myrmidons, devils, demons, and imps, marshalling the hosts of Hell for the terrible oncoming conflict. The tribulation, which will speedily follow the rapture of the Saints, for which we are constantly on the out-look, will be Hell's greatest harvest ever known since Lucifer made the unhappy choice, "to reign in Hell, rather than serve in Heaven."

Noah's flood was a tremendous harvest for the Bottomless Pit, but as compares with the Great Tribulation, is but a drop in the bucket, as there were so few people in the world at that time, contrasted with the sixteen hundred millions at the present day.

When the tribulation sets in, Antichrist will rise at once, and do his best to counterfeit the work of God. I mean the Arch Antichrist of the last days, which the prophecies of Revelations 17th Chapter reveal the Pope of Rome. There we read that he will be the eighth head of the Roman beast. Revelations 13th chapter says that he will be one of the seven heads, and will come up out of the bottomless pit and will go into perdition. The other six heads have all passed away, *i. e.*, the kingdom, the republic, the trumvirate, the dictatorship, the tribuneship, and the empire, which fell A. D. 476, when the barbarians, Goths, Huns, Vandals, and Heruli, conquered Rome. Then followed the papacy, which is the seventh head, and survives to this day. Now, as the eighth head is to be one of the seven, it must be identical with the seventh, *i. e.*, the papacy. The people are not aware that the world is thronged with Antichrists now.

Anti means "instead of;" therefore, *antichrist* simply

means "a substitute for Christ." We have two distinct lines of preaching ringing around the world to-day, *i. e.*, the true and the counterfeit; the former cries, *"Behold, the Lamb of God that taketh away the sin of the world;"* meanwhile, the counterfeit shouts, "Lo here, lo there, come to us, let us baptize you or sacrament you; follow us, if you want to be saved you must have this or that." All such represent antichrist, *i. e.*, they offer you "a substitute."

Our glorious Christ, none other that God Almighty, Who has become our Vicarious Substitute, needs no help to save the whole world, therefore, everyone who offers a substitute of any kind is preaching the counterfeit gospel of antichrist.

The current "Tongues" heresy, substitutes the mystery of an unknown language for the mystery of Godliness, *i. e.*, regeneration and sanctification, which are mysteries indissoluble to all the uninitiated, to those who experience them, no longer a mystery, but so plain, *"That way-faring men, though fools, need not err therein."* (Isaiah 35:8.)

Satan resorts to all conceivable devices in order to play off substitutes on the people, so as to get the eye off of Christ. I was informed by candid, reliable Holiness people, that they actually studied languages in books in the "Tongues" meetings. I do hope many genuine cases will yet develop, but none that I have yet heard of, who have received a foreign language in these meetings have found their people and utilized their language. That is really the decisive test, because we know that God's works are all abundantly competent to bear the test of intelligibility, and utility. But the sad

SPIRITUAL GIFTS. 193

commentary on all these "Tongues" meetings, is the fact of their unfruitfulness in conversions and sanctifications. The best Christians I have ever known have certified to me that they had thoroughly investigated, and in their meetings, while many are at the altar seeking the gift of tongues, they never find one seeking pardon or purity, thus you see the work is on a sidetrack, deflecting the people from the Great Trunk Line, running out from Regeneration Station and reaching Glorification Depot, landing you in the New Jerusalem.

E. There is a sense in which we can all receive the gift of tongues to the infinite enhancement of our usefulness, even if we live and die in our native land, never enjoying the privilege of being a foreign missionary, and consequently, never needing the gift of a foreign tongue.

Our English language with only 23,000 original words, has grown into the enormous vocabulary of one hundred and fifty thousand. The common people only speak three to four hundred words; great scholars, only eight to ten thousand. Therefore, you see what a grand thing a gift of the English language would be to us all.

Before I got sanctified, I could not preach a sermon unless I had studied it out. If I tried it, I would run out of words. When the Lord sanctified me, He conferred on me the gift of the English tongue in a glorious and illimitable enlargement, so as to make me a preaching-machine, never running out of words; the more I speak, the more I have on hand; like the river flowing on, augmented anon by tributary after tributary, till it disembogues into the sea.

Language is the vehicle by which we transmit the wonderful saving message of Gospel grace, therefore, we should all go to God for this gift, which will make us indefatigable talking machines for God, holiness, and Heaven. These gifts are free for all. Oh, what a mistake we make when we do not duly appreciate them! I am praying God to use the current "Tongues" Movement to stir up the Holiness People to appreciate these extraordinary gifts of the Spirit, as they constitute the Christian soldiers panoply invested in which he is more than a match for the enemy. I trow you have read my book on the subject which the Lord gave me nearly a score of years ago, and wonderfully blessed it in the edification of people.

N. B. "Tongues" has no meaning but "languages," as language is the great and indispensable vehicle of thought, therefore, we cannot appreciate this gift too highly. We should with adoring gratitude, so appreciate it that we would all avail ourselves of its invaluable utility, not only receiving it, but developing in the appreciation, and availability of it, at the same time watching lest Satan lead us into fanaticism and infidelity over it, as he is wont to do with every good thing.

These gifts are of so infinite value to us, as God's panoply, with which to fight and conquer the insidious enemy, that we will be foolish, and inculpatory, if we do not appreciatively utilize them; yet when we give them preeminence over the graces, *i. e.*, regeneration and sanctification, "without which we lose our souls," even though we may have all the gifts, in that case we run into fanaticism and idolatory, exalting the gift above the Giver, *i. e.*, the creature above the Creator.

F. We now reach the interpretation of tongues, which is the ninth and the last in the catalogue. The

Lord has let me travel in Greece, the land of poetry, oratory, philosophy, the fine arts, statesmenship, and heroism, brightest on the escutcheon of Ancient history. If you ever visit Athens, you will doubtless go to the Hill of the Muses. These nine Muses were wonderful little divinities, who inspired the true genius, which makes the poet, the orator, the philosopher, the artisan, the inventor, the statesman, the hero, the martyr, and everything calculated to exalt humanity and write the name on fame's fair temple to shine with ever increasing splendor.

The Greeks had no Bible. The great sea rolled between them and the Hebrews, the only people in the world who had a knowledge of the true God. The mariner's compass and the steam engine were entirely unknown, navigation was in its infancy, and very perilous. The Jews had a commission from God, then, to carry their religion to the ends of the earth. Yet the Holy Spirit in the absence of the written Word, so wonderfully illuminated the brilliant intellects and vivid imaginations of these wonderful Greeks, as to enable them to reach much primary truth in its primeval essence, and virtue; *e. g.*, these nine Muses, which are glorious natural substitutes for the nine spiritual gifts. Interpretation is really the normal concomitant of the languages.

Hundreds and thousands of words and phrases in your own language need interpretation and must have it, if the end which language conserves is reached, *i. e.*, the transmission of truth from the speaker to the auditor. But when you are speaking in a language entirely unknown, the interpretation is absolutely necessary.

In my travels among the heathens, I constantly preach

through an interpreter standing by me, and speaking my message to the people in their own language. The blessed Holy Spirit has given me the beautiful languages in which the Scriptures is written, and also the interpretation of the same. A whole generation has passed away since I have used the New Testament in a translation but constantly the inspired original, at the same time serving as my own interpreter, otherwise it would be utterly useless to the people who do not understand it.

God forbids us to speak in an unknown tongue, unless it is interpreted; meanwhile, He positively commands us, (1 Cor. 14:26,) *"Let all things be done to edification."* These commandments are so recklessly violated in the "Tongues" meetings, now prevalent in this country, as to thoroughly convince all honest Bible readers that while the gift of tongues is all right in its place, these meetings are flooded with heresy and fanaticism, calculated to ruin souls by detracting attention away from our glorious Christ, Who saves us by regeneration and sanctification, and focalizing it on the gift of tongues, or anything else, which is not essential to salvation.

The Roman Catholic Church is awfully guilty at this point, having their services all over the world in the Latin language, which the people do not understand, and which is positively forbidden by the Word of God, thus involving them in a fearful responsibility.

Though I preach and teach directly out of unknown tongues all the time, I do not give them to the people, but the interpretation, God in His great mercy, having conferred on unworthy me both the gift and the interpretation. The blessed Holy Spirit wonderfully confers this gift of interpretation.

SPIRITUAL GIFTS. 197

In 1849 A. D., when the Methodists held their first camp-meeting in California, for the salvation of those wicked miners, as Bishop Fitzgerald, who was present, then a circuit-rider, afterward wrote up in the "National Advocate;" among the vast multitudes of all nationalities, the Indian tribe of that region was there in full force, escorted by their venerable chief who, sitting at the root of a tree, listened to the bishop on Sunday morning, while he preached one of the greatest sermons of his life, standing two solid hours, his face literally illuminated with the glory of God, preaching "with the Holy Ghost sent down from Heaven," swaying the multitudes, like the storm bears down before it the bending forests, the vast throng lingering spellbound as from his eloquent lips, wave after wave of sweeping eloquence rolled down from Heaven, inundating his soul and with his stentorian voice inundating the enchanted multitude. Meanwhile, the face of the old Indian chief lit up with supernatural splendor, and his eyes caught the flash and sparkle of preter-natural brillancy, and before the bishop wound up his sermon, his enraptured brother in red, leaped and shouted aloud. What was the solution of the wonderful effect of the bishop's sermon on the Indian chief, who did not know a word of the English language? Why, the blessed Holy Spirit interpreted to him, *i. e.*, imparted to him His own blessed gift of interpretation.

In 1620, when the Pilgrim fathers landed on the Plymouth Rock, John Elliott, their faithful preacher soon immortalized himself preaching to the Indians, and in the history of the United States, this day enjoys the honorable cognomen of Indian apostle. He used to preach to great crowds of the poor heathen savages, right on the ground where the city of Boston now stands, when there was not a stick of this, but all in the wild woods. While he stood before them, his face deluged with sympathetic tears, preaching to them the unsearchable riches of Christ with all his might, there was no one commandable who understood both languages, the Indian and the English. It was impossible for him to preach to them in their own tongue, because he did not know it, neither was it possible for the Indians to have it interpreted into their own language, for there was no one at their command who understood both languages, yet, while he preached to them, just as if they understood him, those ignorant savages, clothed in skins of wild beasts, got so convicted, that falling on the ground, rolling in the leaves, they cried to God for His mercy; He bent the Heavens, and came down and wonderfully converted their souls. Leaping to their feet, they hugged one another, and rejoiced with "joy unspeakable and full of glory."

What was the secret of the wonderful phenomenon? The blessed Holy Spirit imparted to those poor Indians the gift of interpretation. You all need this gift and cannot do without it. It is indispensable to qualify you to understand the Bible and other good books, which you read, explanatory of the Bible. You can have this gift; it does not cost anything. God calls everything by its right name. If it were not a gift, He would not so call it. The very fact that it is a gift involves the conclusion that is is for you, and that, without money and without price.

G. When Jonathan went out with the lonely armor-bearer, climbed the Philistine citadel, shouted uproar-

SPIRITUAL GIFTS. 199

iously, panic-struck them all, they fled from the field, and a great victory subvened. There we see a glorious verification and an illustration of the concomitancy of the blessed Holy Spirit, the Armor-bearer of the Christian warrior on the battle-field.

The ancient warrior went into the battle as light and elastic as the bounding antelope, and free as a bird of paradise, meanwhile, his armor-bearer carried his weapons of warfare, handing him the one he needed in the dint of time. So the blessed Holy Spirit, with His Omnipotent Arm, carries His own weapons; meanwhile the competent has nothing to do but use them.

E. G. This City (Cincinnati), with her 500,000 people on either side of the beautiful Ohio, is invaded by an army. The warriors are safe in their citadels, which they regard as impregnable, consequently, the invading foe must drive them out, and force them to evacuate or meet him on the battle-plain, and settle the matter. Therefore, he selects a lofty mountain, uses the heaviest artillery, and bombards the city, till he forces all the fighting men to evacuate their citadels, and meet him on the open plains, or surrender at descretion. Now, they evacuate the mountain summit, and descend into the plain, and meet the whole army in battle array. They need a goody supply of musketry, powder, shot, bayonets and swords, as well as the heavy artillery. All these are promptly furnished by the government at her own expense, not only all the cannons, muskets, bayonets, and diversified ammunitions of war, but she furnishes the wagons and mules that haul them to the mountain-side, and back to the plain. If the soldiers had to pull the cannon, and lug their arms and ammunition, it would break them down, and disqualify them for the dint of conflict, which they must meet successfully, or suffer signal defeat. Now the embattled host meet on the open plain. Terrible is the conflict; charge after charge, made by the brilliant cavalcades, till eventually the phalanx is broken, and the lines are everywhere waving to and fro in disorganization and consternation, now in the general charges and stampedes, the warriors meeting everywhere in deadly hand to hand combat, the plain deluged with blood and heaped with mountains of the slain, every warrior wants a six-shooter. All these revolvers are furnished by the Republic, at Her own expense; neither artillery, rifles, swords, revolvers, bayonets, shot, grape, canister, nor gattling-guns cost the soldiers a solitary cent; the Republic furnishes them all and the wagons and teams that haul them to the scene of conflict. The soldiers have nothing to do but load and shoot, wield the sword, and bayonet.

Even so it is with the Christian soldier. The Government of Heaven furnished his own whole panoply, consisting of these nine Supernatural gifts of the Holy Spirit, Who is the Executive of the Trinity, and the Executive of the Divine Government. What God does for human souls He does through His Agent, the Holy Spirit; what Jesus does for souls, He does through His Agent, the Holy Spirit. Consequently, the blasphemy, *i. e.,* blasphemy against the Holy Ghost is the only unpardonable sin.

Get this glorious uttermost salvation, so you will be done with yourself and saved to the uttermost; therefore, nothing to do but to save others; then in utter and eternal abandonment, go out intrepid and fearless, to meet the myriad foe, relying on the great Captain of our salvation to go with you, ever condescending to serve you as Armor-bearer. Then enter the conflict, sure of victory, because King Jesus never loses a battle. The Armor-bearer, the blessed Holy Ghost, is by your side, the Custodian of His own gifts; not giving them to you as personal property, lest Satan tempt you to spiritual pride and get inflated, but as the heavy artillery belongs to the Government, and you simply have use of it, not for your own good, but that of your country; so you have a free use of all these spiritual gifts, not for yourself, but for the glory of God, in the salvation of lost people, who will shine like stars in your crown of rejoicing for ever and ever. So do not delude yourself with the idea that you can appropriate yourself with these gifts, but simply utilize them for the glory of God in saving the lost. 1 Cor. 12:11: *"All these worketh in you one and the same Spirit, dispensing unto each one as he willeth."* This is the key which solves the problem, unlocks the mystery, and gives you the clear light, in reference to the reception and utilization of these wonderful gifts. Your attitude is that of utter, unreserved, and eternal abandonment to God, with perfect faith in Him, to give you all the needed help as His promise meets every emergency. *"My grace shall be sufficient for you."*

The moment you need "wisdom," He gives it to you; quick as the flash of lightning, when you need "knowledge" He comes to your relief, so with the "gift of faith," He inspires it according to the emergency; when you need "bodily healing" for yourself, and for others, He imparts it, in the dint of time. He really makes you a moving dynamo, ever full of the dynamite, which is

God's definition of the "Gospel." *"The dynamite of salvation to every one that believeth."* (Rom. 1:16.) Therefore, you are always armed with "dynamite," which is God's explosive, to blow out of the heart the devil and everything he ever put in fallen humanity. The moment you need the gift of "prophecy," which qualifies you to speak to the people, to *"Edification, exhortation, and comfort"* He gives it to you, thus making you a preaching-machine, always ready to tell the people the truth of God, and thus edify them, at the same time overflowing with exhortation to everybody, to be true to God, and make sure of Heaven, and ever ready to comfort them with the precious promises, which are sure and steadfast, and under which all can perfectly rely and, *"Thank God and take courage."*

This blessed Armor-bearer is always ready to impart the "discernment of spirits," the very time you need it, not only giving you grace to try the spirits, (1 John 4:1,) but giving you the discernment, which reads people, like you read books, and discriminates what Gospel they need,—whether Sinai or Conviction, Calvary or Conversion, Pentecost or Sanctification, or the Transfiguration Gospel; to keep them always ready to be translated in the *"Twinkling of an eye."* (1 Cor. 15:52.)

This wonderful Armor-bearer has the very language you need, at the time you need it to glorify God, in the conviction of sinners, the conversion of penitents, the sanctification of believers, the reclamation of backsliders, and the establishment of God's Kingdom in all the earth. He gives you words you need at the very time you need them. He says we need not premeditate what we are going to say, He says the Holy Ghost will give it to us at the time we need it; *"For it is not you that speak, but the Holy Ghost speaking in you."* But this unedifying gibberish, which characterizes the "Tongues" meetings, exciting the people and running into wild fanaticism, to no profit, is not the work of the Holy Spirit, but that of unholy spirits, in order to deceive the people, and to ruin them. Rest assured, all of God's work is full of intelligent edification, everything else belonging to the evil one.

In the Pentecostal revival, we are informed that people were there from *"every nation under heaven."* Therefore, we have no right to conclude that a language was spoken on that occasion, which people in that multitude did not understand, as God speaks no idle words, neither does He allow you or me to speak an idle word. *"Idle"* in that passage, literally means, "inefficient." Therefore, He does not allow us to speak a word that does not accomplish something good. So beware how you impute this senseless, and meaningless gibberish, characterizing the "Tongues" meetings, to the Holy Ghost. I would not dare to do it, lest I sin against him. The very fact that nobody is edified in the meetings by those so-called tongues, is *prima facia* evidence that they are not given by the Holy Ghost, Who positively forbids us to have anything in our meetings that does not edify somebody. It is a well-known fact that this gibberish edifies no one, unless the recipients of these unknown tongues find the people, and use them for the glory of God, the arguments warrant the conclusion that they are given by demons, as in case of the Spiritualists, who are devil-worshippers in this country.

The blessed Holy Spirit, your glorious Armor-bearer,

will go with you on the streets and give you language, so you will never run out; He gives it to me, always and everywhere.

Satan is the sworn enemy of the Holy Ghost, consequently, he and his emissaries are doing everything in their power to counterfeit the mighty works of the Holy Ghost, and thus use them as greased planks, over which to slide people into Hell. Rest assured, it is your privilege to utilize, for the glory of God, and enjoy all of these gifts. We may therefore observe that as a rule in every Christian character, some one predominates. You see the idea that all do not use all of them at the same time, yet 1 Corinthians 12: 31 commands us to covet them earnestly, that shows us it is our privilege to have them, some in greater measure than others.

I do verily believe that since I have entered the sanctified experience, I have enjoyed them all in a measure, some times one more copiously than another. These diversities manifest in the different gifts are somewhat accomodatory to the character of the conflict in which we are engaged.

I close this exegesis with an illusion to an incident in my life, which beautifully illustrates it. The first time I traveled in the Holy Land, in 1895, when we went to Jericho, the Jordan and the Dead Sea, as we had to pass through the wilderness of Judea, which in all ages has been badly infested with robbers, because the caves are so numerous, and so large, in that crowded bed of mountains, innumerable peaks, just dotting all the region, affording so ample hiding that none of the governments have ever been able to exterminate them, and keep them out. This vividity illustrates the case of the traveler beaten by the robbers as he went down to Jericho. (St. Luke 10:25-37.) We had to travel that same road. I have traveled over it six times and always with an armed escort. I was surprised to find our escort a solitary man, tall, active as a catamount, with keen-flashing eye, and riding the fleetest horse I ever knew, his easy walk, keeping all of our horses in a trot. When passing through a deep mountain gorge, the craggy steep mountain above our heads, my guide said to me: "This is the valley of blood, so named, because so many travelers have been killed by robbers," at the same time, calling my attention to five robbers skulking in the mountain with their guns on their shoulders, and observing, said: "I told you, you could not travel this route without an armed escort. Now, you see these robbers; they would be on us quickly if they did not see the escort," (whose uniform and the regalia of his horse were characterized with the most showy colors, so he was identified readily as far as could be seen, and when the robbers see the escort, they are afraid to attack us, because even if they succeeded in robbing us, the whole Bedouin nation, represented by the escort, would turn out against them, hunt and kill them all.)

But as our escort was a lonely man, when I see the five robbers, all armed, I begin to feel a degree of insecurity, and say to my guide: "Interpret for me, while I talk to the escort." Then I proceed: "Now, escort, I see those five robbers, and for aught I know, five hundred are in their caves, and are ready to respond to the report of a gun; then what would you do if a troop were to attack us?" I saw no weapon, but a short gun swinging around his neck, and a sword belted on him. Then he responded, holding up the gun in his hand: "This gun shoots seventeen times, and never hangs fire." The guide intercepting, notifies me that he has revolvers all over him, unseen, hidden by the loose garments, peculiar to the Orientals. "Hence, I am sure he is good for a hundred shots." Meanwhile he encourages me that he never misses; then lifting up his sword, he observes, that when the hundred shots are gone, "I will give them this till I have time to reload; therefore traveler, do not be afraid, for you are in no danger."

Rest assured, the Holy Ghost beats my Bedouin escort out of sight. *"Therefore let not your heart be troubled;"* Take Jesus for your only Leader, the Holy Ghost for your only Guide, and the New Testament for your only Authority, and you are as sure of Heaven as if you were in it.

CHAPTER XII.

GLORIFICATION.

Though this great and final work of the Holy Ghost is indispensable to our admission into Heaven, from the fact that we do not receive it by an act of our own will through repentance and faith, as in case of its two great and indispensable antecedents, *i. e.*, regeneration for sinners, and sanctification for Christians, therefore, we give it the place among the non-essentials so far as preaching the Gospel is concerned. Like pre-natal justification and regeneration, it is normally administered by the Holy Spirit, responsive to the great and glorious vicarious substitutionary atonement, which the Son of God has made for every human being. Confirmatory of the conclusion of its dispensability to admission into Heaven, we refer you to St. Luke 20:36. Our Savior's response to the insidious question of the Sadducees, appertaining to the woman who survived her seventh husband: *"Whose wife shall she be in the resurrection,"* when He answered, *"In that day, they will neither be marrying, nor giving in marriage: but all will be as the angels of God; being the sons of the resurrection."* The word in this response *Isoi angeloi*, i. e., "equal to the angels, or like the angels of God," thus involving the conclusion that angelic perfection precluding all infirmities is indispensable to admission into Heaven.

This third great work of the Holy Spirit, executive of the new creation, is wrought in the human soul and spirit, simultaneously with the evacuation of the body. While it is a truth at once beautiful, grand and climacteric sublime, forever sweeping away the last vestige of infirmity, hereditary from the fall; yet as the human will is not involved in its reception, because the Holy Spirit, pursuant to the normal functions of His office, as the Omnipotent Executive of the Trinity, administers it to all sanctified souls, *nolens volens, i. e.,* "without an act of the will." As the will determines the sphere of human responsibility, therefore, items of Gospel truth, which do not in any way involve it, are not essential to salvation, because we will all receive their benefit, whether we hear or understand them or not, yet they are indispensable to our edification in the Kingdom, and instruction in righteousness.

H. Whereas justification, which is the reversal of the condemnatory sentence, saves us from guilt, giving us a clear record in Heaven, meanwhile its invaluable concomitant, regeneration, resurrects the dead human spirit, making us new creatures in Christ; sanctification saves us from depravity, which we inherit from the fall, —crucifying the "old man," destroying the "body of sin," burying him by the baptism, which Jesus gives with the Holy Ghost and fire, so deep into the death of Christ, *i. e.,* the atonement, that Satan will never be able to resurrect him, thus giving us a clean heart, and gloriously consummating the negative phrase of entire sanctification, which is invariably followed by the positive, *i. e.,* the infilling of the Holy Spirit, in the succession of crucified Adam, the first, now comes to abide, and give victory.

GLORIFICATION.

Therefore, entire sanctification, both positive and negative, constitutes full salvation, which is the normal standard of the New Testament Church, anything inferior dropping you down on the plane of the old dispensation, and putting you back in legal bondage, where, sad to say, the rank and file of the Protestant Churches this day groan under the burden of the violated law. While the first great work of grace, constituting the beautiful globe of conversion, which consists of two hemispheres, justification, the negative, liberating you from the condemnation normal to actual transgression, regeneration, the positive, giving you a new heart, thus making you a *bona fide* citizen of God's kingdom, the normal result of the supernatural birth. (St. John 3:5-7.)

In the glorious and gracious economy succeeded by the beautiful globe of entire sanctification, consummated by the radical expurgation of inbred sin out of the heart by the cleansing Blood of Jesus, administered by the Holy Spirit, thus giving you a clean heart, the blessed Holy Ghost thus having cleansed the temple, now comes in, filling it with his glory to abide for ever, thus flooding the soul with the fulness of God, and verifying the positive hemisphere of this great new creation wrought by the blessed Holy Spirit, responsive to the great vicarious substitutionary atonement, consummated by the Son, with His own redeeming Blood poured out on Calvary. This great consummating work of the Holy Ghost gives you full salvation, illiminating all inbred sin out of the heart and making you holy.

Josephus tells us that it was a common thing at the great annual Passover to sacrifice two hundred and fifty thousand lambs. Oh, what rivers of blood; quantity substituted for quality, and all symbolizing the lamb of God, bleeding on Calvary.

When Solomon dedicated the temple, he sacrificed twenty-two thousand oxen and a hundred and twenty thousand sheep; after this, falling on his knees in the portico, while the myriads of Israel bowed on the Holy Campus in front; he led the dedicatory prayer, hovering over the most beautiful superstructure ever beheld by mortal eyes, to the God of Israel, for His abiding place in the midst of his people who, entering in His glory, filled the temple.

You know, the temple symbolizes the human heart, as it was expurgated by those rivers of blood, typefying the precious redeeming Blood of the Great Antitype, dying on Calvary; so when our hearts are thoroughly expurgated by the Blood of Christ, sprinkled by the Holy Ghost, then He comes in, filling us with the bright cloud of His glory, shining away all our darkness for ever, thus filled with all the fullness of God (Eph. 3:19) we enjoy beautiful satisfactory, normal New Testament saintship, *bona fide* in His kingdom in this world.

N. B. The Divine administration is three-fold. In Hell it is punitive; in earth it is mixed; but Heaven it is glorious.

Entire sanctification confers normal citizenship in his terrestrial administration, but we still need another great work of the Holy Spirit in order to deliver us from all infirmities, which are not sins condemnatory, nor contaminatory, yet they are sins of ignorance, through failure of memory, errors of judgment, and torpitude of our sensibilities, which frequently supervenes from physical conditions. Whereas, John Wesley denominated these troubles, "infirmities," the Bible pronounces them "sins of ignorance," and though not condemnatory, yet they need atonement.

This we see in the Cities of Refuge, which were on both sides of Jordan's swelling flood, so as to be accessible by every person who had accidentally committed homicide. The Mosaic administration had no judiciary, but only the executive department, specifying the nearest relative as the executor of the death-penalty in case of murder. Therefore, in case of accidental homicide, the man-slayer was permitted to flee to the City of Refuge, Kedesh in Galilee, Shechem in Samaria, Hebron in Judea, Ramoth in Gilead, and Gozan in Perea. When the homicide took place, if the slayer did not make his escape to one of the Cities of Refuge, the nearest kinsman of the slain was certain to pursue him, and avenge the blood of his relative. Therefore, if the avenger of blood overtook the man-slayer in his flight for life, he was certain to kill him, whereas, if he could only by the hardest running, reach the City of Refuge, come in time to fall through the gate, come before the avenger overtook him, he was all right, and perfectly safe.

While these beautiful similies so beautifully represent the absolute necessity of the atonement, as well as its perfect expurgatory efficacy, it forever settles the undisputable truth, that even sins of ignorance, *i. e.*, mistakes,—need the atonement.

1. Conversion, the great first work of grace, including justification, by which God, for Christ's sake, cancels all your sins from Heaven's chancery; and regeneration,

in which you are *"born from above,"* and raised from the dead, is salvation.

Sanctification, which includes the elimination of inbred sin, by the cleansing Blood, and the infilling of the Holy Spirit, is *full* salvation.

But Glorification, which sweeps away all infirmities, thus forever saving us from sins of ignorance, is final salvation. (1 Peter 2:2.) *"Therefore having laid aside all malice, and all guile, and hypocrisies, and envyings, and all calumniations, as newly born babes, desiring the pure milk of the Word, in order that you may grow thereby into salvation: if you have tasted that the Lord is good."* This passage beautifully reveals the truth we here enunciate. Here we have the new birth specified, and the subsequent removal of inbred sin, followed by the positive commandment, "To desire and earnestly seek after the pure milk of the Word," in order that we may grow thereby.

This last clause, *eis soterian,* slipped through the fingers of some careless transcribers, and is not in the *Lestris receptus,* from which the English Version was translated. Consequently, that final clause, *"Into salvation,"* is not in it.

This illustrates the indispensable importance of having all the Scripture, and nothing else. For this reason, you need my translation, which is the only one in the world that leaves out all the interpolation and gives all of the lost passages, restored in their places. This final salvation, we all receive, when the Holy Ghost glorifies the soul, by applying the precious Blood to sweep away all the infirmities encumbering the human spirit, through the collateral influence of the fallen mind and body.

GLORIFICATION.

Heb. 2:9: *"But we see Jesus, humiliated somewhat below the angels on account of the suffering of death, crowned with glory and honor in order by the grace of God, He might taste death for every one."* Here we see clearly revealed, the universal redemption of mankind. 1 Cor. 15:22: *"As in Adam all die, even so in Christ shall all be made alive."* Here we see clearly the fact revealed, that every human being is fallen in Adam, and redeemed in Christ. Whereas, the Adamic fall is seminal, as he was the only creation. (Acts 17:26.) When God created him, He created the whole human race, Eve being no exception, as she was but a transformation of Adam's rib. Therefore, when Adam fell, every human being fell; consequently, every one inherited depravity, *i. e.,* spiritual death from the fall.

While the fall is seminal, the redemption, as you see, (Heb. 2:9,) is personal, therefore, the moment soul and body unite—constitute personality, which is some time before the physical birth, that very moment justification and regeneration by the normal grace supervene.

If you do not have the correct translation at this point, *"Born from above,"* (St. John 3:5, 7,) and not "born again," as in English Version, you will get tangled up in contradictions, which abound in the English Version, but not one in the Word of God.

N. B. Here you see the four works of grace, in the great plan of salvation; *i. e.,* justification and regeneration in the pre-natal state, without faith, or without works; then the justification and regeneration of the adult sinner, (which is simply his reclamation from a backslidden state, as illustrated in the case of the Prodigal Son) by faith alone, as the sinner is in the devil's kingdom, where he cannot work for God, as all his work belongs to Satan, and he must get out of his kingdom, and, by the super-natural birth, become a citizen of God's Kingdom, before he can possibly work for Him. Then there is a third justification, which is that of a Christian, in the sense of Divine approval, (James 2,) which is by faith and works.

There is also a fourth justification; when we stand before the final Judgment Bar, (Rev. 22: 12,) which is by works alone, determinative of reward. While our good works have really nothing to do with our salvation, they constitute the measure of our reward in Heaven.

Here you see two great works of grace, which are in no way dependent on the human will, *i. e.*, the prenatal redemption of every human being, including a full and free justification through the atonement of Christ, and concomitant regeneration by the Holy Spirit, and the final glorification of the soul, simultaneously with its disembodiment.

While these great and mighty works of the Holy Spirit, the Omnipotent, Omniscient and Omnipresent Dispensor of the wonderful redeeming grace of God in Christ, through His perfect vicarious substitutionary atonement, are utterly independent of the human will, consequently, not necessary to preach them in order to the salvation of the people, the former having taken place before we knew anything, and the latter in the normal and infallible economy, postponed till mortal life is swallowed up in victory, and is too late for the will to participate in the wonderful achievement which, in the majority of cases, supervenes as a glorious and happy surprise, because the fewest number of Christians have ever heard of it, and even those who have received the most liberal instructions, have but a vague apprehension of the glories that await us.

The conclusion in which nearly all Christians abide, is that we have to go to Heaven to be glorified, which is a mistake, the truth being the very opposite, *i. e.*, we have to be glorified in order to go to Heaven. The mighty work of the Holy Ghost sweeps away all of our infirmities, which must take place before we enter Heaven, (St. Luke, 20:36,) where you see Jesus positively informs us that we are to have "angelic perfection," (my translation.)

J. These infirmities, which are eliminated by the Holy Ghost in glorification, are the scars which sin has left on the soul in the cruel tread of Satan's great rough cloven feet.

I have a big scar on my body, where the Lord healed a cancer ten years ago, after it had troubled me a while, though I had never lost an hour's work for it. Having been notified by a medical authority that I must have it amputated, I turned it over to the infallible Surgeon, to perform the delicate operation. He used no cruel knife, but as He commanded the storm, sweeping over the Sea of Galilee, to acquiesce, and there was a great calm; so, in condescending mercy, responsive to my faith, he commanded the cancer, "Depart and return no more." *Ex neccatate,* it departed, leaving its souvenir, a great scar, which will abide till glorification sweeps it away. In a similar manner, my poor soul, though perfectly healed, is scarred all over, as by small-pox, which renders me odious and obnoxious to the sensibilities of many good people, who pronounce me, "Odd, cranky, crazy, fool, etc." When they meet me on the Shining Shore they will have nothing to criticize, as I will outshine the sun, and they will recognize no dark shadow; the old scars having all evanesced before the splendors of the Sun of Righteousness, in the finishing touches of glorification.

We here see the ineffable manifestations of Omnipotent redeeming grace. The scars forever tell the story of crookedness and meanness, debauchery, and diabolisms, though long ago gloriously healed of all the wounds inflicted by the cruel missles hurled from Satan's quiver. Perfect health is the triumphant achievement of entire sanctification, yet it has no power to remove the scars, which still we carry to our shame, because they mar our beauty, and really make us very ugly. Suppose we carried them into Heaven, these obnoxious souvenirs would reveal to the angels, who have never known sin, nor sorrow, the dark story of our unhappy lives in this world.

Oh, I am so glad the mighty besom of glorification will sweep them all away, so the debauchee, the thug and the harlot will shine with a splendor so beautiful and glorious, that the angels will recognize not a solitary vestige of Satan's heavy tread, and Hell's black smut; but they will gladly take us all in their arms, and hail us, as brothers, and sisters, beloved in the Lord, and not a memento of discount, possibly discernable by those immortalized, which outshine the stars, and never grow dim. Oh, how blessed to contemplate the stupendous victories of redeeming grace, not only settling the sin problem with a shout of victory, which will ring on through the flight of eternal ages, but even those innocent infirmities which so mar the beauty of holiness, while we dwell in these clay-houses, that good people misunderstand and misjudge us, because they cannot look within and see our thoughts, and motives, and realize that we always mean right, and are trying to be good. Oh, it is wonderful how the triumphant grace of God in Christ in the glorious ultimation, after having conquered every foe, and eradicated and exterminated every sin, is going to take away all of the ashes, and give us beauty, that will magnetize and immortalize through the flight of eternal ages.

K. The pre-natal justification and regeneration constitute the normal redemption of every soul, verifying the consolatory fact, that every human being, through the wonderful and stupendous grace of God in Christ is actually born in the kingdom, and only gets out by overt transgression.

Now you see this great and universal redemption, including normal justification and regeneration, supervenes without any reference to the human will. The same is true appertaining to the glorification, which climaxes the great work of final salvation, sweeping away all the scars which the heavy tread of sin has ever left.

These two mighty works, constituting the Alpha and Omega, are wrought by the blessed Holy Spirit for every human being, *nolens volens*. While there is no exception whatever to the justification and regeneration in the pre-natal state; of course, glorification is only for those who are sanctified wholly, all others having forfeited it by actual transgression.

We all understand, that all infants and adult Christians are sanctified by the normal grace of Christ, administered by the Holy Spirit in the article of death. While all Christians should be duly instructed on these great truths, a pre-natal regeneration, and glorification; not only for their own education, but in order to qualify them for usefulness in the salvation of others, yet the great burden of Gospel preaching, should be the salvation of sinners, and the sanctification of Christians, "Without which, no one will ever be the recipient of glorification."

The fact that so many Christians oppose sanctification, upon the allegation that it puts us beyond temptation, and where we cannot sin, is an indirect confession of their own mistake, putting sanctification where glorification really belongs. The same people tell you, there are no sanctified people on the earth, quoting, *"There is not a just man on the earth, who doeth good and sinneth not,"* which is simply a wrong translation. This misapprehension of sanctification, giving it the definition of glorification, can only be successfully relieved by correct information, expository of both these great works. So long as they give sanctification the definition of glorification, they will have no courage to seek it, which involves them in terrible peril, because the Word is positive and unequivocal. Heb. 12:14: *"Without the sanctification no one shall see the Lord."*

The popular idea, that conversion, justification and regeneration, are all synonymous, is incorrect.

"Justification," from *justus, fio,* simply means, "To make you just," *i. e.,* right as before God. This can only be done by imputing to you the righteousness of Christ, which He has freely purchased for you, and you receive by simple faith, exercised after genuine repentance has put you on believing ground.

"Regeneration," is the resurrection of the dead soul into life, as the original positively reveals, thus giving you the super-natural birth, which makes you a member of God's family and consummates your reconciliation, and adoption.

These works of grace are only essential to conversion, in case that they have been forfeited by actual transgression, which has alienated the soul out of the Kingdom of God, in which it was born, having entered it by pre-natal justification.

"Conversion," literally means, "A turning round," from *cum,* "together," *verto,* "to turn." Its normal time and place, is antecedently to the forfeiture of infantile justification, by the commission of known sins. Hence, the great and vital importance of securing the intelligent conversion of every child before it is old enough to know right from wrong, and thus be exposed to the liability of apostasy from God. As the little ones are all weak, spiritually, on account of intellectual non-development, they are very liable to backslide, quickly and inadvertently, therefore, they need constant attention, not only to retain them in the kingdom, but reclaim them, quickly, when they backslide; because abiding in Satan's kingdom will prove awfully detrimental to their spirituality, by hardening the heart, and seriously jeopard their eternal hopes.

As every adult sinner is simply a backslider, pursuant to the prodigal son, therefore, the most of our work is on the line of reclamation. It has generally been called conversion, which probably takes place during the infantile justification and consists simply in turning the little one around (as the depravity, hereditary in the heart, Psa. 51:5, turns its face away from God,) and introducing it to the Savior. Thus conversion, in its right place, does not include justification and sanctification, because the child already has these works of grace, having received them in the pre-natal state. But this popular conversion, which is a simple reclamation from a backslidden state, cannot possibly take place without justification, to break the devil's yoke, which holds the victim fast in his kingdom; and the regeneration, which is the recreation of the Divine life in the soul of a sinner, which was superinduced by his own transgression. Ezek. 18:4, 20: *"The soul that sinneth, it shall die."* As there is no Heaven, without glorification, which saves us from sins of ignorance, and takes away all infirmities, which are incompatible with the Heavenly state, and no glorification without sanctification, and no sanctification without regeneration, therefore, the great burden of Gospel preaching is conviction, repentance, and faith, which constitute the graces, necessarily antecedent to justification, which must, in every case, precede regeneration, because the law cannot be violated with impunity. Christ has satisfied it but this will do us no good, unless we receive Him as our atoning Savior, by the grace of faith, which we never can do till genuine repentance puts us on believing ground. Rest assured, the indispensable *sine qua non* of glorification is entire sanctification, which can only come into a heart freely justified and truly born from above.

CHAPTER XIII.

Our Lord's Return and Glorious Reign on the Earth.

Egypt was the first country to come to the front of the world and stand at the head of the nations, during the reign of the Pharaohs; having reached the preeminence under the administration of Rameses II., known in history under the name of Sesostris.

Phœnicia succeeded Egypt in the leadership of the world, through the boundless wealth, and maritime power of Tyre and Sidon.

Israel under the military leadership of David, and the wisdom of Solomon, was the third to lead the nations.

The Chaldeans, under the wise administration and transient military genius and heroism of Nebuchadnezzar, was the fourth to stand at the front. She was succeeded by Persia, under the brilliant military career of Cyrus, the Great, Medo-Persian.

Greece, under the brilliant and unprecedently glorious military leadership of Alexander the Great, was the sixth to come to the front of the world, having conquered all nations. Alexander is said to have wept because there was not another world to conquer.

Rome was the seventh, after 753 years, spent almost incessantly in the prosecution of the bloody wars and the subjugation of all the nations of the earth, came to the front, and stood a thousand years.

Arabia, under the leadership of the false prophet, Mohammed and his successors, the Caliphs, was the eighth to contest for the pre-eminence and actually almost exterminated Christianity from the earth.

India, under the Mongol Empire, founded by Acbor, the great statesman and Tamerlane, the greatest military chief in his day; was the ninth to reach pre-eminence, and stand at the front of the world.

France, under the brilliant military career of Napoleon Bonaparte, was the tenth to reach the supremacy among all the nations of the earth, and hold the pre-eminence, till the fall of her mighty leader on the battle-fields of Waterloo, and his banishment to the lonely Isle of St. Helena, where he ended his eventful life, while a terrible storm was sweeping over the sea, significantly homogenous to his tempestous career. With the fall of Napoleon, under the prowess of the English armies, led by the Duke of Wellington, England came to the front of the world, where she stands to this day, ruling six hundred millions out of the sixteen hundred millions populating the globe.

In Daniel's chronological image to 3145, he sees the great Chaldean power, under Nebuchadnezzar, rule over the whole earth, for an important time, when this golden kingdom is succeeded by the silver kingdom of Persia, which in due time, gives way.

The brazen kingdom of Greece, which subdues the whole earth, and rules all nations, with a rod of iron, is destined to yield to mighty Rome, the great and invincible iron kingdom, marching her armies to the ends of the earth, and subjugating every nation beneath the skies, till mistress of the globe, her crown radiates the rays of an unsetting sun, and her scepter sweeps the circumberence of the globe. (2:44:) *"And in the days of these kings shall the God of heaven set up a kingdom, which shall never be destroyed: and the kingdoms shall not be left to other people, but it shall break in pieces and shall consume all of these kingdoms, and shall stand for ever."* (Ch. 7:9, 10, 13, 14.) *"I beheld till the thrones were cast down, and the Ancient of days did sit, Whose garment was white as snow, and the hair of His head like the pure wool: His throne was like the fiery flame, and His wheels were burning fire. A fiery stream issued and came forth before Him: a thousand thousands ministered unto Him, and ten thousand times ten thousand stood before Him: . . . . I saw in the night visions, and, behold, one like the Son of Man came with the clouds of heaven, and came to the Ancient of days, and they brought Him near before Him. And there was given Him dominion, and glory, and a kingdom, and all peoples, nations, and languages, should serve Him: His dominion is an everlasting dominion, which shall not pass away, and His kingdom, that which shall not be destroyed."* (Vs. 18.) *"But the saints of the most High shall take the kingdom, and possess the kingdom for ever, and even for ever and ever."*

You see in these prophecies of Daniel, that during the reign of these kings, *"The God of heaven will set up a kingdom, which shall never be destroyed: it will not be left to other people, but will subdue the whole earth and stand for ever."*

Daniel saw the great Roman kingdom, symbolized by the iron legs; the head of Rome symbolizing the Chaldean kingdom, under Nebuchadnezzar; the breast and arms, of silver, the Medo-Persian, under Cyrus; the brazen abdomen and thighs, the Grecian, under Alexander the great, and two feet on which the image stood, representing Rome and Constantinople and the ten toes, the ten kingdoms of the Middle Ages, into which the great Roman Empire was disintegrated when it fell under the destroying wars of the Goths, Huns and Vandals. Those ten kingdoms are still standing with little modification.

Then he says: *"I saw a stone cut out of the mountain without hands, strike the image on its feet, and it fell to pieces and became as the chaff of the Summer threshing-floor, but the stone filled the whole earth."* This is certainly none other than the kingdom of the Lord, which is destined to cover the whole earth, as the waters cover the sea, and as Daniel says in the days of these kings shall the God of Heaven set up a kingdom, which shall never be destroyed.

This prophecy did not receive its fulfillment in our Lord's first Advent, because it says that He will come in the clouds of Heaven, whereas in His first Advent, He came into the world, a babe, born in Bethlehem. Hence you see, the decisive difference between His two Advents. Again, in His first Advent, He refused to take the Kingdom of Israel; responding, *"My Kingdom is not of this world."* If He would have taken the Kingdom of Israel, they would not have crucified Him, but would have rallied round Him and fought for Him. Truly, He came the first time, a Man of sorrows and acquainted with grief, to suffer and die, to redeem the world. But He will come the second time, as you see here, in the clouds of Heaven, and come to the Ancient of days, *i. e.*, God, the Father, receive the Kingdom, ascend the throne of the world and reign forever. You see (Vs. 18,) that the saints of the most High, will receive the Kingdom, and possess it, for ever and ever. Daniel and John saw the same visions.

L. Rev. 20:6: *"Blessed and holy is He that hath part in the first resurrection: for they shall be kings and priests unto God, and reign with Christ a thousand years."* Satan's Post-millennial invasion of the earth (Vs. 7-9), will prove an utter failure, as you see, and consequently occasion no real interregnum in the reign of the saints. We read in Daniel 7:18 that the saints of the most High will possess the kingdom for ever and ever, and there is perfect harmony in God's Word, whether by the hand of Daniel or John.

The eternal reign of Christ, and that of the saints is in perfect harmony, because the latter will simply rule subordinate to the former, *i. e.*, our glorious Lord is going to rule the whole earth, and we know not to what extent other worlds, through the instrumentality of the saints constituting the Bridehood.

Here in the Fourth Chapter of Daniel, we have a measuring-line, felicitously revealed, by which we are enabled to approximate the time of the end. Though we found that no one knows the day of His coming, yet, we may proximately know the time of the end.

When the Theocracy went down, B. C. 587, with the Fall of Jerusalem, the destruction of the temple, by Nebuchadnezzar, human rule supervened; Nebuchadnezzar, enjoying the honor of God's successor in the administration of the earth. I trow, he was the most competent, and hence, when the world got so wicked that they would not submit to Divine rule, God, in mercy, selected the most competent man in all the earth to rule all nations. In this Fourth Chapter, you see how his gigantic intellect, which had so expeditiously conquered the world, that inspiration symbolizes him as a flying eagle; having become weary, reels, totters, and falls from the throne of the world. Hence, in his demented condition, utterly incompetent to administer his world-wide kingdom, thus leaving it to his royal cabinet and their coadjutors, he wanders away and dwells with the wild beasts, roaming over mountain and plain, in the delirium of his demented, though gigantic intellect, till seven years have passed away. Then God touches his body, and re-enthrones his masterly mind, restoring back his mighty ratiocination. When the news of his restoration reaches the palace, his people wait on him; wash, trim, and re-invest him with new royal apparel, and splendid regalia, mount him on the litter, borne high on the shoulders of his mighty nobles, amid the melodious clarion of every musical instrument, known to the world, with royal banners waving in the air, and triumphant shouts, they re-enthrone him, to rule all nations, as in bygone years.

These seven years constitute a decisive interregnum in his reign, thus symboliing the human interregnum, in the Divine administration. Verily, the Theocracy, which thunder-claps, lightning-shafts, and earth-quakes inaugurated from Sinai's melting summit, is not dead, but only indulging a short nap. Soon she will rise, refreshed by the invigorating slumber, resume her scepter, and crown, never to have another interregnum.

We have three methods of measuring time: by the

revolutions of the moon around the earth, the revolutions of the planets around the sun, and the revolutions of the earth around the sun. Of course, the heavenly bodies never vary in their periodical peregrinations through the void immense; but human calculations are not infallible, however, they certainly may be proximately relied on, according to the lunar chronology.

The Gentile times are 354 lunar years, multiplied by the seven years of Nebuchadnezzar's insanity equals 2478. The calendar year 360 by 7 equals 2520; while the solar year 365 by 7 equals 2555. The time which has elapsed since the fall of the Theocracy, B. C. 587 plus 1907 equals 2494. Now if you will substract from this sum 2478 you will have 16 years remaining. Hence, you see, according to the lunar chronology, the Gentile times have already passed away, and sixteen years more. 2520 less 2494 equals 26. You see, according to the planetary chronology, we still have twenty-six years of Gentile times. 2555 less 2494 equals 61. And you see, according to Solar Chronology, which is longest, we still have sixty-one years of Gentile times. Daniel 12:11 gives us 1290 years, for the desolation of Jerusalem by the Mohammedans. They subjugated the country in A. D. 634. Now, if you will subtract this number from 1290 plus 634 you will have 1924. Sow 1924 less 1907 equals 17. Hence, you see from these prophecies, the Gentile times only have seventeen years.

The twelfth chapter of Daniel says: *"Blessed is he that waiteth, and cometh to the end of the thousand three hundred and five and thirty days."* (1335.)

Now, let us from this number, 1335, subtract 1290, and you have the tribulation period, forty-five years.

Now, let us see when the tribulation is due, according to these chronologies.

N. B. The tribulation, forty-five years, belong to the Gentiles times. You have already seen that the lunar chronology expires the Gentiles times already, and sixteen years more, therefore 45 plus 16 equals 61. Consequently, you see, that according to the lunar chronology, the Rapture of the saints, which takes place immediately before the Tribulation sets in, is already over-due sixty-one years.

Let us proceed to consult the Planetary Chronology, which, as you see above, has twenty-six years of Gentile times yet to come. So, 45 less 26 equals 19, establishing the fact, that according to this Chronology, the Rapture of the saints is already over-due nineteen years.

Now, let us proceed to hear from the Solar Chronology, which gives sixty-one years of Gentile times yet to come. 61 less 45 equals 16. Hence, you see this Chronology, which is the longest of all, makes the Rapture of the saints due in sixteen years. Therefore, you see, the Lunar Chronology has the Rapture over-due sixty-one years; the Calendar over-due nineteen years, and the Solar due in sixteen years.

"Now, Brother Godbey, which one of these Chronologies are the more reliable?" I can only answer, the Lunar Chronology is generally used in Asia and Africa by the Jews and Mohammedans; the Planetary Chronology is generally used by the Nations of Europe; while the solar Chronology is currently used in America.

As an American, of course, I bow to the Solar Chronology; yet, am not disposed to criticise either of the others. It is certain, that the revolutions of the heavenly bodies are perfectly reliable in their periodicity, but, while astronomers have done their best to make perfect calculations, you know, they are not infallible. However, the legitimate conclusion crowds on us that we must be living in the time of the end, and our Lord is assuredly very nigh. Consequently, I am on the incessant outlook for His glorious appearing to call away His waiting Bride; in that case, He will not come to the earth, but in calling distance. 1 Thess. 4: 16-18: *"The Lord Himself will descend from heaven with a shout, with the voice of the archangel, and with the trump of God: and the dead in Christ will rise first: then we who are living who are left will be caught up along with them in the clouds, to meet the Lord in the air. So exhort one another by these words."*

Our Lord here is exceedingly plain and explicit in His positive affirmation, through inspired Paul, that He will, in Person, descend from Heaven with a shout with the triumph of God, and the voice of the archangel, and the dead in Christ shall rise first, *i. e.,* before the living are translated and caught up to meet the Lord in the air. After the resurrection of the buried saints, throughout the whole earth, we, living saints of the Bridehood, who are still left on the earth till that blessed and glorious epoch in the history of God's Kingdom, will be caught up to meet the Lord in the air, and thus be forever with Him.

Here the conclusion, that He will come to the earth this time, is not deducible, from the plain statement of the inspired Word, but, that instead of His coming to the earth, we will be caught up to meet Him in the air. Whereas, before our Rapture, the buried saints will already have risen and ascended to Him; you see we will be the last in the Rapture, and, consequently immediately with the Lord ascend into Heaven, to the Marriage Supper of the Lamb, where we will remain during the Tribulation Period, which Daniel gives forty-five years, but the Lord says, will be shortened, lest no life should be left on the earth, (however, that statement directly applies to the Jewish Tribulation, which lasted seven years, A. D. 66-73,) but we could not safely reject its application to the Gentile Tribulation; which, some think, will be just seven years, the period of the Jewish Tribulation; but as our tribulation will reach doubtless a thousand times as many as theirs did, I do not infer that it will drop much short of Daniel's forty-five years, because its great utility will be the elimination of the unsavable and incorrigible people out of the world, leaving only such as will do for the glorious Millennial Reign.

M. The Scriptures abound, and superabound with clear and explicit revelation, confirmatory of our Lord's glorious and personal return to reign on the earth. The statement, *"The Lord Himself,"* (1 Thess. 4:16,) cannot be twisted into a misunderstanding. The conclusion that the glorified Jesus, in Person, is coming back for His Bride, is absolutely irrefutable. Acts 1:11: *"And they said, Ye Galilean men, why stand ye gazing up into heaven? This same Jesus, Who has been caught up from you into heaven, will so come in the manner in which you saw Him going into heaven."* He went up in white clouds, accompanied by multitudes of angels, hence, you see positively and unequivocally the identical glorified Jesus is coming back, accompanied by multitudes of angels. Hence, the return of the personal Son of God, with the same body that was born in Bethlehem, and preached throughout Palestine, suffered under Pontius Pilate, and was crucified, arose from the dead, and ascended up to Heaven, amid multitudes of angels, is coming back, accompanied by the mighty hosts. St. Luke 19: 11-27: *"They hearing these things, putting forth a parable, He said because He was nigh to Jerusalem, and they think the Kingdom of God is about to appear immediately."* This shows that He is not speaking of the Gospel Kingdom, which was preached by John the Baptist, and Jesus, and His Apostles, and dispensationally inaugurated on the Day of Pentecost, only fifty days from that time.

"Then He said, A certain nobleman departed into a far country to receive for Himself a Kingdom and to return." Himself is the Nobleman; Heaven the far-off country, and the glorious Millennium He was going to receive and bring down to this world and extend it over the whole earth.

"Having called His ten servants, He gave to them ten pounds, and said to them, Trade till I come." These ten servants are His Disciples, in all ages. He gives us all an out-fit for business, capital, resources, and facilities, and thus a chance to make a fortune.

"But His citizens hated Him, and sent an embassy after Him, saying, We do not wish Thee to rule over us." These citizens are the people of the world, who fell out with Him when He was here the first time, persecuted and killed Him. They have never changed, consequently, they are as hostile to Him, and as much opposed to Him now, as ever.

"And it came to pass, when He came, having received

the Kingdom, and said that the servants to whom He had given the money should be called, that He might know what each one had made. But the first came, saying, Lord, Thy pound has gained ten pounds. And He said to him, Well done, good servant: because thou hast been faithful in the smallest matter, have thou authority over ten cities." Here you see the clear corroboration of the truth revealed, (Rev. 20:6,) and many other places, that the transfigured saints will rule the whole world sub-ordinate to Christ during the Millennium.

"And the second came saying, Lord Thy pound has gained five pounds. And He also said to him, Be thou ruler over five cities." Here you see a glimpse of the endless diversity, that will characterize the reign of saints on the earth sub-ordinate to Christ.

"And the other one came, saying, Lord, behold, Thy pound, which I have laid up in a napkin: for I was afraid of Thee, because Thou art an austere man: Thou takest up what Thou hast not laid down, and reapest that which Thou hast not sown. He says to him, Out of thine own mouth I will judge thee, O thou wicked servant. Didst thou know that I was an austere man, taking up what I have not laid down, and reaping what I have not sown: why indeed didst thou not give my money to the bank, truly having come I would have received the same with the product? Indeed He said to the by-standers, Take the pound from him, and give it to him who has ten pounds. (And they said to Him, Lord, he has ten pounds.") You see they were astonished that He gave the pound to the ten-pounder, instead of the five-pounder. But you see this is precisely correct, because he will make twice as much out of it, as the five-pounder would. So

if you want the Lord to flood you with grace, go ahead and just get more religion than anybody else, then He will exactly give you waters to swim in. (Ezekiel 47:1-12.)

"*I say unto you, That to every one that hath shall be given; but from him that has not, shall be taken away even that which he hath. Moreover, bring hither, these My enemies, who are not willing for Me to rule over them, and slay them here in My presence.*" This is the Great Tribulation, and will immediately follow the Rapture of the saints, in all the earth. The Lord is neither stingy nor unjust, as this man, who wrapped his pound in a napkin said, but He simply turned his own false testimony against him.

The man represents a very large class, who now make the mistake of putting the standard too high, consequently, like him, they dispair of reaching it, and do not try. Besides, he was encumbered with Satan's theology, "Once in grace, always in grace," and you see in his case, a literal test, clearly developing its utter falsity. This man actually kept the pound, *i. e.,* he did not squander it, yet, he lost his soul, because he was too lazy and cowardly to add to it.

N. B. These prophecies in Daniel and John are identical. Therefore, it is perfectly legitimate to expound them simultaneously. The Tribulation will be the third and last woe (Rev. 9:12), and inaugurated, perpetuated and consummated by the last *"bowl of wrath."*

N. Doubtless we are now about the close of the period occupied by the sixth *"bowl of wrath."* (Rev. 16:12.) "*And the sixth* (angel) *poured out his bowl from the great river Euphrates; and his water was dried up, in order that the way of the kings from the rising of the sun may be prepared."* Four Turkish sultanies border on that great river, representing the power of the false prophet, destined along with the Beast (the papacy and the dragon), Paganism, to figure so conspicuously in the latter days, *"And I saw the three unclean spirits like frogs come out of the mouth of the dragon, the Beast and the False Prophet; for these, the spirits of demons working miracles, which are going forth to the kings of the whole earth, to gather them together to the war of the Great Day of God Almighty."*

You see these three unclean spirits coming out of the mouth of the Dragon, *i. e.*, Paganism, the Beast, *i. e.*, the Papacy, and the False Prophet, *i. e.*, Mohammedanism, are all the spirits of devils, going forth to work miracles and stir up this trinity of Satanic power against God Almighty.

We have already had a vivid prelude of it, in the Japo-Russian War, in which Russia is the Beast; Japan, the Dragon, and Turkey, which was simultaneously belligerent, the False Prophet.

We have now constantly fresh manifestations of this demonical work, *i. e.*, in the counterfeit "Tongues" movement, etc. When the glorified Christ reached Heaven, triumphant from the bloody heights of Calvary, and reported His work, the Father said, "Well done; it is all satisfactory; you have conquered, and shall have that world forever, sit down here on My right hand, till I make thine enemies Thy foot-stool." (Acts 2:34.) He is sitting there to this day, administering the mediatorial kingdom, but such in the culmination of the prophecies, that we are every moment expecting the Father to descend and verify this promise to the Son.

Dan. 7:9: *"I beheld till the thrones were cast down, and the Ancient of days did sit, and a fiery stream went before Him: and a million minister to Him."* The fire symbolizes the awful destruction of the Tribulation. These million are the destroying angels, who will execute righteous judgments against the wicked nations and fallen Church in all the earth. The thrones which will be cast down during the Tribulation, are now occupied by all the rulers of the earth, secular and ecclesiastical. They must all fall, preparatory to the coronation of the glorified Jesus, King of kings, and Lord of lords.

Now continue, Rev. 16:15, *"Behold, I come as a thief."* The thief comes at midnight, when all are asleep, and always comes to steal something. Oh, when has there been a sleep so deep in the wicked nations and worldly churches as at the present day. Surely it is the midnight slumber, yet the Bride, Whom He is coming to steal, is wakeful and watching.

"Blessed is the one watching, and keeping his garments, in order that he may not walk about naked, and they may see his shame." Oh, how the people are everywhere waking up and putting on their Blood-washed robes, that they may be ready at His coming, and the shame of their carnality not be seen.

"And He led them together into the place called in Hebrew Armageddon." Here you see the sixth angel winds up his work with the inauguration of the terrible Armageddon wars, which will deluge the world with blood and heap it with mountains of the slain, and thus

clear the way for our Lord's coronation and glorious Millenial Reign.

o. We now reach the "pouring out of the last bowl of wrath, by the seventh angel." Hitherto the infections of the six preceding bowls were somewhat local, now in case of this seventh and last, it is universal, as he simply pours it out upon the air, which envelops the whole earth, and, consequently, disseminates the infection throughout every nation under Heaven.

The Seventh Chapter gives the history of the rise of Antichrist. As "Anti" means "Instead of," therefore, for Christ, *i. e.*, the Savior, because Christ alone can save, as God out of Christ is but a Consuming fire. (Heb. 12:18.) Therefore, all vain substitutes for salvation are preached by Antichrists. They abounded in John's day and superabound in our day. They are constantly interpenetrating the ranks of the Holiness Movement in sheep's clothing, palming off some vain substitute for the Christ, Who saves to the uttermost, and sanctifies wholly. While the Antichrists abound already, a great special autocrat, leading the army of Antichrists, will rise, immediately after the Rapture of the saints, and simultaneously with the inauguration of the Great Tribulation.

You see above, how the Lord comes to steal away His Bride, meanwhile those three unclean spirits are agitating the three great departments of Satan's kingdom on the earth, *i. e.*, as they come out of the mouth of the dragon, *i. e.*, Paganism with its thousand millions; the Beast, *i. e.*, the Papacy with three hundred and fifty millions, and the False Prophet, *i. e.*, Mohammedanism, with its two hundred millions. Such is the culmination of prophetical fulfillments, as you have seen the Lunar Chronology has the Rapture of the saints over-due already sixty-one years; the Calendar nineteen years, and the solar, makes it due in sixteen years; while John stirs us up, to look for it immediately after the Japo-Russian War. Consequently, we are literally inundated by prophetical inspiration to be constantly on the outlook for His glorious coming to snatch away His waiting Bride.

At the same time, the Father, the Ancient of Days, (Dan. 7:9,) descends, accompanied by the million destroying angels, and shakes down every ruler in the globe, both political and ecclesiastical thus vacating all the kingdoms of the earth, which have been occupied by usurpers ever since the Fall of the Theocracy with the capture of Jerusalem by Nebuchadnezzar, B. C. 587.

In this Chapter 17 of Revelation, we see Antichrist rise and take a seat upon the usurped throne of the world, here designated as the eighth head of the Roman Beast. It is also said, that he is one of the seven, and that he comes up out of the bottomless pit and goes into perdition, *i. e.*, comes from Hell for the emergency, and after his signal defeat, of course, goes back. Here you see John testifies, that five of these heads of the beast have already fallen and one is, and another is to come. This Beast, (Rev. 13th Ch.,) which John sees rise up out of the sea, *i. e.*, from the people, had seven heads and ten horns.

The kingdoms, the republic, the triumvirate, the dictatorship, and the tribuneship, are the five, which had fallen before John's day; the empire, which was the sixth head of the beast, at that time current; whereas, the Papacy, the seventh head, could not rise till the Empire fell, A. D. 476. This seventh head, the Papacy, still exists, and is the only one, as five out of the seven had fallen before John's day, nineteen hundred years ago, and the sixth head fell A. D. 476, leaving none surviving but the seventh, *i. e.*, the Papacy, which continues to this day, therefore, the eighth head, which will be the Antichrist of the Tribulation, and is one of the seven, must of necessity be that seventh head, which is none other than the Pope of Rome the most influential character in Satan's kingdom on the earth, and in the very nature of his office, none other than Antichrist, because he audaciously claims to be the vice-gerent of God and the Vicar of Christ on the earth, thus diabolically usurping the throne of Christ.

When the Barbarians conquered the Roman Empire, A. D. 476, after a two-hundred years' war, they spent a whole week gathering the gold and silver from the palaces, temples and shrines, as the Romans had conquered all nations, spoliating them and they brought the precious metals to Rome, the Emperor actually living in a golden house, and looking out upon five thousand Senators, living in silver houses. Thus, having captured the gold and silver, they returned to their native land, common soldiers having become millionaires, and leaving the throne of the world vacant, as they were satisfied with the money. This, the Pope ascended and occupied, during the thousand years that followed, really Satan's millennium, in history known as "The Dark Ages," because Rome was the only upholder of ancient civilization; hence, with her fall, it passed away and her barbarian conquerors took the whole world. The Pope and his coadjutors even to this day, look back upon the Dark

Ages as the brightest period in the history of the world, because they ruled it, and had things their own way. Therefore, when the kings of the earth fall, during the Armageddon wars of the Tribulation Period, the Pope will simply avail himself of the open door to resume his place on the throne of the world, from which he has been largely driven by the secular powers. Then, as he already claims the right to domineer human conscience, and command universal homage, he will simply proceed to enforce his claims as during the thousand years of his millennium, while he martyred one hundred thousand saints, *i. e.*, all who dared to contravene his despotic rule, sternly conservative of its own Antichristhood, in which his cardinals, Archbishops, Bishops, and priests were his sub-ordinate participants.

p. Rev. 18th Chapter, gives us the Fall of Babylon, accompanied by the utter destruction of Rome, by the inundating sea, the normal result of tremendous earthquakes.

The word "Babylon" means "confusion," and fitly includes all counterfeit religions, which confuse people with the delusion that they are on their way to Heaven when they are going straight to Hell. I must here say, with sadness and sorrow, while the three hundred and fifty millions constituting the Greek and Latin Churches, are with an exception here and there in spiritual Babylon, the rank and file of all the great Protestant Churches, clerical and layical, as I awfully fear, have actually been carried by Satan into spiritual Babylon, within the last sixty years.

Verily, God's true people follow Jesus only, led by the Holy Ghost, and recognizing no authority, but His precious Word, to which they cling with the pertinacity of a drowning man. When Satan succeeded in blotting out the lights of ancient civilization and bringing on the Dark Ages, his own millennium, *i. e.,* a thousand years, during which not one man in a thousand, or not one woman in twenty thousand could read or write, his administration became so heavy that he simultaneously raised up two sub-ordinates, (A. D. 606,) the Pope to rule the West, and Mohammed the East. They have both served him heroically from that day to this, leading the people into the captivity of spiritual Babylon, the old harlot mother, so conspicious in the prophecies, whose daughters are prominent in all the great Protestant Churches. You see, in this chapter, the angel descending, and you hear the clarion shout, "Fallen, fallen is Babylon." So here Babylon falls, to rise no more forever, *i. e.,* counterfeit religion, which includes all, except the genuine of the Holy Ghost, is smashed into smithereens and evanesced forever, henceforth to be known only in the black chronicles of the bottomless pit.

God has raised up the Holiness Movement to restore the genuine Bible Holy Ghost religion to the whole world, which will fill the earth during the glorious Millennium, shine and shout forever. Here you see the proclamation, *"Come out of her my people, come out of her my people,"* revealing to our consolation, that God has many savable people in Babylon. Some give this a fanatical construction, involving the conclusion that the Holiness people are to come out of all the fallen churches, which would defeat the very end for which God has sanctified them, *i. e.,* that they might preach the Gospel to the whole world, of course, including Babylon, which this day contains the great majority of the people on the earth professing to serve the God of the Bible. We are to stay in Babylon, perfectly free from her contaminations, which cannot reach us from the outside, and never can get in while we are filled with the Holy Ghost, meanwhile thus abiding, we are to preach to them the everlasting Gospel, with the *"Holy Ghost sent down from heaven."* This we are to do heroically till God smashes old Babylon into smithereens, then we are to come out, and still labor to save the millions of savable but unsaved elect souls, who, if not sooner will felicitously receive it, when the glorious millennium sets in.

N. B. The great utility of the Tribulation, is to hackle out of the world the unsavables and incorrigibles, who now actually rule, not only the nations but the worldly churches, and are simply incompetent and unavailable material for the glorious Millennial Kingdom. They are the conservators of the wild beast governments which now fill the earth and have no conception, nor possible congeniality for the Millennium, which will be a government not enforced by armies, policemen, the hangman's rope, penitentiaries, jails, etc., but by righteousness, peace, love and holiness. Therefore, all the people who are unmanageable in that way will evanesce during the Tribulation.

The Bible positively says that when the Millennium comes, the nations *"will beat their swords into plowshares, and their spears into pruning-hooks, and learn war no more."* Suppose we would, with the present population of the earth, do away with all physical force, *i. e.*, wild beast governments, having no fire-arms, nor weapons of any kind, no policemen, or soldiers, jails nor penitentiaries, you know, thieves and desperadoes would absolutely take into hand every nation under Heaven, and turn the world into a hell. Therefore, the wisdom of God, Who knows every person on the earth who cannot be managed by the power of righteousness, peace, love and holiness, will simply eliminate them all away, leaving none on the earth unsusceptible of the Millennial administration. You must not think our Lord will take away our freedom in order to manage us, as in so doing, He would delimitize us. On the contrary, every human being on the earth, during the Millennium, will still be a free moral agent, yet, perfectly susceptible of the glorious reign of righteousness, peace, love and holiness, in the utter absence of all physical force through the whole world. Do not fanatically leap to the conclusion, that all of the wicked will perish during the Tribulation, of whom multiplied millions, especially in the heathen lands, where they have had so little light, are susceptible of salvation and adoption to the perfect Divine rule, which will characterize the reign of Christ.

Q. Chapter 19 gives us a brilliant panorama of the great final conflict of Armageddon. Here we see all the kings of the earth in battle array against the Lord Jesus Christ, vividly portrayed as a mounted warrior, riding forth amid the thunder of battle, and the din of conflict, His garments sprinkled with the blood of His enemies, as He presses the battle, till all the kings of the earth go down in blood, with their mighty men and their marshalled millions, promiscuously heaping the earth with mountains of the dead, till every foe has fallen, *i. e.*, (the nations of the earth will thus kill out one another.)

OUR LORD'S RETURN. 243

Drop your eye down to the middle of the chapter and you see an angel standing on the sun, (a convenient place from which to see the whole world, as he rolls his chariot round;) shouting to all the carnivorous beasts, and ferocious birds to come to the grand carnival and eat the flesh of fallen kings, principals and potentates, with their millions of soldiers and servants, throughout the whole world. This really winds up the terrible bloody work of the Great Tribulation. A little farther down the column, you see the Pope, the beast, and Mohammed, the false prophet, the right and left powers of Satan, ever since the inauguration of the Dark Ages, verily the two armies of Antichrist, arrested and both cast alive into the Lake of Fire, actually arriving thither before Satan, thus winding up their brilliant career of, *"A time, times and a half time,"* frequently mentioned in the prophecies, *i. e.,* twelve hundred and sixty years, which, dating from A. D. 606, actually ran out in 1866; but as fifty years elapsed after the Pope proclaimed his spiritual prerogative, before he augmented it by the temporal, thus consumating the verification of his Antichristhood, we may pertinently add it, which gives 1866 plus 50=1916, which will, as you see, run out nine years from this date.

Oh, how significantly all the prophecies now force on us the conclusion that we are living in the Saturday evening of the Gentile times, meanwhile the glorious millennium ushers in, the moment we pass the midnight culmination.

The last verse of this 19th chapter, *"And all the rest were slain by the sword proceeding out of the mouth of Him that sitteth on the horse."* Here we have a wonderful and transcendently encouraging revelation of the consolatory fact, that all of the people, who survived the elimination of the Great Tribulation, will be evangelized and saved.

This follows as a legitimate conclusion, from the plain and unmistakable revelation of this verse. "Sword" in the Bible constantly means, "The Word of God." Heb. 4:12, describes God's Word as, *"A sharp two-edged sword;"* the salvation edge so keen, that if we heroically hug it, it is certain to cut out of us everything we cannot take to Heaven with us, meanwhile the damnation edge is equally sharp and if we do not give the salvation edge a chance, will certainly cut out forever our hopes of Heaven.

R. This beautiful and consolitory truth so felicitly revealed in this verse is copiously augmented and confirmed in the verdict of the Jerusalem Council of Apostles, elders, and brethren, relative to the attitude of the Gentile members of the Gospel Church.

James, the brother of the Lord, presiding over that Council, referring to a decisive speech, which Peter had delivered, referent to his own ministry at the house of Cornelius, when God honored him with the prerogative of breaking down the partition-wall and bidding the Gentile world welcome to *bona fide* membership in the Gospel Church, which He abundantly confirms, by sending on them the Pentecostal baptism of the Holy Ghost.

(V. 14.) *"Simeon hath expounded how God in the first place interposed to take from the Gentiles, a people in His Name. And to this they agree the words of the prophets, as had been written, After these things I will return, and will build again the throne of David, which has fallen down; and will build again the ruins of the same, and will set it up again: in order that the survivors of the people may seek out the Lord, even all the Gentiles, upon whom My Name has been called upon them, saith the Lord, Who doeth all things known from the beginning.*" Here you see the revelation clear and explicit, confirmatory of the conclusion, that all of the people who shall in the providence of God survive the Tribuiation, will seek and find hte Lord, as we have seen in Rev. 19:21, *"Be slain by the sword, proceeding out from the mouth of Him that sitteth on the horse."* "The sword" here means, "The Word of God." To be slain by it, could mean nothing but a blessed and glorious case of personal, and e--perimental salvation, *i. e.,* the old man of sin is slain by the sword proceeding out of the Lord's mouth, *i. e.,* you get gloriously sanctified, with the baptism of the Holy Ghost and fire, which crucifies old Adam, and buries him into the atonement, *i. e.,* the death of Christ, to rise no more. (Rom. 6:1, 6.)

In this Jerusalem Council, James says that the great end for which God is now taking for Himself a people out of the Gentiles, *"In order that the survivors of the peoples may seek out the Lord;"* not as the English Version, *"Seek after the Lord,"* which is an incorrect translation, as *ekzeotesoosi,* from *ek,* "out," and *zetsoo,* "to seek," means, *"Seek out the Lord;" i. e.,* seek Him till you find Him, which means a glorious case of personal salvation every time. You may, *"Seek after the Lord,"* all you like, never find Him, and in the end lose your soul, whereas, if you, *"Seek out the Lord,"* you find Him every time.

The Word of the Lord in these passages, to our

infinite consolation, assures us that all people who survive the Tribulation will be saved. Facts with good reason come to corroborate this conclusion. As we read in Rev. 20, at the conclusion of the Tribulation, Satan having lost all of his churches in the Fall of Babylon Ch. 18) and all of his kingdoms with the fall of his kings (Ch. 19), the Pope and Mohammed, having already been arrested and cast into the Lake of Fire, is trembling for his own awful impending doom, when the Apocalyptic angel ascends from Heaven with a great chain in his hand, lays hold of him, arresting him like a common criminal, leads him away and casts him into the bottomless pit, thus making him a hopeless prisoner the next thousand years. Though, after the expiration of the Millennial decade he is loosed and permitted to come back and heroically try his hand for the recovery of this world, he simply returns to get a whipping, suffer signal defeat, and final ejectment into the Lake of Fire, whither Pope and Mohammed have proceeded him a thousand years.

When the devil is arrested by the hand of God's angel policemen and taken out of the world, certainly his myrmidons will all share the same fate, yea, knowing their cause is forever lost, their king arrested and cast into Hell, they will have no courage to perpetuate the war.

I traveled throughout the great South soon after the close of the Civil War, when I was repeatedly informed that when General Lee surrendered to Grant at Appomattox, and the lightning couriers leaping over the wires, carried the news into all parts of Dixie Land; every Confederate soldier laid down his gun, and said, "The war is over, and I will shoot no more." The same was true, when lord Cornwallis surrendered to Washington at Yorktown. Now the simple fact, that there will be no devil in all this world to hold them back authenticates the conclusion that all who survive the tribulation will find the Lord and get saved. This is abundantly corroborated by Dan. 12:12, *"Blessed are they that come to the end of the one thousand five and thirty days."* This is simply another statement for the end of the Tribulation. The reason why all who reach it are blessed, is because they will get saved. The old prophets get exceedingly eloquent, describing the Millennium, certifying *"A nation shall be born in a day."*

N. B. The first work of the transfigured saints, who go up with the Lord in the Rapture, and enjoy that long Supper for forty-five years, meanwhile that wonderful adjudication, organizing them for their glorious work on earth, during the coming Millennium will transpire, giving every one of us our appointments, so when we accompany the Lord with His return to the earth on the throne of the Millennial Theocracy we will all know our places and be ready to proceed at once to our delectable participation in the Millennial administration, subordinate to our beloved Lord, once humiliated, now exalted Lord and King. Mutiplied millions of people will be on the earth, will then spread out before us, white for the sickle. The evangelizing of the whole world will be the first great work inviting the transfigured saints to glorify God, preaching the Gospel to every creature. The prevailing impression, that we are to convert all nations to Christianity, before the Lord comes, is a great mistake. You see in the above Scripture (Acts 15 Ch), that the work of the Church is just to preach the Gospel to every nation, so as to get the Bride ready, before our Divine Spouse shall come to take Her away to the Marriage Supper.

Matt. 24:14, He tells us positively, that so soon as we preach the Gospel to every nation, He is coming back. The reason why we must preach the Gospel to every nation before He takes away His Bride, is because He is going to rule the world, through the instrumentality of the transfigured saints.

Rev. 20:6: *"Blessed and holy is he that hath part in the first resurrection: for over such the second death hath no power, but they shall be kings and priests unto God, and shall reign with him a thousand years."* Here you see the fact clearly revealed, that the Lord is going to rule the world, through the instrumentality of the transfigured saints: among whom, the Apostles will enjoy the pre-eminence.

St. Matt. 19:27, 28: *"Then Peter responding said to Him, Behold we have left all, and followed thee; then what shall be to us? And Jesus said unto them, Truly I say unto you, That you who have followed me, in the regeneration when the Son of man may sit upon the throne of His glory, you yourselves shall sit upon twelve thrones, judging the twelve tribes of Israel."* Here you see that the Apostles will be the first rulers in the glorious Millennial Theocracy, sub-ordinate to Christ. All the people on the earth will still be mortal and the world will move on, much like it does now, with the exception of sin, which will not be permitted to break out and become ruler over it, and as no devil or demon will be here to tempt the people, delude them and keep them away from God, the trend of the popular mind will be Godward, and Holinessward. The reason why a nation can *"be born in a day,"* is because the Gospel will be preached by the transfigured saints, who will have no weight, and can move at will, with angelic velocity, and, consequently, a hundred thousand transfigured saints lighting down on Ohio, and beginning with the rising sun, can preach the Gospel to every soul, and bring them all to God in time to wire to New York at night-fall the glorious news, "All Ohio brought to God." The same day a million of transfigured saints do similar work in the State of New York. Meanwhile similar achievements are reported from the British Isles, France, China, Japan and all parts of the earth. Of course, the living saints will constantly co-operate with the transfigured in the great work of the world's evangelization. As the sanctified people will all be transfigured, and go up in the rapture, there will be none left on the earth to pass through the Tribulation and greet us when we come back.

There is no doubt but the work of sanctification, as well as salvation, will go on during the Tribulation, despite the terrible antagonism of Satan through the Antichrist, who will do his utmost to get the people to follow him and persecute dissenters, even unto death, as we see in Rev. 20:4, *"I saw thrones, and judgment was given unto them."* This refers to the thrones occupied by the transfigured saints, who shall rule the world in the capacity of Judges. Then he says, *"I saw the souls of those who had been beheaded for the witness of Jesus, who had not worshipped the beast, nor his image, nor received his mark in their forehead, nor in their hands:*

and they lived and reigned with Christ a thousand years. But the rest of the dead lived not again till the thousand years were fulfilled." Here is an allusion to people who had been sanctified during the Tribulation and suffered martyrdom at the hands of Antichrist, and by our Lord admitted to a place in the first resurrection, along with the transfigured saints; thus received as a supplementary addition to the first resurrection. Whereas, the great Tribulation will be the most copious harvest Hell will ever reap on the earth, even eclipsing Noah's flood, as there will be so many people in the world. Meanwhile Satan, through the powerful and influential reign of Antichrist, and his innumerable coadjutors, will do his utmost to press the work of destruction, laying under contribution earth and Hell and pressing every conceivable agency to expediate the damnation by the wholesale, when the awful tornadoes of death and ruin, temporal and eternal shall have exhausted their energies, deluging all nations with the sword, pestilence and famine, yet, amid all, the hand of the Almighty will preserve countless multitudes in all nations, especially heathens, Mohammedans and even Greek and Roman Catholics. Of course, the overwhelming majority of the people, who in the finale, shall survive the rivers of blood, and mountains of the dead, will be still living on the earth, when the Lord returns from the Marriage Supper of the Lamb, accompanied by the transfigured saints of His Bridehood. While the tribulation will be Hell's greatest harvest, the long run of the Millennial thousand years will be Heaven's greatest harvest. Meanwhile, the awful sufferings and sorrows of bygone years will be forgotten, amid the glorious prosperity, which will everywhere brighten the world, while the glory of the Lord shall cover the earth, as the waters cover the sea.

As already expanded, and authenticated by the precious Word, the first work of the transfigured saints will be evangelization of all the world. These transfigured saints will represent every nation under Heaven, as we see in St. Matt. 24:14, the Lord is not coming back till we have preached the Gospel to every nation, in order to give all a chance for the Bridehood, as He is going to rule the world through the instrumentality of the transfigured saints, constituting his Bridehood, who will be the charter members of His glorious Millennial Kingdom.

Here we see the great reason why we must preach the Gospel to every nation, in order that He may have a nucleus of transfigured saints, to evangelize and rule that nation. Just as He must have enough in Ohio to manage this country during the Millennial Reign, so He must have enough in England, France, Italy, Greece, Germany, India, China, Japan, Thibet, Africa, Australia, and every land beneath the skies.

s. When the Lord returns, accompanied by all the transfigured saints of His Bridehood, and finds this world without a devil in it to keep anybody away from God (Rev. 20th Chapter), he will be chained, and taken out of the world, when, of course, all of his myrmidons will retreat from the earth *nolens volens,* willing or unwilling. The old prophets get eloquent describing the wonderful revivals that will sweep over this world, when the Millennium sets in, and, *"A nation shall be born in a day."* The prophetic eye recognizes great multitudes of unsaved people at their toils, rising up and saying, "Do you not know that those holiness people, whom we missed quite a while ago have come back and are preaching with all their might in Cincinnati, and I am going to the 'Mt. of Blessings' to get religion, will you not go with me?" You find the Bible phraseology, *"Let us go up to the mountain of the Lord's house and worship the Lord."* This gives us an idea how the popular mind, even unsaved, in the absence of all devils and demons, will yield to the Holy Spirit, and spontaneously rise up and go to seek the Lord.

The transfigured saints can move with angelic velocity, and will neither need a boarding-house, nor a ticket, as we will never again eat mortal food. Neither will we need any more sleep.

Sunday afternoon is the celebrated hour for the holiness meetings in all parts of the earth. We hold it here on the "Mount of Blessings," till the day declineth; then we have nothing to do, but drop back to Denver, Colorado with lightning velocity, where we have ample time for another meeting before nightfall; then to San Francisco, California; then to Tokyo, Japan; then to Shanghai, China; then to Bombay, India. From there drop back to John Wesley's Church in London; then fly over the great Atlantic to New York City, and then back to Cincinnati without ever seeing the sun go down as we have been moving toward his setting, and thus perpetuating the day, till we circumnavigate the globe. The transfigured body will never get tired, nor sleepy, nor hungry for *mortal* food; neither will it get old; but bloom in immortal youth forever. As we will be preaching the Gospel to mortal people in this world, when there is an alternation of day and night, we can either, as above, change our location, moving easterly, so as to have day-light all the time, or at night-fall, just retire away to Heaven, where there is no night, and spend the time among the angels, and return the ensuing day, and resume our work.

The first great work, after we reach this world will be the evangelization of all the nations of the earth; not impeded by devils and demons, excarnate and incarnate, and all of the diabolical machinations of earth and Hell, as in the present age, and I may add the terrible impediments of diseases, small-pox, cholera and pestilential fevers, such as prevail in Africa, and India; but the transfigured will have their immortal bodies perfectly free from all diseases impossible to get sick, or to die, and, therefore, the facilities of prosecuting the work, will be wonderful beyond conception. Besides, all the people in the world will be willing and gladly yield to the blessed Holy Spirit. We read, *"They shall be willing in the day of His power."* The entire Millennial Reign will be "The day of His power." Now just conceive a thousand transfigured Chinese, lighting down in Pekin and begin to preach to the four millions of people, with the wonderful facilities, peculiar to the transfigured state, as above described. Oh, what a revival will break out, and run like fire in dry stubble, everywhere sweeping everything before it! When we go there, a thousand difficulties attend us, because we are foreigners, and unadapted to the country, and the work in so many respects. You certainly see the wonderful wisdom of our Lord in calling out the Bride from every nation under Heaven, so that when the glorious Millennium sets in, every nation will be supplied with its own people, perfectly adapted in all respects to the evangelization of their kindred friends and countrymen. As the transfigured saints, moving with angelic velocity through the air, perfectly independently of all mortal appurtenances and environments, can so quickly reach all the people; oh, what wonderful revivals will break out everywhere, as the transfigured saints will all come back to their own countries and nationalities!

As salvation is the great end in view, transcending everything else, of course, this will be our first enterprise, precedent to our normal administrations, for the amelioration of all mankind, subordinately to the glorious reign of our wonderful King.

> "For He shall have dominion,
>   O'er river, sea and shore,
> Far as the angel's pinion,
>   Or dove's light wing can soar."

CHAPTER XIV.

SIGNS OF HIS COMING.

When I contemplate this theme, I am lost in unutterable bewilderment. Having, in the providence of God, enjoyed three tours through the old world, beginning my Oriental travels in 1895, and only having returned in 1906 from my last tour through both hemispheres, I am actually inundated with signs of His coming on all sides, whether traveling among Pagans, Mohammedans, Catholics or Protestants, verily the whole earth is luminous with omens of His near approach.

The signal defeat of the Moslem army of three hundred thousand veterans, flushed with a thousand victories, flashing over Europe, Asia and Africa, electrifying them with the glowing anticipation of the speedy surrender of the whole world to the Islam Prophet, now coiling around Vienna the greatest stronghold in Christendom like a huge boa-constrictor, cutting off all ingress and egress, perfectly sanguine of victory, and with the Fall of Vienna, the surrender of the entire fragment of Europe, then the only survival of the Christian cause; their signal and crushing defeat, by John Sobeiski and his seventy thousand Poles, begins the fulfillment of Dan. 8:25, *"He* (Mohammed) *shall be broken without hand."*

All Christendom united, spent two hundred years in

bloody crusades against the False Prophet, though actually capturing Jerusalem and holding it eighty-eight years, when finally defeated in the Battle of Hattan, were driven out of Asia. From this victory at Vienna in 1683, the Moslem power has been constantly waning, ever and anon relaxing her grip from this country, that and the other, till a whole dozen great kingdoms and empires have been wrested from her serpentine coils.

In my three tours in the Turkish Empire, her only survivor, in the perpetual observation of eleven years, I have seen the star of her hope constantly fading from the national firmament. Even now, the iron grip of the Sultan, hitherto so tight in Palestine, is relaxing with marvelous rapidity, so the Jewish emigration back to the Holy Land, which has met apparently inseparable obstructions from the beginning of their power, in that country, to the astonishment of all observers, is becoming periodically lenient.

Similar phenomena we find in the Papacy, from that memorable epoch (A. D. 1870), when Victor Emmanual, king of Sardinia, (what a significant name!) entered Rome with his triumphant army and shook the Pope down from his temporal throne, which he has never regained, his power has been obviously relaxing in all the earth.

Rome now abounds in Protestant Churches whose ingress is but of yesterday. The Holy Father daily, in his Vatican Palace, when he looks toward the east, is constrained to behold the monument of Victor Emmanuel, who shook him down from his throne. When he looks toward the west he cannot evade the odious splendor of the monument erected to commemorate the victory won by Garabaldi, who fought and conquered the French army, sent thither to reinstate him on the throne of his temporal dominion, spoliated from him, by Victor Emmanuel.

We sadly contemplate the deplorable fulfilment of the latter day Pauline prophecies, in the current apostacy, now patent in all the great Protestant denominations. 2 Tim. 3rd Chapter: *"But know this, that in the last days perilous times will come. For the people will be lovers of themselves, lovers of money, arrogant, proud, speaking evil, disobedient to parents, ungrateful, unholy, without natural affection, covenant breakers, devilish, incorrigible, furious, opposed to the good, traitors, headstrong, puffed up, lovers of pleasures rather than lovers of God; having the form of godliness, but denying its powers; indeed from these turn away."* You see plainly that this awful description applies to professors of religion, and not the people of the world; because they have a form of godliness, which is all right, but utterly worthless without the power.

The manifestation of the sad fulfillment of this prophecy at the present day is distressing and even appalling. Fifty years ago, the orthodox Protestant Churches all rang with beautiful testimonies and reverberated triumphant shouts in their ordinary meetings, and preeminently so in their revival campaigns.

All this has given way to lifeless ritualism and icebergy ceremony actually destitute of Gospel, Satan having so prevailed, as to despiritualize and degospelize the churches. This is not criticism, but candid statement of an awful reality, and abundantly sustained by God's own definition of "Gospel" (Rom. 1:16), *i. e.*, *"The dynamite of God unto salvation."*

Dynamite is the greatest explosive in the world, and really the only definition of Gospel you find in the Bible.

т. St. Matthew (24:14), and Mt. Mark (13:10), assure us that when the Gospel of the kingdom shall be preached in the whole world, to all the heathens, then the end will come. This is necessary, in order to give all nations a chance for the Bridehood, because our Lord is going to rule the world through the instrumentality of the transfigured saints. (Rev. 20:6.) Therefore, our great work is to get the Bride ready in all the earth so that through her instrumentality, all the people in the world when the Millennium sets in, will hear the Gospel and be saved. Therefore the wonderful progress of the Gospel among the heathens, at the present day, and the paradoxical increase of its availability in reaching and saving them, is strikingly ominous of His near coming.

The first missionaries toiled, suffered and waited many years to see a convert. Adoniram Judson and his good wife preached to the Burmans seven years before they saw a convert. When the angels came for them, at the end of thirty-seven years they had seen but a few dozens. When I was there, last year, they had eight hundred churches, four hundred and seventy thousand members, and a great publishing house flooding the country with Bibles and good religious books.

A similar phenomenon characterizes great India. Long did a few missionaries toil, with almost no encouragement. Now the heart of the missionary is cheered by oft recurring old-time revivals.

Signs of His Coming. 259

I traveled six thousand miles by rail, and preached three months in that country, witnessing more conversions and sanctifications and calls to the ministry than ever before in my life in the same length of time.

The same may be said of Japan, which, forty years ago, did not contain a dozen people professing Christianity.

While the work in great China is not so demonstrative, yet it is in every way encouraging.

The same may be said of great dark Africa and beautiful Oceanica. Truly, the mighty Orient is shaking with the tread of a spiritual earthquake. Truly, *"Ethiopia is stretching forth her hands."*

u. The signs of His coming are strikingly phenomenal among the children of Abraham, in their worldwide dispersions among all the nations of the earth, who lost their kingdom, as far as this world was concerned when their King was born in Bethlehem, responsive to the prophecy of Jacob. Gen. 49:10: *"The sceptre shall not depart from Judah, nor the lawgiver from between his feet, till Shiloh come."*

Though the Romans fought seven hundred and fifty-three years to conquer every nation under heaven, with no other end in view but to take the government, subjugate, and rule them forever, yet, when they conquered the Jews (70 B. C.) how strange they did not take their kingdom, but just let them have it, and even protected their king on his throne. This strange freak in their administration illustrates the fact that all nations *nolens volens,* fulfilled the prophecies. The reason why the sceptre departed from Judah, when Jesus was born, was because it went to Him, and He has it yet. While

He was a fugitive infant in Egypt, King Herod died and was succeeded by Archelaus (St. Matt. 2:22,) who did not dare to wear his father's crown till by imperial hands it was placed on his head; therefore having gone to Rome and presented himself at the feet of Augustus Cæsar, feeling sure that he would crown him king of the Jews, in the succession of his father, how was he surprised, when the emperor utterly refused to give him his father's crown, and immediately proceeded to take the kingdom from the Jews, turn India into a Roman province, and send away Coponius to take charge of it, as a Roman governor. From that day to this, the Jews have been without a kingdom, roaming among all the nations of the earth; long ago driven from their country, which God gave them, and looking for their Christ to come, and gather them back.

St. Luke 1:31-33: *"And the Lord God will give unto Him the throne of David His father; and He will rule over the house of Jacob forever; and of His kingdom there shall be no end."* The house of Jacob includes all the tribes of Israel, who will be restored during the Millennium. You see this clearly revealed in the last eight chapters of Ezekiel. While Jesus stood before Pilate, and he asks Him if He was King of the Jews, He answered in the affirmative, but said, *"My kingdom is not of this world, as in that case my servants would fight, in order that I might not be delivered to the Jews."* Some have inferred from this that His kingdom will never prevail over this world, which certainly does not follow as a logical sequence. When Daniel says, during the days of these kings, *i. e.,* those revealed to him in the chronological image, *"The God of heaven*

Signs of His Coming. 261

shall set up a kingdom, that shall never be destroyed," He also sees that kingdom as stone cut out of the mountain without hands, which struck the feet of the image and utterly demolished it, till it became as the chaff of the summer threshing floor, meanwhile the stone kingdom enlarges, and fills the whole earth, and stands forever.

Though the golden head of the image evanesced with the Chaldean Empire; the silver breast and arms, with the Medo-Persian; the brazen abdomen and thighs, with the Grecian; the iron legs, with the Roman, the ten toes, representing the kingdoms developing out of the Roman Empire, after its destruction, by the Goths, Huns, and Vandals (A. D. 476), are standing to this day, awaiting the stroke of the stone that shall utterly demolish them, when the Ancient of days shall descend (Dan. 7:9,) and execute righteous judgments against the wicked nations, and fallen churches; when all the thrones, political and ecclesiastical, will be cast down. Then you see, Daniel saw in his vision *"One like unto the Son of man come to the Ancient of days, and receive a kingdom, which will never be destroyed, but stand forever."*

This cannot be identified with our Lord's first coming; born of the virgin, in the manger of Bethlehem; as He now comes, " *in the clouds of heaven."* We see in this same connection, "the saints of the Most High" possess the kingdom, "and will, forever and ever," in harmony with John, (Rev. 20:6,) who assures us that the transfigured saints will reign with Christ in His glorious coming kingdom.

The reason why the scepter had to depart from

Judah when Shiloh came, (Gen. 49:10), was because it went to Him, and though He told Pilate that He was King of the Jews, and His kingdom was not of this world, was because the Theocracy, which is His kingdom, will not extend over this world till the Gentile times expire and the thrones shall all fall, thus vacating all the kingdoms of the earth for the succession of His glorious kingdom, which shall stand forever.

Rev. 11:15: *"And the seventh angel sounded; and there were great voices in heaven, saying, The kingdom of the world has become the kingdom of our Lord, and His Christ; and He will reign forever and ever."*

Ch. 16:12-16, you read prophecies, which have literally been fulfilled in the late Japo-Russian war. (However, prophecies frequently receive more than one fulfillment, developing, and to human observation, apparently upsetting themselves in order to exhaust the vision of the prophet.)

V. 15 you see the Lord actually comes to take away His Bride, pronouncing His blessing upon every one who is robed and ready. Then (V. 16) the Armageddon war breaks out. Now read on, and you see the seventh angel pours out his last bowl of wrath upon the air, which is all infected, and consequently the terrible catastrophe reaches the whole world. Verily, the chronologies and fulfillment of the prophecies unanimously concur in the enforcement of the conclusion that the time for the seventh angel to pour out his bowl of wrath, which will finish the awful castigatory judgments of the Almighty against the wicked nations and fallen churches is at hand, and staring us in the face. We should all be listening for the trumpet to sound, which will proclaim the Rapture of the saints, inaugurate the Tribulation whose work of illumination will sweep from the earth every rival kingdom, thus clearing the way for the coronation of God's Son, King of kings, and Lord of lords.

As you see from these prophecies, "kingdom" is in the singular number, because there will be but one, *i. e.*, the Theocracy, which has shadowed forth in the days of Moses, and the prophets, and especially David and Solomon, but finally evanescing with the fall of Jerusalem under Nebuchadnezzar's dream of the depreciating scale, beginning with the golden head, depreciating to silver, then brass, followed by the iron and finally the iron mixed with clay, till the strong kingdom which God in the Bible has denominated "Rock," finally supervenes, thus bringing back the Theocracy, that is none other than the Divine government, having been symbolically adumbrated during the typical dispensation.

v. During their awful Tribulation, those memorable seven years of blood (A. D. 66-73), pursuant to that memorable edict of Vespasian, proclaiming the denationalization of the Jews, because having tried their best a third of a century to manage them and keep them peacable, and signally failed, purusant to their notorious universal policy of rule or ruin, finally, feeling that they had borne with them till forbearance ceased to be a virtue, the Emperor, in his golden house, far away at Rome, issued the irrevocable decree that the Hebrew nation should be blotted from the escutcheon of their universal empire. Consequently, the armies were sent to different parts of Palestine, to enforce the edict of extermination, by subjugating and selling all into slavery, who survived the sword, pestilence and famine.

As Jerusalem is so impregnably fortified by nature, an immense army under Gallus Celceus, was sent thither to carry out the awful edict of Hebrew denationalization. Having done his best, two years, he gives up in despair, when the old Emperor, in person, vacates his golden palace, comes to Jerusalem, takes command of the army, presses the war two years and dies, succeeded on the throne of the world by his son Titus, and in the command of the Jerusalem army.

Titus presses the siege three years longer, takes the city and destroys it, the desolating armies in all parts of the country having some time previously completed their work of extermination. As at that time all nations had slaves, they came from the ends of the earth, to supply themselves at the great auctions which followed every victory, till they were all supplied, the market flooded, and the prophecy of Isaiah and Ezekiel, *"They will sell you and no one will buy you,"* was literally fulfilled, leaving a great host of captives on their hands, whom they led to Rome, and there enslaved.

As Rome ruled all nations, this captivity of the Jews actually put them in bondage to all the nations of the earth. Hence the pertinency of this prophecy, revelatory of their current conversation after their final gathering from the ends of the earth into their own land, never more to go out, *"You will no longer say, The God of our Father brought us up out of the land of Egypt, nor out of Babylon; but out of every nation under heaven, and established us in our own land never to go out."*

Signs of His Coming. 265

You will find these predictions substantially enunciated. So autocratic and irrefragible were the Roman laws enforcing the imperial edict that it was not only a penalty of death for a Jew to be found in Palestine, but anywhere else in all the world, if traveling with his face toward Jerusalem, those cruel laws required him to be arrested and put to death.

These laws, of course, became effete after the fall of the Empire (476 A. D.). But during those four hundred years so many generations passed away, never having seen the Holy Land, they became alienated from it, though everywhere reading the Old Testament, and worshipping the God of Abraham, Isaac and Jacob.

The thrilling mementoes of their ancestry and the home their God had given them, still lingered in their melancholy wanderings over the face of the whole world: meanwhile the fall of the Empire and other revolutions had broken their chains of slavery, yet, perhaps, as a result of long years in the chains of bondage, they became the byword of odium and contempt in all the earth.

When the Moslems conquered Palestine (A. D. 634) and took possession, which they have held till this day, except those eighty-eight years of Christian rule of the Crusaders, who, after generations of blood and slaughter (A. D. 1099) captured Jerusalem and held it till it was wrested from them by the Moslems at the battle of Hattan (A. D. 1187). They claim to be the children of Abraham, through Ishmael and Esau, and a right to that country through the Abrahamic Covenant, pursuant to the patriarchal law, which gave the birthright to the elder son, as Ishmael was Abraham's eldest son, and Esau his oldest grandson. Therefore, ever since they got possession of that country they have done their utmost to obliterate and even annihilate the vaguest probability that the Jews will ever get it, as they look upon them as their uncompromising rivals, pursuant to the old controversy between Esau and Jacob; not only making their sojourn in the land as difficult as possible, but utterly prohibiting them from the Holy Campus (thirty-five acres of holy ground, surrounding the temple) and the temple, by the penalty of death. As the centuries rolled on the Jews began to come back, stay a little while and leave, and eventually some of them managed, with great difficulty to remain in the country, especially by bribing the Turkish officers.

In 1885 only ten thousand were in all the Holy Land. A great change came over them throughout the world, turning their hearts toward the sacred mountains. When I was there, in 1895, there were a hundred thousand. In 1899, when I again visited that country, I found two hundred thousand. In 1905 there were so many that I was unable to reach an adequate estimate, as the persecutions are so rife, and so much difficulty tending even their sojourn in the land that no census is taken.

In Jerusalem, in a population of a hundred thousand, our missionaries told me, there were seventy-five thousand Jews. Rolla Floyd, a Christian American, who came thither forty-two years ago, told me that on his arrival there was not a house outside of the wall. Now the outside city is much larger than all within the wall.

Jer. 16: 14-17: *"Therefore, behold, the day is come, saith the Lord, that it shall no more be said, The Lord* liveth, that brought up the children of Israel out of the land of Egypt; but, the Lord liveth that brought up the children of Israel from the land of the north, and from all the lands whither He had driven them; and I will bring them again into their land that I gave unto their fathers. Behold, I will send for many fishers, saith the Lord, and they shall fish them; and after will I send for many hunters, and they shall hunt them from every mountain, and from every hill, and out of the holes of the rocks. For mine eyes are upon their ways; they are not hid from my face, neither is their iniquity hid from mine eyes."

The great Russian Empire, occupying the northern world, is said to contain one-half of all the Jews on the globe. You see this prophecy refers directly to the gathering of the latter days. The fishers are the eleven great colonization societies, constantly at work, gathering the wandering children of Abraham back to their delightful home, meanwhile, the hunters are their persecutors, even rising up in armies, almost revolutionizing the Russian Empire, driving them out.

Jeremiah and also Zachariah give an especial prophecy in reference to their work at Jerusalem, certifying that they will build the city from the tower of Hananneal by the outer gate (Joppa gate), to the Fullers' field, to the hill Gareb to the wine-press. The hill Goash, to the Valley of dead bodies (*i. e.*, the Valley of Hinnum); yea, it shall be built and never thrown down.

Rolla Floyd told me, in 1905, that it had all been built in the last forty years, this great and beautiful city, outside of the wall, the edifices all valuable hewn stone, and it is mainly the work of the Jews. They are also colonizing and rebuilding in substantial magnificent stone edifices, all of the ancient cities. We have very recently a thrilling phenomenon of the greatest encouragement appertaining to the return of the Jews. It is the sudden and paradoxical clemency of the Sultan, whereas hitherto he has been so rigid with them, and seemed to do everything in his power to embarrass and impede the immigration of the Jews.

When I was there, in 1905, the most formidable difficulties obstructed. As early as 1874 a law was passed utterly forbidding Jews to citizenize in the Holy Land. Consequently, they all had to hold citizenship in other countries, and only abide as sojourners for a specified number of days, at most ninety. It is now reported by the papers, and it seems to be confirmed and authentic, that they are coming in vast numbers hitherto utterly unprecedented, and that the Sultan seems perfectly lenient, putting no obstruction in their way. So all Christendom is astounded and electrified over this encouraging new departure in the Turkish administration.

While I was traveling around the world, and constantly associating with the English people, I heard much talk about an effort on the part of the British Government to settle the Jews on her territory in the rich valley of the Congo, in Africa; she kindly, characteristic of her notoriety as the greatest colonizer on the globe, proposing to donate them land, thus relieving them of their Russian troubles, and settling them in her own territory. When I heard it, I did not believe they would take it, when, behold, my anticipation was, in due time, confirmed by the report of their non-acceptance of the kind offer.

w. I now refer you to the last eight chapters of Ezekiel, which beautifully and elaborately reveal the re-organization of Israel, with all the tribes in the Holy Land, during the Millennium.

The first chapter of Joshua gives us the boundary of God's gift to Israel, bordering on the great sea, on the west, the desert, Arabia and Euphrates on the East, and the Northern boundary including Mesopotamia and extending from the Great Sea to the Euphrates.

You will find that he locates Dan on the North, extending the entire width of the boundary, from the sea to the Euphrates; then Naphtali, Zebulon, Issachar, Ephraim, Manasseh, Benjamin, Asher, Judah, Simeon, also giving Reuben and Gad their portions. Whereas, Joshua only succeeded in appropriating comparatively a small portion of the inheritance; David, in his wonderful military career, doubling the conquered territory; yet leaving the larger portion of it unappropriated. But an examination of the above prophecies will show you that it will all be appropriated, after the return of Israel from the long exile of world-wide dispersion upon the face of the earth.

I am aware that not a few of the Lord's people accept the hypothesis that the Anglo-Saxons are the lost tribes of Israel. In this, I verily believe they are mistaken, because, in the first place, those tribes were not lost, as is generally supposed.

On the Day of Pentecost (Acts 2nd Chapter), we see they were all present, from every nation under Heaven, a number of which are there specified, and none other than the leading nationalities of the world-wide Chaldean Empire into which they were carried captive. Among the multiplied millions, only fifty thousand returned in the Nehemiah Exodus, because they had dispersed abroad and were so engaged in business that they preferred to remain. However, when the great annual national Pentecost came off, they came and sent their representatives from all parts of that old world-wide empire, as you see verified in the inspired report. (Acts 2:6, 8.) While those ten tribes were not lost, we must admit, they had lost their tribehood, having been there two hundred years, all mixing up, while Judah and Benjamin, having only been there seventy years, still retained their tribehood. Doubtless, many of the other ten tribes returned in the Exodus, but not in their tribal organization. Whereas, the advocates of the Anglo-Saxon identity, with the ten tribes, as soon as they left Asia, came into Europe, crossed the Continent, and settled in the British Islands. It is decisively more plausible that they remained in their native Asia, and traveled eastwardly.

In my tour around the world I saw their footprints. The Afghan, a great nation, actually claim identity with those so-called lost tribes. So I found a similar klan, in Japan, identifying themselves with the lost tribes of Israel, and heard of it in other localities.

The eye of God is on them in all their meanderings and peregrinations. It will be no trouble for Him to identify them. I find also a difficulty involved in the trinity of races eminating from Noah's family, irreconcilable with the Anglo-Saxon identity. "Shem" means, "red;" "Ham," "black," and, "Japheth," "white." The most ancient history, *"Viri Romae,"* beginning with creation, descends and winds up with the Roman age.

Signs of His Coming. 271

I do not know that this book has ever been translated into English. I am familiar with it, but only have it in the Latin. It says, Noah upon evacuation of the ark divided out his estate, the whole world, among his sons; pursuant to a patriarch law, which gives the first-born the double portion, he gave Shem, Asia; Ham, Africa, and Japheth, Europe. America, then unknown in the prophecies, is included with Europe, which means "West;" Asia, meaning, "East," and Africa, "South." Hence, you see, this is incompatible with the Anglo-Saxon claim to identify with the lost tribes, as they are Shemites, while the Anglo-Saxons are all Japhethites.

x. Ezekiel 37 Chapter shows clearly that the gathering of the Jews will take place antecedently to their conversion to Christianity. Facts are constantly verifying that conclusion. While not a few of the Jews are already converted and the work is progressing among them, yet, the rank and file of those gathering into the home-land, are still members of the old covenant.

Rom. 11:25, 26: *"For I do not wish you to be ignorant, brethren, that blindness in part happened unto Israel, until the fullness of the Gentiles may come in. And thus all Israel shall be saved: as it has been written, A Leader shall come out of Zion, and turn away ungodliness from Jacob."* That "Leader" is none other than the glorified Savior, Who, in the Rapture, will come from Heaven, which is often called Zion, and turn away ungodliness from Jacob.

I was recently sitting by a cobler, and preaching to him, while he mended my shoe. When he notified me that he was a son of Abraham, I asked him if he believed that Jesus is the Christ, he responded in the negative, and said he was looking for another. Then I asked him if Jesus were to come down from Heaven in a cloud of glory, would be believe that He was the Christ. Tears came in his eyes, and he responded in the affirmative. There is no doubt, but when He comes for His Bride He will reveal Himself to His long-blinded and mistaken consanguinity. You see this blindness is going to be on them till the fulness of the Gentiles shall come in.

We know not a nation upon the earth, to-day, with whom we have not some missionaries preaching the Gospel. Of course there must be some whom we know not, for the Lord would come at once, and take away His Bride to the Marriage Supper of the Lamb; because He so certifies in St. Matt. 24: 14, and St. Mark 13: 10, that He will come so soon as we preach the Gospel to all nations, not to all people in every nation. From the fact that the transfigured saints of the Bridehood will not only constitute the nucleus of the Millennium Kingdom, but the rulers of the same, subordinately to King Jesus, we must preach the Gospel to every nation in order to call out the Bride, and get Her ready for the coming of Her Heavenly Spouse to reign in righteousness forever.

Hence, this exceedingly rapid gathering of the Hebrew nation from the ends of the earth into the Holy Land, is exceedingly ominous of the Lord's near approach. From the fact that we must reach all other nations before the Jews, and we have already so far succeeded, that we know not a nation in the whole earth who has not been reached, no wonder there is such a wonderful shaking of the dry bones!

Ezek. 37: 11: *"These bones are the whole house of*

Israel." As they are now moving and rattling so, surely the time of their resurrection is at hand. He says here, *"I will take you up out of your graves and clothe you with flesh and you shall live again."*

They have been buried throughout the Gentile world 1834 years, ever since the Romans blotted them from the roll of nations. Soon they are going to rise and take their place among the nations of the earth. They are even now ready and waiting for the nations to recognize their nationality, which nearly all of the nations on the globe have consented their readiness to do, aye, all except great, cruel Russia, and Papal-ridden Italy.

Zechariah tells us in his last chapter that our Lord's feet will again stand on Mt. Olivet, where He walked so much in the days of His humiliation. When that whole country is thronged with His people, as in the olden time, and He, in His glory, shall return and stand upon Mt. Olivet; oh, what a shaking in the Hebrew valley of dry bones we will then assume, and what an uprising! This same chapter speaks of terrible troubles in the land of Canaan during the Tribulation, meanwhile, he says, *"Two parts will be cut off,"* but the surviving third, having passed through those terrible ordeals of blood and fire, which will inundate the whole world, will in the glorious finale when the King shall return from the Marriage Supper of the Lamb, on the throne of the Millennial Theocracy, crowned and sceptered, and accompanied by the transfigured saints of His Bridehood, having been adjugated and organized, during the Marriage Supper, so all will know their places and work in the perfect adjustment of the glorious Millennial Kingdom, so that, with perfect order and Heavenly symmetry, the administration of the restored Theocracy will run with angelic beauty and symmetry. Then on His triumphant decension to the earth, the surviving third of the elect, who are now gathering out of all nations, having passed through every fiery ordeal, which the persecutions of Antichrist can superinduce, intact and unscabbed, with the shouts of victory from all the battle-fields of earth, they will enjoy the brightest honor ever conferred on people this side the pearly gates, *i. e.*, the reception and coronation of their own glorified Brother, Jesus, long ages hidden from them, and unknown, but now revealed in Heavenly splendor, glory and majesty.

Behold, the sunburst of unutterable glory, which descends on them, thus permitted to receive their own Brother—Heir of the royal Son of King David, the Shiloh of prophecy, the Redeemer of Israel, the Christ of God, and the Savior of the world, and now crown Him King of kings, and Lord of lords. Then and there, the long procession, marching under the blood-stained banner of King Immanuel, the Jews having been long relegated to the rear for rejecting their own Christ, are now called to their ancient place at the front, the honored consanguinity of the King, His standard-bearers, and diplomats forever.

The Jews, in their world-wide dispersion, by their contact with all the nations in the earth, are in a wonderful mysterious way preparing for the cosmopolitan-ship of the world. Even now it is well certified the temple is in process of building in Petersburg, Moscow, Berlin, Vienna, London, Paris, Rome, Naples, etc., ready for transportation to the Holy Land, and be set up like its great predecessor, in the days of Solomon, without the clanger of the saw or the sound of the hammer, when Jerusalem will be built out over the great interior highlands of Palestine and henceforth be the capital and metropolis of the whole world, delightfully, and conveniently located at the center of the old world, where Asia, Africa and Europe all come together, and the beautiful Mediterranean Sea, two thousand miles long, straight as an arrow, and blue as indigo, for the especial benefit of us Americans, who will sweep over the Atlantic, and down through the sea, landing at Joppa, and ascending the sacred mountain, enter the world's metropolis, and capital, and behold wondrous, ineffable patriarchs, prophets, and martyrs, and *mirabile dictu* (wonderful to tell), Jesus in His transfigured glory. Peter, James and John actually thus saw Him, with their mortal eyes. When the glorious Millennium sets in, pursuant to infallible light, and leadership, all Israel will be reconstructed and located on their allotted possessions, occuping the entire claim our Lord gave them.

Besides, the seventy millions of Jews now known, immense multitudes known only to the God of Israel, will be gathered and restored to their inheritance, as specified in the first chapter of Joshua.

v. Among the innumerable signs of our Lord's coming, we must refer briefly to the morning star, the faithful herald and precursor of the rising sun. In this case, we simply mean the Holiness Movement, dative from 1874, though, by Divine intervention, scattered over vast regions of country, antecedently received the experience, *e. g.*, your humble servant, six years previously. Though beginning like the drops before the coming shower, the clouds have accumulated, spread abroad, and actually enveloped the globe.

In my recent journey around the world, I was with the holiness people incessantly, finding them in every land; representing many nationalities. Truly we are living in the robing-time of the Church, when the Bride is responding to the mandate of Her Lord, speaking down from the throne of His glory: "Hearken, my Beloved, it is high time for you to wash and dress, as I am coming quickly."

St. Luke 18: 1-8: *"And He spoke a parable to them, that they should pray always, and faint not; saying, There was a certain judge in a certain city, who neither feared God, nor regarded man: and there was a widow in that city; and she continued to come to him, saying, Avenge me of mine adversary. And he was not willing for a time: but afterwards he said within himself, If indeed I fear not God, nor regard man, yet because this widow gives me trouble, I will avenge her, lest coming to the end she may smite me in the face. And the Lord said, Hear what the unjust judge saith. Must not God execute vengeance in behalf of His own elect, who cry day and night unto Him, even though He bears long with them? I say unto you that He will avenge them speedily. Moreover the Son of man having come whither shall He find faith on the earth?"* The answer is in the negative, involving the conclusion that faith will be exceedingly scarce. In this parable, you will, perhaps, be surprised when I tell you that the unjust judge emblematizes God the Father. You think He ought to represent the devil, but that is not true in this parable, as the adversary against whom the widow is seeking protection is Satan.

N. B. In medicals, the similitude, as a rule, only applies to a few salient points, and frequently only one. We must constantly watch, lest we commit the error in logic designated, "Pressing the metaphor too far," and making it walk on all-fours. In this parable the unjust judge only represents God in His sovereign independency. Then the similitude is perfect, because he is absolutely free, dependent on no one, so that he neither fears God nor regards man, at the same time, he is the very incarnation of selfishness, and in all respects, except that of his absolute independent sovereignty, he is the very opposite of God. The poor widow is the Bride of Christ, the true Church, left in widowhood by Her ascending Husband, and will so remain till He returns in glorious triumph.

During His absence, Satan, her implacable adversary, persecutes her incessantly, tempting, wounding and killing her children on all sides, meanwhile, night and day she is pleading with God to send Him back, that He may whip the devil, and give her victory. God is still delaying, yet, He is sure to answer her prayer, and do it quickly, as you see the conclusion is irresistible, though like the unjust judge, who said, while he neither feared God nor regarded man, she never would let him rest, but would just come on forever and in desperation smite him in the face. So God sees that the widowed Church is never going to give up, and ignore His promise to return to send back Her ascended Husband to protect Her Children, and all the interest of His Kingdom against the constant cruel ravages of Satan, and his merciless myrmidons, and if He desists much longer, she will actually come to the end of all endurance, and in desperation smite Him in the face, as the literal gives it *hupoopiazee*. This word means, "To smite the cheek-bone directly beneath the eye," and a free translation, would simply read, "Give me a black eye." It reveals the importunate prayer and the actually incorrigible enthusiasm on the part of the waiting Bride, for the return of Her ascended Husband. When our Lord came the first time, the morning star, which the wise men saw in the east, and the greatest astronomer, Kepler, by his wonderful calculations for which he received the cognomen, "The legislator of the skies," identified to be the conjunction of the great planets, Jupiter and Saturn, thus producing this wonderful splendor, and glory, which attracted the attention of the wise men, who are teachers of astronomy and astrology, and other phases of wisdom. So glorious and brilliant was the phenomenon, that they, mounting their camels, start out out to find the King of the Jews, pursuant to their enchantments revealed to them by this extraordinary star.

In the providence of God, the great Holiness Movement is now serving the function of that morning star, girdling the globe with their testimonies to full salvation, and also the proclamation, *"Behold, our King cometh."*

Daniel tells us in his last chapter, so soon as He shall have accomplished to scatter the fire of the holy people then the Lord will come. Oh, how obviously and significantly this sign of His coming is manifest in all the earth.

In thirty-four years, the Movement, with no prestige on the earth to help it, by introduction, and no financial resources, has actually circumnavigated the globe, interpenetrated all nations and filled the world with people professing an uttermost salvation, and shouting to the ends of the earth: "Get ready, the Lord cometh!"

CHAPTER XV.

The Post-millennial View of Our Lord's Second Coming Untenable.

This view assumes that we must bring the Millennium into the world by our educational, moral, religious and philanthropic enterprises, thus making a Millennium, and getting it ready to present to the Lord when He comes. Suffice it is to say the very opposite of this view is true.

The Lord is going to bring His own Millennium with Him, and give it to us. The Millennium is none other than His glorious reign on the earth. Verily, His presence is our Paradise.

> Not all the harps above, can make a heavenly place,
> If God His residence remove or but conceal His face.
> To Thee, and Thee alone the angels owe their bliss,
> They circle round the blazing throne and dwell where Jesus is.
> To Thee my spirits fly with infinite desire,
> And, yet, how far from Thee I lie, Oh, Jesus raise me higher."

The Post-millennialist applies his optimism indiscriminately to the whole world, assuming that it is all getting better, when the powers of evil are weakening. This is a mistake; everything finite is progressing, Satan is no exception; he is getting worse all the time, progressing in diabolical shrewdness and torpitude. The truly saved people in the world who have the victory and keep it are progressing constantly in wisdom and holiness.

The Bible is better understood now than ever before, increasing light is simply radiating from its inspired pages. The Bible constantly reveals the downward trend of mankind, in the absence of redeeming and sustaining grace. He began his career in Paradise with a perfect spirit, soul and body, and the whole world at his command, for he owned it all; yet, he proved a failure, and, as you see, gets worse and worse as the Bible reveals, till wickedness filled the whole earth, except one righteous family, and God was of the necessity, either to interpose and destroy them all, or let Hell devour each revolving generation forever. It seemed that man would have profited by the awful failure he made before the flood. He did endeavor so to do; sanguinely resolving this time to make a success, as he was constantly reminded by the bones everywhere so bleaching unburied or plowed up while cultivating the alluvial soil. The people were so large, doubtless, comparatively with us, giants in stature, that their bones must have been very conspicuous. Yet, all these warnings were not sufficient to arrest the downward trend.

A few generations have flown and we find him in hopeless slavery,—a failure again. God, in mercy, interposed, with ten terrible judgments against the enemy emancipating His elect from bondage. The law, which had been given in the beginning, is now proclaimed in thunder and lightning, and earthquake, striking panic to the people; oh, how all tremble, and quake, and promise to be good. Though with miraculous intervention, repeated over and over with the on-rolling centuries; oh, how even the elect nation blackened their history with failure, wreck, ruin and deportation into captivity to their enemies. Yet, after a regular Bible School of fifteen hundred years, they are so full of hereditary depravity in all its phases, despite all its professions of Holiness to the Lord, and so are they blinded by Satan, and led captive at his will, when their own Christ, for Whom they had been looking and praying for four thousand years, came among them, instead of hailing Him their glorious Deliverer, and receiving the highest honor this side of Heaven, the commission to go to the ends of the earth, preaching to the Gentile world, they rejected and killed Him, crying out to the authorities: *"Give unto us Barabbas, the robber."*

Now, let us see if it is any better when we come to the Gentile world. Daniel, in his Chronological image, sees and reveals Gentile rule from beginning to end. Read it for yourself.

The 2nd Chapter you find begins with gold, *i. e.,* "the golden head of the image;" then deteriorates to silver,—decidedly inferior in value; then to brass, still going down; then to iron, the cheapest and most common metal; finally, to iron mixed with clay, thus bringing in that utterly worthless element of weakness; therefore, you see that constantly progressive downward trend to utter deterioration.

St. Luke (18:8), referring to our Lord's appearing on the earth, propounds the question: *"Yet the Son of man having come, shall He find faith on the earth?"* involving a negative answer, and authenticating the sad conclusion that genuine faith will be an exceeding scarce article when the Lord appears on the earth. The world will be full of religion of which faith is the baseful grace, but it will be Satan's counterfeit, and vanish before the splendor of his glory, as the morning gossamer evanesces before the rising sun. Oh, how we see the churches now literally carried away with pride, vanity, follies, trivialities, frivolities, hilarities, fashions, styles and worldliness in all its forms and phases. The solemn assemblies actually exhibiting the phantasmogoria of vanity fair.

z. The commandment which our Lord repeats more frequently than any other in all His ministry is "Watch." It is a verb in the imperative mode, giving us a very simple commandment in a plain monosyllable, with the simple meaning to be always on the lookout for His glorious coming.

When I was on the other side of the world, sailing on the sea, and enjoying the godly conversation of one of our noble bishops, and simply stated to him, my constant expectancy and outlook is for the glorious appearing of my Lord and King, he had the candor to confess that such was not his attitude, and that he was not looking for the Lord now. When I repeated these commandments, and as I had my Greek Testament in my hand, ready to read the very words of Jesus, assuring us of His return to the earth and commanding us to look for Him incessantly; the dear brother received it very appreciatively. He said he would prayerfully consider the matter. You know any doctrine whatever that antagonizes the plain Word of God and puts you in an attitude irresponsive to that Word, is bound to be untrue. We should deal with them very kindly, and lovingly, at the same time asking the Lord to use our humble instrumentality to relieve them of the mistake.

Again the Lord enforces His commandment to watch incessantly, *i. e.*, be constantly looking for His glorious appearing by the terrible warning, actually denouncing woes and calamities on the unwatchful.

With the closing verses of St. Matthew 24, how withering and blighting those woes He pronounces on the servant who says, *"My Lord delayeth His coming."* He says, the Lord will come in a day he does not expect, in an hour he does not anticipate, cut him off and appoint his portion with the hypocrites and unbelievers, where there is weeping and wailing and gnashing of teeth.

IT IS PERFECTLY CLEAR AND UNMISTAKABLE THAT THE TRUE ATTITUDE OF SAINTSHIP IS CONSTANT EXPECTANCY OF THE LORD'S INCARNATE APPEARING ON THE EARTH.

During the old dispensation His true people were constantly looking for Him all the four thousand years which antedated His birth in Bethlehem. At that time, the devout people in all the earth, *i. e.*, the wise men of the East, were on the outlook. All the prophets, from the days of Adam and Eve, through the rolling centuries, lived and died in constant expectancy. When He ascended, the angels assured the gazing multitudes that He was coming again in the manner in which He ascended, *i. e.*, amid brilliant white clouds and accompanied by hosts of angels. The New Testament is perfectly clear and indisputably confirmatory of the conclusion, that all of the Apostles and their contemporaries were on the incessant outlook for His glorious appearing.

A. The whole Church, without a dissenting voice, the first three hundred years, looked for Him incessantly, as we clearly see in the writings of the Anti-Nicene Fathers. The whole Bible, Old and New, confirms the fact of His second coming; not after we have made a Millennium and gotten it ready to give Him, but to bring with Him His own Millennium, which is none other than His glorious reign upon the earth, and a dogma antagonistical to the constant expectancy, was never heard of; then whence originated the Post-Millennial view? The solution is found in the fact that when the Emperor Constantine was suddenly and to the surprise of all converted to Christianity (A. D. 321), (history imputes it to the appearing of a golden cross shining in the sky before him, while he was traveling at the head of his army, and on it the words, *En touto nika,* "Conquer by this;" when he suddenly halted his army, took down the ensigns of idolatry and unfurled that of the cross;) such was the tide of holy joy that swept over the Church like a heavenly cyclone everywhere filling them with rapture; and the suffering, persecuted saints were suddenly promoted from the burning stake and the lion's mouth to the royal palace, and the very council chamber of the world's autocrat, that amid these tempests of holy delight, which swept over hitherto persecuted and down-trodden pilgrims in their, even then, world-wide dispersions, that giving way to the sweeping rapture of this joy, they leap to the conclusion that the Lord had actually come back in the person of the Emperor, thus acquiescing in a symbolic fulfillment of those wonderful prophecies, setting forth, and in that way discontinued their expectancy of His personal advent.

Post-Millennial View Untenable. 285

We must certainly say to his commendation that the Emperor was exceedingly zealous for Christianity, actually doing his best to make it the religion of the Empire, which then claimed the whole world. In his enthusiasm for the success of Christianity and its establishment as the religion of the world, he even changed the capital from Rome to Constantinople, because the former was full of magnificent pagan temples, and even in the exercise of his despotic power, he was unable to carry out his laudable enterprise in converting them all to Christianity.

During the first three centuries, the Church had no creed but God's Word, especially the New Testament, and preached constantly the great fundamental doctrines of the supernatural birth, entire sanctification, and the return of the glorified Savior, to reign over the whole earth.

In A. D. 325 the Emperor called the first Ecumenical Council at Nicæ, Bithynia, over which he presided in person, sitting in a golden chair. History says it truly looked like a council of martyrs, as there was scarcely a sound man in it, one minus an eye, another an arm, another a leg, and others maimed in sundry ways, thus bearing the marks of the persecutions through which they had passed. They, during their session, formulated the Nicene Creed, which is still used by the Greek and Roman Catholic churches of which the Episcopal is a modification, and the Methodists a modification of that.

The Nicene is the mother of all the creeds of Christendom. It originated from the purest motives, but misguided judgments, superinducing the great mistake which

Satan has so adroitly used to side-track the Church from the King's Highway of Holiness.

N. B. During the Dark Ages, the creeds were born and multiplied rapidly, with the breaking day of modern civilization, and as a normal result they generally favor the Post-Millennial view of our Lord's coming, which we know to be a mistake, innocently made by not a few of our elect brethren, whom we dare not discount an iota, yet we must be true to God and all mankind, and shout as we go, *"Behold, He cometh."*

B. The Post-Millennial view assumes that the world is getting better and that the ameliatory agencies, now in progress, *i. e.*, education in the wonderful achievements of the arts and sciences, philosophy, and especially and pre-eminently in the progress of Christianity into every nation under heaven, that as the normal result, light, truth, righteousness and holiness will so prevail in the whole world as to bring in the reign of righteousness, peace, love, and holiness as an inevitable logical sequence, pursuant to the reciprocal relation of cause and effect, and thus practically bring on the Millennium. This conclusion is not only unsustained by the historic facts of all ages, which positively reveals moral and spiritual deterioration characteristic of every antecedent age, *i. e.*, the antediluvians most obviously, as revealed by the inspired history, constantly deteriorating from bad to worse, finally culminating in the necessity of a great flood to destroy them all.

The Post-diluvian ages have exhibited the same sad retrogression, and deterioration, showing us no exception to the rule, so mournfully manifested in the antediluvian times, *i. e.,* moral and spiritual retrogression and deterioration from generation to generation.

The Greek poets, historians and philosophers in the absence of the revealed Word, actually corroborate Daniel's prophecy so perfectly that it seems that they must have had a Bible, whereas, the facts refute such a conclusion. They describe the whole, beginning with the golden age, in which flowers without seed springing up beautified the whole earth, symbolic of the universal prosperity that prevailed.

Meanwhile, they describe the gods descending from heaven, and dwelling with men, making their lives a glorious sunshine. Then this moral and spiritual deterioration so prevailed that they grieved away the gods so that they would only visit them anon, and bless them, and thus the silver age came on, which was a decisive depreciation, contrastable with its felicitous predecessor.

But this downward trend, alienating the gods more and more from human abodes, still continues, bringing on the brazen age, in which the nations made war on one another, and so grieved the gods that they no longer came among them, but only descended on the mountain tops, and rebuked them for their wickedness and threatened them with awful judgments.

Still this retrogression and moral and spiritual deterioration continues, till it brings on the iron age, in which the people became rough and ferocious, and degenerated into barbarism, deluging the world with their mutual blood, and heaping it with the slain, so grieving the gods that they ceased to come down and bless them with light and wisdom and warn them of the awful calamities which they were thus entailing upon themselves and their posterity.

Paul, in the 1st chapter of Romans, gives us an inspired history, which precisely corroborates the above which has reached us through paganistic tradition. He there certifies that the heathens are without excuse, because they once had a knowledge of God, but turned away from the light, and walked after the inclinations of their own evil hearts. He there vividly describes this progressive, moral and spiritual deterioration, describing the first stage of apostasy into intellectualism, idolizing human wisdom and rejecting the true knowledge of God. The second stage of this downward trend lands them in idolatry, worshipping the sun, moon, stars and many other creatures, *"More than the Creator, who is blessed for evermore."*

Finally, this downward trend culminates in brutality, which Paul describes in language appalling in the extreme. So far as the arts, sciences and learning are concerned, instead of ameliorating the people morally and spiritually, facts sadly confirm the contrary. These arts, sciences, and inventions are all utilized by the wicked in the prosecution of their diabolical enterprises, with infinitely greater success than the possibilities of ignorant barbarians would guarantee.

When I was preaching in Pittsburg, a few years ago, a railroad officer rode out in a carriage to a place in the vicinity of Washington, where two or three hundred men were laboring, making a cut in the Wabash railroad, having with him a large sum of money, which he had taken out of the bank to pay off those hands.

While the buggy passed over a culvert, a dynamite

explosion tore it into smithereens, instantly killing the man and his comrade by his side, and tearing the horse to pieces. Several days had elapsed before he left that country, all efforts to get on the track of the murderers having failed. Where the thief used to come at midnight, and steal a few dollars' worth, now in the person of an elegant gentleman with a finished collegiate education he becomes your companion in business and deliberately robs you of all you have. Verily, all of these wonderful improvements, which were such a blessing to God's true people, are with the profoundest shrewdness and diabolical chicanery, brought into availability in the perpetration of the vilest theft, robbery, debauchery and murder incessantly.

The true attitude is optimism on grace and pessimism on sin, this involving the terrible conclusion that the good are getting better and the bad worse. Therefore, this universal reign of righteousness can never supervene, but by supernatural Divine intervention.

The only hope of the world is on the line of the supernaturalism which God excuses in the regeneration of sinners, the sanctification of Christians, and the glorious ushering in of the Millennium, which He will bring in person and give it to us to enjoy forever, instead of us making a Millennium, and giving it to Him, as the Post-Millennium view assumes.

c. This problem is easily and forever solved by simple heed to the words of Jesus. St. Matt. 24: 37-41: *"But as the days of Noah, so shall indeed be the coming of the Son of man. For as they were in those days before the flood, eating and drinking, marrying and giving in marriage, until the day on which Noah entered into the ark, and they knew not until the flood came and took them all away; so indeed shall the coming of the Son of man be. Then two men will be in the field; one is taken, and one is left; two women will be grinding at the mill, one is taken, and one is left."*

St. Luke 17:28-30: *"Likewise as it was in the days of Lot; they were eating, they were drinking, they were buying, they were selling, they were planting, they were building; and on the day on which Lot went out of Sodom fire and brimstone rained from heaven, and destroyed them all; according to the same things will it be in the day of the Son of man is revealed."*

You see the plain and unmistakable words of Jesus, clearly refutes the hypothesis of the world's gradual amelioration, till the normal reign of righteousness shall supervene as the logical sequence of Christian enterprise.

You know the Bible clearly reveals that the antediluvian world got worse and worse till the end. God finally calling His Spirit away (Gen. 6:3), and in mercy resorting to the only remedy for the coming millions of mankind, *i. e.*, the destruction of that generation, that the world might take a new start.

You know, Sodom and Gomorrah had actually gotten so bad that, though Lot had preached there twenty-three years, there were not ten righteous people in that teeming population.

One of the decisive signs of the Lord's near coming is the incorrigibility and, consequently, hopeless estate of multitudes all around us. You know, the Word reveals that He will come at midnight, when the wicked world and the fallen Church are all wrapped in profound slumber, but the Bride is on the house-top looking for

Him. It does seem strange that the man, in this reference of our Saviour, cannot convince his fellow-laborer in the field with him and get him ready for the glorious Rapture of the saints. I know he has done his best, because the very fact that he goes up in the Rapture is demonstrative proof that he is all right—saved and sanctified. Of course, the sanctified woman does her best to get her sister-comrade-in-labor at the mill robed and ready for the glorious Rapture, but you see she, too, makes a failure.

The steam engine reached Jerusalem before I ever saw it. Yet the people in that country use the little old-style hand-mill of the patriarchal age, to grind their bread. Instead of keeping flour in their houses, they keep wheat and barley, and when they want bread, two women sit down on a bench, on either side of the mill, the one turning and the other feeding and taking care of the flour. This, of itself, is ominous that He is very nigh, and they are holding on till He comes. Verily, the universal increase of wickedness, with the onward march of the arts, sciences and literature, is a striking fulfillment of the latter-day prophecies, confirmatory of His near coming.

While the Post-Millennial view, as you see, is utterly untenable for two reasons, the one because it positively contradicts the Word of God in multitudes of passages, and the other because its normal effect is to keep the people from obeying that positive and copiously repeated commandment of our Savior, to watch, *i. e.*, to be always on the outlook for His appearing.

The theory, which contradicts the Word of God and keeps the people from obeying Jesus cannot have any truth in it. Yet we should be full of love for the dear good people who entertain it. Of course, they are innocent, it being simply the normal effect of a wrong education. When we tell them the truth in the plain words of our blessed Savior, which are so copious on this subject; and still they persist; let us be patient, pray for them, and love them none the less, remembering that they are God's servants, and not ours. *"Who art thou that judgeth another man's servant? to his own master he stands or falls. But he shall stand; for the Lord is able to make him stand."* (Rom. 14:4.)

D. The most important consideration in connection with this momentous problem is that we should all be ready when the trumpet sounds and the Lord descends to snatch away His waiting Bride.

St. Matthew 25:13 gives you a clear solution of the problem. Those ten virgins, representing the kingdom, are all truly and genuinely born from above, as you see abundantly confirmed in the fact that their lamps are all lighted. Every sinner is a citizen of Satan's kingdom, wrapped in spiritual midnight, unrelieved by a solitary ray from the Sun of righteousness. The dear man, though he has eyes, sees nothing.

I need not tell a Bible reader that every sinner is a spiritual corpse. In regeneration the Holy Ghost creates the Divine life in that dead spirit (Eph. 2:1), then the heavenly daybreak dawns upon the vision, and the Sun of righteousness shines away the midnight darkness.

So these ten were all genuinely converted. While five of them, fully appreciative of the glorious work already received, believed that will suffice every need and consequently rest satisfied with it, determined to hold it at any cost and they certainly did, especially to their credit.

If Dr. Clark had seen the true reading, which is, "*Our lamps are going out,*" he would not have consigned the foolish virgins to perdition, because a lamp that is "going out" is not yet out; it still has a small amount of oil, much needing replenishing.

The wise virgins are only so denominated, because they prudentially thought on the future; as the word *hronimoi* reveals and concluded, they had better provide for coming emergencies; therefore, they went to the market and had their vessels filled with oil.

"The vessel" is the heart, and "the oil," the Holy Ghost. We all came into this world full of depravity. (Psa. 51:5.) Therefore we must first get emptied before we can be filled. The cleansing blood procures the former, and the incoming Holy Spirit Himself the latter.

During the tarrying of the Bridegroom, which is still continuing, nodding spells ever and anon come over the wise, as we have clearly revealed by *anustoxan*, in the imperfect tense, reveals "a continual slumber," from the aorist tense, revealing a sudden nod, and then waking, and resuming vigilance; whereas, *ekatheudon*, the part of the foolish.

You see clearly how the foolish virgins forfeited a place in the Rapture, and at the Marriage Supper of the Lamb by neglecting the second work of grace. Therefore, we should all profit by their sad mistake, lest we be left on the earth with the wicked to take chances in the awful Tribulation.

Daniel 12th chapter says this time of trouble has never before been equalled on the earth, but "*every one shall be delivered* (from it) *whose name is written in the book,"* i. e., on the roll of the Bridegroom, as the wholly sanctified members of the Bride, *i. e.*, as you see revealed in this parable, those who not only enjoy the genuine regeneration, but the radical sanctification, which empties them of sin, and fills them with the Holy Ghost.

Therefore, with this clear Bible standard before us, as we peregrinate this wicked world, we are forced to the conclusion that comparatively few are actually robed and ready to meet the Bridegroom at His coming.

"Is there no hope for the foolish virgins?" We have to respond in the affirmative. Rev. 20:4: *"And I saw thrones, and those that sat on them, and judgment was given unto them."* These are, doubtless, the thrones to be occupied by the transfigured saints of the Bridehood, who shall co-operate with Christ, as His subordinate rulers of the world, as you see revealed in V. 6.

Now let us continue this quotation. *"And* (I saw) *the souls of them who had been beheaded on account of the witness of Jesus, and on account of the word, who indeed did not worship the beast* (Anti-christ), *nor his image and did not receive his mark on their forehead and on their hand, and they lived and reigned with Christ a thousand years."*

There you see clearly a lot of people who got sanctified during the Tribulation and suffered terrible persecutions by Anti-christ, even having their heads cut off.

The pope, in bygone ages, has slaughtered a hundred millions of God's people according to history. Therefore, when he gets the throned world during the Tribulation, he will doubtless resume his ancient policy,

Post-Millennial View Untenable. 295

and make it awfully hard for those who will not worship him and his image.

That these people were sanctified is unquestionable, from the fact that Christ honored them with a place in the first resurrection, to that which preceded the Rapture, and took in all of the varied saints, meanwhile the living were all transfigured through the translation; as we saw exemplified in the Mount of Transfiguration (St. Matt. 17th ch.), where Moses represented all who were transfigured through the resurrection, and Elijah those who were transfigured through the translation. These foolish virgins represent all the real Christians in the world on the regeneration plane, when the Lord comes for His Bride. They are not hopeless apostates, as the English version, *"Lamps gone out;"* but to their great credit, had held on to their justification by a hard struggle with inbred sin, though excluded from the Marriage Supper, as you see (V. 13,) the Lord says, *"I know you not,"* i. e., know you not as members of the Bridehood, yet they had not forfeited their citizenship in the Kingdom; though left on the earth to take chances with all the wicked in the awful Tribulation, and exposed to the awful persecutions of Anti-christ.

Doubtless, millions of the justified people, under the terrible temptations and persecutions, will fall during the Tribulation; yet you see, some of them will heroically resist it all, and even press on into entire sanctification, despite all formidable difficulties, and the incalculable loss they have sustained in the Rapture of the saints, which will leave not a solitary sanctified person in all the earth. Reader, be sure that every moment you are under the Blood, robed and ready, filled with the Holy Ghost, watching and waiting His glorious appearing.

CHAPTER XVI.

The Eucharist.

This is the survival of the Passover, and a very precious souvenir. Josephus says that it was not uncommon for two hundred and fifty thousand lambs to be slaughtered at a single Passover. Multiply this by fifteen hundred, and you have the enormous result of three hundred and seventy millions of bleeding lambs on Jewish altars slain, all typifying *"the Lamb of God, that taketh away the sin of the world,"* who bled and died on the cross of Calvary for the redemption of every soul by His precious blood.

Our Lord instituted this Supper (St. Matt. 26: 26-29; St. Mark 14: 22-25; St. Luke 22: 19, 20; 1 Cor. 11: 23-25) as a souvenir of His expiatory work, which He consummated by His suffering and death on the rugged cross. Some think He gave it to Judas, with the rest. This is a mistake; He did not administer it, till after Judas had gone away.

While it is the privilege of all regenerated people to participate in this memorable feast of His dying hour, the deplorable fact that the great majority, actually *"eat and drink condemnation to their souls,"* when thus partaking of the emblems of His shed blood without a spiritual discernment of the same, should alarm the giddy, carnal millions, who throng the communion table, throughout Christendom. 1 Cor. 11:29: *"For he that eateth and drinketh, not discerning His body, eateth and drinketh condemnation to himself."*

Some of the churches hold a series of services on communion seasons, very judiciously, in order to prepare the people for this solemn occasion and the great responsibility. Epecial efforts ought to be made to bring all the communicants into such a devotional state of mind and communion with God, as to enable them to spiritually discern the Lord's body, as a means of grace —we cannot afford to neglect it.

The Pentecostal saints took it every day, after a time dropping to every fourth day, and then to once a week, *i. e.*, the Lord's Day, and eventually to once a month, and then, as now, once in three months. As this is really the surviving souvenir of the Passover, which, with all the bloody sacrifices, typified the expiatory work of Christ in the vicarious substitutionary atonement, which He made of His own body of the sins of the whole world, and, is thus, the procuring cause of universal salvation; therefore, we cannot appreciate it too highly, yet it has long ago been idolized by the Church—the three hundred and fifty millions of Greek and Latin Christians in all the earth actually worship it, to the awful detriment of their souls, while many Protestants have followed them in the same flagrant idolatry.

The Lutherans claim seventy millions of members in the world. This idolatry with them is lamentably prevalent, arising from the fact that their noble founder, so wonderfully used of God in bringing light to millions who had idolized the ceremonies of the church, and drifted away into dead formality, lead away by the cunning devices of Popery, prelacy, and priest-craft, till, with the exception of one here and there, they seem to have lost sight of vital godliness.

But this great man, while used of God as a sunburst on the world, and a luminary to the church, and really a heroic iconoclast, smashing into smithereens the idols which had crept into the church during the long night of the Dark Ages; this one, *i. e.*, trans-substantiation, in which the priest plays off on the people, claiming that when he consecrates the bread, it is turned to the real flesh of Christ, and when he consecrates the wine, it is turned to the actual blood of our Lord, and they, to this day, so teach, and the people so believe, and think they are saved by the sacraments, which is really a form of idolatry.

While Luther grandly delivered himself and got the victory, at every other salient point, he failed at this, and, instead of utterly repudiating and disproving the idolatrous heresy of trans-substantiation, he only modified it, recognizing the presence of the real body and blood, though discarding the literal dogma of the transmutation of the bread into the real body, and wine into the literal blood.

His failure at this point was manipulated by the enemy as a greased plank, over which he used to slide the people back into the Catholic idolatry.

We have but two sacraments in the Christian Church. (Beware of the popish heresy of the seven sacraments.) The Eucharist symbolizes *the entire work of Christ,* and symbolic baptism typifies *the entire work of the Holy Spirit.* A heresy somewhat prevails, robbing the Eucharist of this complete symbolism of the Lord's burial and resurrection, and giving it to water baptism, in order to sustain the unscriptural mode of immersion. It is of the greatest importance that we should vigilantly and joyfully leave everything just where God has put it; as we always suffer detriment to our own spirituality and afflict it upon others more or less by any departure from Divine order.

CHAPTER XVII.

Symbolic Baptism.

This is the cognate symbol, along with the Eucharist, which represents the stupendous vicarious substitutionary work of Christ, typifying the mighty works of the Holy Ghost. We are not living in the dispensation of types, shadows and ordinances, but that of the Holy Ghost, in His Pentecostal official power and glory, the personal successor of the risen, ascended, glorified Saviour.

St. John 14:16, 17: *"And I will ask the Father, and He will give you another Comforter, that He will be with you forever, the Spirit of truth; whom the world is not able to receive; because it does not see Him, or know Him; but you know Him, because He abideth with you, and shall be in you."*

Again our Lord gives the office of His successor in the Holy Ghost (V. 25): *"I have spoken these things to you, abiding with you. But the Comforter, the Holy Spirit, whom the Father will send in My name, He will teach you all things, and will remind you of all things which I have spoken unto you."* Thus you see, the blessed Holy Spirit is the successor of the glorified Saviour, administering the benefits of His great atonement to every appreciative soul.

While we are lost in unutterable bewilderment, con-

SYMBOLIC BAPTISM. 301

templating the copious magnitude of bloody symbo.isms, deluging the Holy Land, the fifteen hundred years of its occupancy by His chosen people, Oh, what rivers of blood do flow!

Those passover lambs, though according to history, aggregating at least approximating three hundred and seventy millions, were but a fraction of the aggregate, when we contemplate the innumerable goats, heifers, oxen, and the innumerable bleeding birds on Hebrew altars slain.

When Solomon dedicated the temple, he slaughtered twenty-two thousand oxen and one hundred and twenty thousand sheep—all these rivers of blood teaching the people the enormity of sin, and the verity of that Scripture (Ezek. 18:4, 20), *"The soul that sinneth, it shall die."* All this is souvenired to us vividly in the simple Eucharist, not a great feast, but a crumb of bread and a sip of wine.

When we contemplate the symbolism of the Holy Ghost, contemporary with that of Christ, through all the typical ages, we find them, if possible, equalling copiously His works, as to apply the blood, and eliminate every vestige of hereditary depravity from the spiritual organism in the great work of the new creation, giving us the supernatural birth into the Kingdom of God, and entire sanctification, *i. e.*, the expurgation of every living taint from the immortal spirit, actually investing us with the snowy-white robe.

The Levitical law specifies the sacrifice of the red heifer, without spot or blemish, and a drop of her blood, in water, thus making it ceremonial, rendering it expurgatory. As that would be both laborious and costly, on every occasion, when ceremonial defilement had been contracted, the law provided that they should utterly consume the entire animal, with fire and then drop a dust or two of the ashes into a quantity of pure water, thus preparing the water of purification, which any ceremonially clean person was competent to sprinkle on the subject of ceremonial defilement, thus expurgating all pollution and qualifying the recipient again to enter the tabernacle for the temple and enjoy its services.

E. Ceremonial defilement was susceptible of contraction in so many, many ways, *i. e.*, by contact with unclean animals, *i. e.*, the camel, the donkey, and the dog; the most useful, common and superabounding, or if they came into contact with lepers or dead bodies, or a grave; and in that case, they were prohibited from the tabernacle service till expurgated by the water of purification sprinkled on them by some person who had not come in contact with defilement, and was consequently ceremonially clean.

On the ratification of the Sinaic Covenant, in the wilderness, Moses sprinkled all the people (three millions) at the tabernacle door, thus qualifying them to enter the tabernacle and participate in its sacrifices, and enjoy its services. If you will read about this transaction (Heb. 9: 1-19), if you will drop your eye on verse 10, *"Which stood only in meats and drinks and divers washings."* The word here is *baptismos,* and should read "baptisms," as you find in my translation, where everything is just as the Holy Spirit gave it. In that translation you will find great help on the controversy of baptism, from the simple fact that I just let the word remain, and transferred it into the English Version;

which is the true rendering, because "baptism" is an original Greek word, and has been thence transferred and adopted into the English language.

N. B. We have only twenty-three thousand original English words; whereas, our language now contains one hundred and fifty thousand words; thus one hundred and thirty-seven thousand have been brought in from other languages.

Among these is "baptism," which is elegantly serving us in our language, though a foreigner. Here you see Moses was a great baptist, and equally great sprinkler; for he sprinkled all the people at the tabernacle door— two millions of adults and a million infants.

St. Mark 7: 2-4: *"And seeing some of His disciples eating bread with defiled, that is, unwashed hands. (For the Pharisees, and all the Jews, do not eat, unless they wash their hands thoroughly, holding the tradition of the elders; and when they come from the Forum, they do not eat, unless they be sprinkled; and many other things, which they have received to hold, the baptism of pots, and cups, and brazen vessels.)*

In this passage you have the inspired history of the ancient practice of the Levitical law, appertaining to the sprinkling of the water of purification of the subject of ceremonial defilement. In the market-place, transacting business, they were not only brought in contact with unclean animals, and horses, as everything in that country come and go on the back of a camel or a donkey; they use no wagons, from the simple fact that the camel carries as much on his back as they can haul on a wagon, and it is much cheaper and more convenient—so tall and sure-footed that he can go anywhere with a wagon-load,

Besides they were constantly brought in contact with the Gentiles, all of whom were ceremonially unclean. Now, these ceremonial purifications which they practiced incessantly, as you see clearly, and always by sprinkling, as you see in this passage, are called "baptisms."

The quotation I have given is from the latest edition of the critical Greek Testament, the concensus of all the critics, published by the British and Foreign Bible Society in the Bible House of Bagster Bros., Pater Noster Row, London, England, which I purchased in 1905, on my journey around the world. It has *van-ti-soon-ti*, whereas, the Sinaic Tischendorf, the oldest New Testament in the world, has *baptisoontai*, showing clearly that these two words, "sprinkle" and "baptize," are synonymous and used interchangeably in the Bible. In this passage, where the English Version has "washings," the Greek *baptismons;* while the same statement certifies that they were administered by sprinkling. The ordinance of baptism in its origin is not Christian, but Jewish; having been instituted and practiced by Moses. It superabounded in all the practice of the Levitical ministry. Many a devout Pharisee was actually baptized a hundred thousand times in his life. As a matter of universal convenience, not only adapted to public, but private life, the law permitted any ceremonially clean person to administer it: *i. e.*, sprinkle the water of purification on the subject of ceremonial defilement, which they observed at home and abroad, and without which they dare not enter the tabernacle and enjoy its services.

This explains the otherwise paradoxical possibility of baptizing three thousand on the Day of Pentecost,

SYMBOLIC BAPTISM. 305

during the morning service, and five thousand in the afternoon, with no special appointment, *e. g.*, going to the water or anything else.

I have been in Jerusalem early in June, the very time of the year when that took place, and if I took a drink of water I had to buy it, as it is a mountain city, above the water-line, too high to dig wells, and the supply which they harvest in tanks and cisterns under their houses during the rainy seasons, becomes so scarce during the summer that it is bought and sold.

They did not go to the Pools of Solomon, which supplied the city from twelve miles distant, and if they had, they would not have been permitted to immerse in them. The Jordan was the nearest immersion water, and it was about fifty miles distant. They did not go to it but administered it right there on Mount Zion, where the Pentecostal fire fell on the people, thus baptizing them.

The inspired history reveals that they did the same things with water. If they had immersed them, it is certain the Holy Ghost would have revealed it with a different word. Really, all of the hundred and twenty disciples, and the eight hundred thousand converts on that day, so quickly as they received the ceremonial expurgation were competent to administer it to others. Revelation 19:13 describes our Saviour in the great final battle of Armageddon, in the capacity of a mounted warrior, commanding His armies on the battle-field, while all the kings of the earth are pressing to war against Him, is portrayed by the Holy Spirit, with His garments sprinkled by the blood of His enemies, as it splashed on Him amid the conflict.

My London Version, latest concensus of all the critics, has *bibamenon*, the perfect participle, from *baptoo* "to baptize," whereas, the Sinaic Tischendorf, oldest in the world, has *pevivevamenon*, which means "to sprinkle round," vividly describing the blood of His enemies in the terrible conflict, gushing and splashng on all sides, and sprinkling His garments, but you see here *baptoo* "to baptize," and *vantizoo*, "to sprinkle," used synonymously and interchangeably, as in Mark 7:2. We have already shown you this synonymy of *baptizoo* and *vantizoo*, "to sprinkle," also the noun *baptismos*, used in the same verse, revelatory of those expurgations from ceremonial defilement, which were constantly performed by sprinkling, as you read throughout Leviticus.

F. The reason why the English Version is so exceedingly water-logged is because King James' translators had all been immersed three times, as this was the prevailing practice throughout the Dark Ages, which followed the Fall of Rome (A. D. 476), when the barbarians—Goths, Huns, Vandalls, and Heruli. after a three hundred years' war, finally succeeded in her destruction, thus barbarizing the world, which she had ruled one thousand years. With her fall, ancient civilization passed away, as she was its only upholder, and all nations went into barbarism, superinducing Satan's Millennium, a dismal one thousand years.

Of course, when all nations retrogressed into barbarism, the Church went with them, sinking deep into ignorance, superstition, and fanaticism; meanwhile the Arian and Trinitarian controversy was so rife that, as the latter prevailed, and felt it so important to enforce its principles any possible way, they administered trine

SYMBOLIC BAPTISM. 307

baptism, either dipping or sprinkling three times, in the name of the Father, the Son and the Holy Ghost.

When I was in India, in 1906, preaching in the largest leper asylum in the world, at Purulia, India, I witnessed the baptism of about one hundred persons by the native pastor, and administered by trine-effusion. It was very beautiful and impressive, and I realized the Divine approval and presence.

The Emperor Constantine, when converted to Christianity, became so zealous, that he actually did everything in his power to make it the religion of the world, and convert all the paganistic churches. Consequently, they poured in by myriads, great heathen temples becoming Christian churches, the priests turning preachers and the people Christians. If you ever travel among heathens, and see how they worship the holy rivers, and the great artificial tanks, formed by much labor, and consecrated by the priests, you would see them immersing in holy water all the time, everywhere in order to wash away their sins, repeating it indefinitely, as the painful conscience of sin still survives.

In this way trine-immersion became the prevailing practice of the Church, and so continued through the Dark Ages, consequently, the forty-seven men, who translated for King James, all having been immersed three times, and really having no information on the subject, as learning was then in its infancy, believing it to be the Apostolic practice, they bent their translation toward immersion, though never venturing to use the word.

All of those statements of "going down into the water and coming up out of the water," are simply gratuitous and without warrant in the original; the inspired Word being fully satisfied by the simple statement *"to"* and *"from."*

I have heard many a great sermon on the baptism of the eunuch by Philip, to prove immersion, as the only valid mode. I have, six times, been permitted to visit the place, where it occurred, as confirmed by all authorties. It is simply a waterspout, about one inch in diameter, shooting out of the rock, and so appreciated that every time I saw about a dozen women standing with water-pots, each waiting their turn to put the pot under its mouth, and hold it till it ran full. As they use all the water there is none left to run away and immersion simply out of the question.

In my second tour, in 1899, when the carriage halted, and my young men who had never seen it, curious to investigate, went to it, caught the water, and drank and brought me a drink, I saw them both "go down into the water, and come up out of it." After they took their places in the carriage, I asked them if they had got their feet wet. They responded in the negative, though they both had shoes. The water stands around it, two or three inches deep, having fallen while no one is there. However, they endeavor to economize even the waste waster, catching it in a stone trough for the use of animals.

To the English reader, that is the strongest case of immersion, whereas there is not the vaguest presumption that it ever took place. If you will examine, you will find the "down and up" have simple reference to Philip getting "up" into the chariot, and "down" out of it, and no allusion to the water.

Symbolic Baptism. 309

In the providence of God, I have three times travelled in the Holy Land—in 1895, 1899, and 1905,—and made a specialty to investigate everything, and can frankly say before God, and all the world, that I found not a trace, or a track of immersion. "Yes, but you had prejudice against it." In that you are mistaken. I had received it in good faith, like multiplied thousands, led astray by preachers, who were innocently mistaken, especially by the errors in King James' translation, which with all their extravagance, do not prove it, but only lead the reader to infer it. It does not say that, "Jesus went down into the water," but does say, "He came up 'out of it;'" whereas, the Greek word *apo* never means "out of," but simply "from;" thus refuting even the implication that He was in it.

c. We here give you the testimony of John and Jesus, in reference to the baptisms which they administered. The fact that they both used the same word is positive proof that they did the same thing, differing only in the element. It is superfluous for me to tell you that when Jesus baptized them, upon the day of Pentecost, He poured on them the Holy Ghost and fire.

Read every other Scripture referring to that glorious transaction.

If John had not done with water the very thing that Jesus did with the Holy Ghost He would have been under the necessity of using a different word. Pouring and immersion have opposite meanings, and are never synonymous. We know Jesus poured on them the Holy Ghost and fire. If John the Baptist told the truth, you know equally well that he poured on them the water. John had at his command two Greek words which mean nothing but "immerse" and are both used in the New Testament; *i. e., katapontizoo* (St. Matt. 18:6), and *buthizoo* (1 Tim. 6:9). Either of those words would have perfectly served his purpose, if he had immersed the people. The very fact that he did not use them, but used the same word *baptizoo* to reveal his baptism with water, and that of his Lord with the Holy Ghost and fire (St. Matthew 3:11) is positive and indisputable assurance that He did with water the very thing that Jesus did with the Holy Ghost and fire.

Then, as the Holy Ghost inspired John infallibly we simply know without the possibility of a doubt that he effused those people.

N. B. We begin his baptisms in the wilderness, where there is no immersion water, as I have traveled through it six times. When his fame spread abroad and the multitudes came, he went to the Jordan, just as we always want plenty of water for a big camp-meeting.

I read the inspired Greek, as readily as you do the English, having used nothing else the last thirty years, and been using it fifty years, The only argument for immersion is deduced from the prepositions. The Greek language is so strong that it does not need them. Now take four Scriptures, St. Mark 1:8, St. Luke 3:16 and Acts 1:5; 9:16. In these there is no preposition at all to become the point of controversy. In them John says, *"I indeed baptize you with water."* Jesus says, *"John indeed baptized you with water,"* as there is no preposition used in these four passages, it is impossible to bring in the controversy about them. It is simply the known dative of instrumentality. John certifies that he handled the water and not the people.

Symbolic Baptism. 311

I believe him without a doubt. Jesus certifies that John handled the water and not the people. "What about being buried by baptism?" Turn back to my chapter on "Christian baptism," and you will find everything fully cleared up. The only way they can prove immersion is to rob Jesus of His glory and give it to the water-god. It nowhere says that baptism is a burial; but, on the contrary, certifies that the baptism is the burier, *i. e.,* the undertaker that digs the grave and buries the corpse. Read Rom. 6 and Col. 2, and you will find a simple statement that the baptism which Jesus gives crucifies old Adam, buries him into his own death, the fountain filled with blood, the receptacle of all sin, which have by the grace of the Lord escaped the interment unto Hell, and leaves him there forever.

In immersion you raise up the same thing you bury. In this baptism which Jesus gives, the old man is buried and the "new" resurrected.

V. 3: *"Know you not, that so many of us as have been baptized into Christ, have been baptized into His death.* Also Gal. 3: 27: *"So many as have been baptized into Christ have put on Christ."*

These Scriptures which have been usurped by the immersionists, taking the glory from Jesus, which He purchased with His blood, and giving it to an idol, the water-god, describe transactions grand, momentous and even miraculous, which all intelligent people, if not blinded by sectarian heresy, cannot fail to see utterly alien to an incompatible myth the ordinance of baptism. You see this baptism puts you in Christ Jesus, and you actually put him on. *"If any one be in Christ Jesus, he is a new creature, old things have passed away, behold, they have become new."* (2 Cor. 5:7.) If you are a new creature, you have been born of God, and are now a member of His family. 1 John 3:9: *"Every one who has been born of God does not commit sin, because His seed remaineth in him he is not able to sin, because he has been born of God." "In this the children of God are manifest and the children of the devil."* You know, to your sorrow, that water baptism does not keep people from committing sin, which is demonstrative proof that they are still children of the devil. Here you see this is the descriminating line between the children of God and those of the devil, that the latter commit sin, and the former do not. Hence, if you take the plain Word of God, you are forced to conclude that these, and many other Scriptures which have been turned over to the water-god, who has signally failed to verify them, because he is "weak as water," legitimately belong and only find their fulfillment in the baptism which our blessed Saviour gives.

II. The reason why we do not find baptism in the Old Testament, is not because they did not have a thousand times as much of it as we do, as theirs was the typical dispensation, and water is simply a type of the Spirit throughout the Bible; but because the Old Testament was written in Hebrew and "baptism" is not a Hebrew word, but Greek.

Consequently we have it in the New Testament from beginning to end, mentioned here and there. In a number of places it is rendered "wash" by all the versions, but mine. In this respect, and others too numerous to mention, you read my translation, if you do not in the providence of God read the Greek, independently, as is not the case with one in a million.

While "baptism" is a Greek word, which, with many others, has been adopted into the English language, "immersion" is a Latin word, which has also found a welcome in our vast vocabulary.

It is a well known fact that the Bible was translated into the Latin in the second century, known as the Itala, i. e., in the Apostolic Age, and recognized as having Apostolic endorsement. St. Jerome revised it in the fourth century, after which it has been known as the Vulgate, and was almost the only Bible in circulation during the Dark Ages.

This translation was made in the Apostolic Age, when the people did know the primitive mode; rest assured, if it had been immersion, that word would have been used by the translators, as it is native in the Latin language. Consequently, the significant fact that they did not use it, is demonstrative proof that it was not the Johanic and Apostolic practice.

I have used the Latin Bible all my life, and looked in vain for that word, revelatory of baptism. Instead of using it, they simply baptized the Greek *baptizoo* and adopted in into the Latin language. They had good reason for so doing, and that was that immersion was not the thing they did. This argument they cannot possibly answer, from the simple fact that the truth is against them.

1. "Is not 'immerse' a definition of *baptizoo?*' We certainly respond in the affirmative, and so is "effuse" with its synonyms. But the best dictionaries in the world, *e. g., Schleusner,* who has given us an exhaustive

New Testament Lexicon in two volumes, which I have, defining *baptizoo*, "immerse," "plunge," "sink," etc.; then proceeds to state, but in this sense it is never used in the New Testament, then going on to define it, and "effusion."

The same is true of Robinson's large New Testament Lexicon, which I have before me. Therefore, while "immersion" is one of the definitions, it is restricted to pagan literature, and unknown in the inspired Word.

Daniel, describing Nebuchadnezzar's locks wet with the dew of heaven, gives us *ebaphee* (Septuagint) was baptized, from *baptoo*.

Origen, the most learned man in the Church in the post-apostolic age, who wrote in Greek, expounding the notable controversy of Elijah with the prophets of Baal on Mount Carmel (1 Kings 18th chap.), describing Elijah pouring the water on his altar, uses this word *baptizoo* all the time, when you know it was no immersion. The drought of three and one-half years had rendered water exceedingly scarce (barrel in the English Version is the regular word for pitcher.) It is certain that they poured the water on the sacrifice, and it is equally certain that Origen says they baptized it, using the identical word, "*baptizoo*," on which the whole controversy hangs.

J. We find a number of immersion historians who lived and wrote in our own times; Mosheim, Neander, Orchard, and Wilson, certifying that immersion was the Apostolic practice; but their *ipse dixit* is not worth anything from the simple fact that they quote no ancient author. Therefore, it is nothing but their own opinions.

The single dip is really quite modern and easily traced to its origin, the triune immersion in a state of nudity and identified with superstitious ceremonies is much more ancient, but cannot possibly be traced beyond the third century. The most ancient historian Lactantius, who lived and wrote in the third century, contemporary with Origen, who certifies baptism by pouring in case of the Mt. Carmel altar; has left in his own Latin, *Johanes Baptites tenxit, Petrus tenxit; et Christus misit Apostolos, ut yantes tringerent;* "John the Baptist sprinkled, Peter sprinkled, and Christ sent His Apostles, that they might sprinkle the nations." This is the earliest historic voice on the subject, and dates early enough for the whole matter to have survived in the memories of the people, who in that day very frequently lived a hundred and fifty years.

In that age, a contemporary historian in Rome, certifies, that one hundred and fifty men one hundred and fifty years old, were living in that city. All the ancient statuary represents Jesus standing, and John pouring the water on His head. This corroborates His own words, (St. Matt. 21:23, 27; St. Mark 11:27-33, and St. Luke 20:1-8), where they demand His authority for exercising the office of High Priest, and He refers them to His baptism at the hands of John,—positive proof that John in that way anointed Him for the High Priesthood; *i. e., did to Him with water just what Moses did to Aaron, when he poured the anointing oil on his head.*

K. "Who has a right to symbolic baptism?" None but those who have the thing symbolized, *i. e.*, the saving grace of God in the heart, begun in regeneration and perpetuated in sanctification. For anybody else to receive it would be like a man advertising goods which he did not have, thus lying and deceiving the people. How grossly heretical those people who preached and practiced water baptism in order to remission of sins, when no one who has sins to be remitted has any more right to it than a man in Cincinnati has a right to put up a grocery sign when he has none of the goods in his house, and can only fool and deceive the people.

A misconstruction of Peter (Acts 2:38), *"Repent, and let each one of you be baptized unto the remission of your sins; and ye shall receive the gift of the Holy Ghost,"* has led people into this dangerous error. "Repent" in this passage is in the imperative mode, aorist tense. Hence, it is a positive commandment, which all must obey or lose their souls.

The word literally means, "Change your mind," *i. e.,* "get rid of the carnal mind," which is "devil nature," and get the mind of Christ, which alone can fit you for Heaven. This commandment includes, not only the repentance of a sinner, but that same repentance perpetuated into the higher order, identical with the consecration of a Christian, which puts him on believing ground, where he can receive entire sanctification by simple faith.

God always forgives when a man repents, and in this passage, He commands them to repent unto the remission of their sins, which is confirmed by St. Luke 24:46, 47: *"Then it is written, that Christ shall suffer, and rise from the dead the third day; and repentance unto the remission of sins shall be preached unto all the Gentiles beginning at Jerusalem."*

Peter is here preaching under the commission (St.

SYMBOLIC BAPTISM. 317

Luke 24:47), which promises the remission of sins to all nations, under the solitary condition of repentance, which puts every soul on believing ground for regeneration and sanctification.

"Baptism" in Acts 2:38 is not a commandment, but an exhortation to them to appreciate the precious privilege. The true translation is, *"Let each one of you be baptized,"* i. e., each one who has repented and received remission of sins.

In my boyhood, I heard obedience to the commandments preached all the time, when baptism was so emphasized, that the people all the time thought of it when they heard the word mentioned, whereas, it is not a commandment at all, but the privilege of every Christian, whereas, those people who are, making so much of water baptism, emphasizing it as a saving commandment, which is not true at all, were actually in the midst of their own members, living in disobedience to the decalogue, *i. e.*, neglecting the ten commandments, to their own ruin, and compassing *"sea and land"* to get people to receive immersion, in order to remission on the ground that it is a commandment, which is simply untrue.

"Have infants a right to this symbolic ordinance of the Church?" They certainly do. "Why?" Because they are Christians. Whereas, as all inherit evil nature from the fall (Psa. 51:5), *"I was shapen in iniquity, and in sin did my mother conceive me."* 1 Cor. 15:22, *"Whereas in Adam all die, in Christ shall all be made alive."* Generation is in Adam the First, but regeneration in Adam the Second. As Adam was the only creation (Acts 17:26), Eve being no exception to that statement that she was but a transformation of Adam's rib. Therefore when Adam fell, the whole race fell and became corrupt and passed under condemnation. Whereas, the fall was seminal; the redemption is personal, coming into availability the very moment the soul and body united, constitutes personality, which is in the prenatal state. Heb. 2:9: *"In order that by the grace of God, Christ might taste death for every one."*

Here you see the vicarious substitutionary atonement come into availability the very moment personality supercedes the fœtal state, which is really antecedently to the physical birth. (Mark the error in the English Version, St. John 3:5-7, *"born again,"* whose true rendering is *"born from above."*) This great and fundamental truth of pre-natal regeneration is confirmed by the case of the prodigal son and his elder brother, who were born in their father's house, *i. e.*, the Kingdom of God, and, whereas, the younger sinned out, the elder never did. This great Bible truth of pre-natal regeneration settles the fact that by the redeeming grace of God in Christ, and not native purity, every human being is born a member of God's family, *i. e.*, a Christian, and that is the reason why they all have a right to God's family-mark in this world, *i. e.*, the ordinance of baptism.

If you exclude infants on the allegation of unbelief, you send them to Hell, which you know is the doom of all unbelievers. The hypothesis that an infant is an unbeliever simply because of its immaturity involves the dangerous heresy of intellectualism, *i. e.*, the sad mistake of substituting mentalities for spiritualities. *"With the heart man believeth unto righteousness."* (Rom. 10:10.) Hence, you see, saving faith is a spirituality.

SYMBOLIC BAPTISM.

St. Matt. 18: 1-6: *"At that hour the disciples came to Jesus, saying, Who then is the greater in the kingdom of the heavens? And He calling a little child to Him, placed him in their midst, and said, Truly I say unto you, Unless you be converted, and become like little children, you cannot enter into the kingdom of the heavens. Therefore whosoever shall humble himself as this little child, the same is the greater in the kingdom of the heavens. And whosoever may receive one such little child in My name receiveth Me; whosoever may offend one of these little ones who believe in me, it is better for him that a millstone may be hanged about his neck, and he be drowned in the depth of the sea."*

These were infants. Mark says, *"He took them up in His arms."* Jesus certifies that they were citizens of His Kingdom, even making them paragon members—assuring adults that we must be converted and become humble, simple, and innocent like the little ones. He also recognizes them as believers in Him. You say they could not have faith in Him, because of their immaturity. That is true, in reference to intellectual faith, which is all in its place, but as you see, from the above Scripture, the faith that saves is spiritual, *i. e.*, that of the heart, and perfectly compatible with the apparent disabilities of childhood.

Let us believe the Word of Jesus in reference to the little ones. Here He says, *"Who believe on Me."* The conversation, and the whole transaction simply appertains to those infants. Oh, what an awful woe He pronounces on those who offend them, *i. e.*, tempt and cause them to backslide, and thus forfeit their infantile justification, with which they were born, and which they had received, as above explained, in their pre-natal state.

The word "offend" in the New Testament, constantly means *"to backslide."* It is from the noun *scandalon*, which means nothing but "a stumbling block," over which a person stumbles and falls. The Bible is perfectly clear and explicit, that while all are generated in fallen Adam, and thus inherit depravity; but the wonderful redemption of Christ, which comes into availability in the pre-natal state, the very moment soul and body united, constitutes personality, so every one is born from above, before the physical birth, and, consequently, actually comes into the world a Christian, Christ having already defeated the devil.

"Conversion" literally means simply "a turning around." This hereditary depravity (Psa. 51:5) which is born in every human being, turns the face away from God, so the child is prone to go into sin, and will, if it is not turned around and introduced to the Saviour and cultured in His grace, and love and instructed in His precious Word, so instead of starting away from God, as it will in every case if not converted, it starts toward God, Heaven and Holiness.

The ignorance on the part of Christian parents, Sunday school teachers and even preachers, in reference to the infantile relation to the Divine economy superinduces the neglect of the little ones to their serious detriment, and in millions of cases, their eternal ruin. It is really imperative that all Christian parents should so introduce their little onces to the Saviour, pray for them, teach them to pray, and culture them for God, that they would get intelligently converted before they lose their infantile justification, and then lead them on into entire sanctification before they backslide. In that case, oh, what gigantic Christians would soon succeed the pigmy generation that now makes Christianity a byword and a hiss among the unbelievers.

You see that infants have a right to baptism, for the same reason adults enjoy that right; *i. e.*, because they are Christians. Baptism is God's mark on His own people, who alone have a right to it. Yet, a sheep is as real and worth as much in the market without the mark as with it, as the mark has nothing to do with making the sheep; it must be a sheep before it has a right to the mark. God alone can make a sheep; we can put the mark on it; but how foolish and inconsistent to put the mark on Satan's hog.

You may invest him in a sheep-skin, the wool white as snow, but he will pitch into the first mud-hole he comes to, and ruin the sheep-skin.

Christian parents certainly have a right to dedicate their little ones to God, in His appointed ordinance, which will augment their efficiency in the great and responsible work of bringing them up in the nurture and admonition of the Lord, and prove a constant inspiration to the little ones, and a perpetual means of grace.

Only Christian parents who will assume these obligations to bring up their children for God and Heaven have a right to dedicate them to Him in baptism, for others to do so would be sacrilegious mockery.

My infant baptism was wonderfully used by the blessed Holy Spirit as a constant inspiration to my feeble childhood faith and precarious obedience. It would have been a vast and a greater blessing to me if my parents had understood the Bible truth you are now reading.

The popular idea that children are sinners and have to go ahead and sin a while before they can be converted to God was hatched in the bottomless-pit, and has proved the delusion and damnation of millions. The great Bible truth of pre-natal regeneration, by the redeeming grace of Christ, dispersed by the Holy Spirit, so that every human being is born into the kingdom, a Christian and not a sinner, but born with his face away from God by reason of hereditary depravity, pursuant to which when he reaches responsibility, as in the case of Paul (Rom. 7:9), he will violate the law and sin out of the kingdom; therefore, the *imperative* necessity of conversion, *i. e.,* turning him around and introducing him to the Saviour, before he is old enough, so to know right from wrong, as to forfeit his infantile justification by aactual transgression.

Little children are easily converted, and easily deflected from the way and turned into sin. Therefore they need constant watching to reclaim them every time they backslide, as Satan will quickly harden their hearts, if permitted to remain in his kingdom.

The saints of God peregrinating this world of temptation and sorrow should never forget, in the footprints of Jesus, to give especial attention to the little ones, turning them to God, getting them intelligently converted and laboring for their establishment, leading them on into sanctification, as early as possible, and always ready to reclaim them from a backslidden state.

It is a recognized fact that early impressions are the most lasting. Hence, the great importance of not only keeping the rising generation out of evil company, but doing our best to environment them by salutary heavenly influences.

L. "Bro. Godbey, as you so clearly show up the fact from the blessed Scripture that the mode of symbolic baptism is effusion, should we immerse people when they desire us to do so?" By all means. While the type normally harmonizes with the anti-type, yet as it is a non-essentiality, we should not lay too heavy emphasis on it. 1 Pet. 3:21: *"Which anti-baptism doth now save us, not the removal of the filth of carnality, but the seeking of a good conscience toward God."* The great anti-type, baptism, which Jesus gives with the Holy Ghost and fire, is the Archamedian lever which elevates us to the good conscience toward God, which is void of offence toward God and man, now actually redeemed from the maladies of the fall.

The Jews constantly sprinkled the people with the water of purification, to remove ceremonial defilement, here denominated *"the filth of the flesh,"* and constituted their typical baptism, which symbolizes the great anti-type, *i. e.*, which Jesus administers with the Holy Ghost and fire.

Here you see the water is the type, and the Spirit the anti-type. The normal order, of course, gives the one the form of the other. The Bible clearly undisputably establishes the fact that the typical baptism was always in the form of the anti-type, *i. e.*, effusion, *e. g.*, in case of John the Baptist, who we are told baptized all the multitudes who came to him from Jerusalem, all Judea and the regions about Jordan, which, at that time had a population of about six millions. He only held one protracted meeting, which continued about six months.

Meanwhile, his great work was preaching the Gospel. He certifies *that he handled the water, and not the people,* which abundantly harmonizes with the impossibility for a man to stand in Jordan's swelling flood, moving with the velocity of a mountain torrent, and of his own physical ability, of immersing them in that river, and not have time to do it.

Therefore, like Moses, who sprinkled all the people at the tabernacle door, in the ratification of the Sinaic Covenant (Heb. 9: 19), thus baptizing them all, (V. 10) "washings," (Greek, baptisms); I trow, he baptized the multitudes in a convenient wholesale way, as he himself says, and as Jesus Himself says (St. Mark 1:8; St. Luke 3:16; Acts 1:5, and Acts 11:16), where we have *hudati,* "water," in the dative of instrumentality without a position. Showing, positively, he handled the water, instead of the people.

Of course, in case of Jesus, he took Him alone, making a personal specialty of Him, pouring the water on His head, as Moses poured the oil on Aaron's head. (St. Matt. 21; St. Mark 11; St. Luke 20.)

While it is utterly impossible to find the vestige of argument in favor of immersion, unless you take those beautiful and powerful Scriptures, Rom. 6: Col. 2, Gal. 3:27; 1 Pet. 3:21; 1 Cor. 12:13, etc., and spoliate them from the crown of Jesus, which He purchased with His blood, and turn them over to the water-god, thus drifting away into hydrolatry, the most fatal idolatry of the Christian Church, you actually cannot find a trace or track of immersion in the Bible; yet, as symbolic ordi-

SYMBOLIC BAPTISM.

nances, really have nothing to do with salvation, since they are only the shadows, and the shade of timber-tree is of no value; therefore, if you have the true life, we should not waste the Lord's time controverting about the shadow.

For these, and many other reasons, I exhort you to discount none of the Lord's people for holding an error in these non-essentials. Faithfully give them the truth, in all of its ramifications; but lay all of your burning emphasis on the essentials of salvation, *i. e.*, the supernatural birth, and entire sanctification.

The one baptism which Jesus gives (1 Cor. 12:15) actually unifies all of His people in His mystical spiritual body.

While it is impossible to emphasize these *sine qua nons* too greatly and forcibly, truly we should never let up, but be always at it; meanwhile we should avoid the mistake of an undue importance to non-essentials.

Therefore, give all the people all the water they want and just the way they want it, serving them patiently for Christ's sake. *"Him that is weak receive, but not to doubtful disputations."*

We should remember there is danger on both sides. While we are to make no compromise with error, but contend heroically for *"the faith once delivered to the saints"* (Jude 3), we must keep in the middle of the road. The King's Highway is encompassed with dead formality on the one side, and wild fanaticism on the other. If we do not heroically retain the truth, under all circumstances, the enemy will develop a fatal heresy, which will ruin many.

It is even now a heresy appertaining to immersion

in certain localities doing exceeding detriment to the cause of holiness, consequently we dare not compromise with every form or phase; yet we must humbly, heroically and faithfully walk in the light which God has given us, in the example of His holy apostles, and especially His infallible Son, our great Exampler.

Paul circumcised Timothy after that ordinance was utterly effete in order to render him acceptable to the Jews, who knew that though his mother was a Jewess, his father was a Greek. For the same reason a godly Methodist preacher immersed me a short time after I was gloriously converted, and was under conviction for sanctification, but in the absence of living witnesses and exponents, I did not know what was the matter with me, meanwhile, so much preaching on immersion had led me to the conclusion that perhaps it was the thing I needed. Though that good preacher knew to the contrary, when his effort to convince me proved futile, he acquiesced and nobly served me. I was disappointed, because the aching void was not filled. So I hungered on till nineteen years rolled away, and Jesus, in His condescending mercy, baptized me with the Holy Ghost and fire, thus satisfying my hungry soul and giving me the fullness of God, for which I sighed, though fifteen of those years I spent endeavoring to preach the Living Word.

You readily conclude that as I was disappointed in the anticipated satisfaction of my spiritual hunger, I received no blessing. In this you are mistaken. Then and there the utter futility of church ordinances to satisfy my soul was so clearly demonstrated to enable me to

SYMBOLIC BAPTISM. 327

pass the water-line forever, and begin in good earnest to climb Mt. Zion.

In the absence of a guide, ever and anon finding the way hedged up by craggy steeps, frightful, deep, yawning chasms, so as to necessitate retracing my steps, and often in my bewilderment, crossing my track, till finally reaching the Pentecostal summit, when the fire fell.

As Paul was *"all things to all men that he might save some,"* let us cast away none, since His mercy is boundless and free for all. Therefore we must not let this harmony in non-essentials refugerate the order of the perfect love that burns in all truly sanctified hearts. We must be sure that none of these non-concurrences in matters non-essential to salvation shall conduce to the depreciation of our brethren who do not in all things see as we do. We must not only keep the fires of perfect love always burning on the altar of our hearts, but we must see that we do not discount their labors of love in the common cause of saving a lost world. We must bid them perfectly welcome to the battlefield, fellowship them heartily, and never give them any chance to feel that we discount them an iota. *"Who art thou that judgest another man's servant?"*

N. B. They are not our servants, but God's. There is power and security in the truth, even appertaining to non-essentials, lest Satan may creep in, like a weasel, and sidetrack us on some of these non-essential truths, which he and his adversaries misconstrue, and magnify into essentialities, and actually in that way gradually get us deflected more and more from the main line—Holiness to the Lord, until a mountain will tower up, and gradually hide from us the glorious Sun of Righteousness; then Satan will loom up a dog-sun, such as I have seen in northern latitudes, shining so bright that I had to bring my intellectual diagnosis into availability to discriminate from the true sun and the dog-sun.

While church ordinances have nothing to do with salvation, Satan has always been raising up false prophets, who, in different ages clothed them with the majesty of light and salvation to the detriment and destruction of millions.

I have immersed multitudes of people in water, and if I were young and could live again I would continue to do the same. I have always done it patiently, lovingly, and even gladly for Christ's sake, at the same time telling them to look to Jesus alone for salvation. As in the providence of God He gave me a classical education, and enabled me to investigate His Word, as comparatively few of my contemporaries have enjoyed opportunities so broad, He has put it in me, for His sake, and for His glory alone, to dig up, and to expose doctrinal heresies without distinction or mercy, yet, we must discriminate between the heresy and the heretic. The former is Satan's hell-trap, and we must do our utmost to exterminate it; while the latter is my brother in the family of Father Adam, and I must love him none the less, because Satan has caught him with his lasso; but, on the contrary, do my utmost to rescue him.

While my writings are characteristic of a regular gatling-gun, fire on all forms and phases of doctrinal error, I have the consolation that I am shooting with none but the Lord's guns, *i. e.*, the blessed truth, which He has given me to proclaim to the ends of the earth; and I am using no ammunition but love.

Therefore, it is impossible to shoot out of human souls anything but what Satan has put in them. Truth, and truth only, can eliminate spiritual ailments and restore to the soul that perfect health which brings down a heaven in which to go to Heaven.

I trow that my writings by some are misunderstood and misconstrued. For those that make this mistake and fire back, I have nothing but the love which is ready to lay down my life for my brother. When they differ from me, I love them none the less, yet cannot subtract an iota from the truth or depreciate the glorious light of this wonderful full salvation a solitary scintilla, to win the approval and commendation of all my critics.

While the battle-cry of the Holiness people in every land and clime is *perfect love, entire sanctification, holiness to the Lord,* and this is our only bond of union, yet, in non-essentials we differentiate, without the slightest depreciation, either of the other. (1 Cor. 1:17.) Hear the great Apostle to the Gentiles: *"For Christ sent me not to baptize, but to preach the Gospel; not in wisdom of words, lest the cross of Christ be made of non effect."* This statement clearly proves the non-essentiality of water baptism. We are not sent to preach it, but the one baptism (Eph. 4:5) which Jesus gives, and by which all of God's children are unified in one body, utterly regardless of denominational sect color, national, or race line, shouting, as we go and singing as we go,

> "Brethren, all who disagree,
>   That would have charity to please **us**,
> Union there can never be,
>   Unless we be one in Jesus."

One as He is—one in God, in spirit and disposition. This the Holy Scriptures teach; it is plain without an exposition. 1 Cor. 1:10: *"But I exhort you, brethren, through the name of our Lord Jesus Christ, that ye may all speak the same thing, and that there be no schisms among you; but that you may be perfected in the same mind and disposition."*

Here is an error in King James, which has "judgment." This wonderful experience of Christian perfection does not put us where we all have the same judgment, but it does give us the same disposition, which is a beautiful constituency, characterizing the mind of Christ, which we receive in regeneration, but it is made perfect when the last residium of the carnal mind is eliminated in entire sanctification; thus filling us with the meek, lowly, loving mind of Christ, and superinducing in us the same disposition, however we may intellectually differ in judgment.

CHAPTER XVIII.

Apostasy.

St. Luke 2:41-52. Here we have an item in our Lord's puerile biography quite isolated, the curtain having dropped on their arrival home at Nazareth from an absence of about three months, spent at Bethlehem and Egypt, and on the road, traveling with the tardy gait of the donkey. Now, at the age of twelve, having accompanied His parents to the annual Passover at Jerusalem, the magnitudinous symbolic precursor of His own stupendous work of the world's redemption from sin, death, and Hell, for whose execution He had laid aside His crown and condescended to sojourn in this world of sin and sorrow a third of a century, in order so to identify His humanity with Adam's race, as to render it historic indubitably and indisputably forever, thus leaving infidels without the shadow of excuse for their own damnation.

Tarrying in Jerusalem after the departure of His parents, a brilliant administration of that super-human wisdom which constantly characterizes His ministry, there dropping down from Heaven through the intervention of the Holy Spirit, who at the age of thirty, descending in His personal symbol of the lovely, innocent dove, rested on Him, when John baptized Him, thus qualifying His humanity for His wonderful ministry, entering into the temple He taught the grave theologians, whose boasted erudition in God's revealed Word had rendered them the paradox of the nation, abiding with them three days, meanwhile astounding all by the infallible wisdom which characterized His revelations, and elucidations of the precious word, which His Father had given to the patriarchs, Moses and the prophets. During all this time His parents having started home, three days antecedently, as was customary, using a forenoon in preparation, had journeyed with the crowd of relatives and acquaintances a dozen miles, to Beeroth, where they halt about an hour by sun, spread their tent for the night's lodging, look for their Son, now twelve years old, and unobserved in the journey taking it for granted He is with the group of children walking along in the great crowd, as it was customary thus to make their peregrinations to the annual festivals, for the sake of company and safety, large numbers traveling together, when, behold! they fail to find Him. Consequently, they walk all the way back to Jerusalem, inquiring along the road, and ransacking the city, tortured with solicitude and clamorous to all they meet, hunting their lost boy, when, behold! entering the temple, they find Him in the midst of the learned clergy and cultured theologians, holding all spellbound by the paradoxical manifestations of His super-human wisdom.

With His return home to Nazareth the curtain drops, and eighteen years roll away, with a word,—a signal manifestation of Divine wisdom, as in case that His biography through these years had been written, it would have made the New Testament so large that it would require too much time and labor to learn it. Its brevity is a great blessing, because it has all the truth which we need for salvation, so condensed and focalized, that an ordinary mind, reading it over and over can substantially take it all in, and actually, like Apollos, become mighty in the Scriptures.

M. As Apostasy is the subject of this chapter, I have given you this item in our Lord's biography to illustrate the possibility of our losing Him, as you see the actual occurrence, even in the case of His own parents, who loved and appreciated Him in the superlative degree; yet, they lost Him and were actually three days without Him.

This illustrates the liability and the fearful probability on the part of every disciple to lose our Leader and Savior. 2 Thess. 2nd Chapter, the word, "Apostasy" is the prominent theme, warning us and also pronouncing it one of the prominent signs of the Lord's near coming.

There Paul predicts it as a necessary predecessor of Antichrist, really essential to prepare the world for His rising. In that chapter, the *anomos, i. e.,* "*the lawless one*," English Version, "*That Wicked*," refers directly to the Papacy, which is the seventh head of the Roman beast.

Paul says, "*The mystery of iniquity is even now working: only he that hindereth even till now, must be taken out of the midst. Indeed then the lawless one will be revealed, whom the Lord Jesus Christ will destroy by the breath of His mouth, and exterminate by the brightness of His coming, whose coming is according to the working of Satan with all dynamite and signs and wonders of falsehood, even in every delusion of iniquity to them that perish; because they did not receive the Divine love of the truth, in order that they might be saved. And on this account God sends upon them the working of delusion, that they might believe a lie: in order that all may be condemned who did not believe the truth, but were delighted with unrighteousness."*

This prophecy, at the time Paul enuniciated it, referred directly to the succession of the Emperor by the Pope. The world could not have a Cæsar and Pope both at the same time, as in that case, the former would have killed the latter. Therefore, Cæsar must fall before the Pope could rise.

The Apostasy here mentioned, succeeded the vast influx of the heathen world into Christianity, superinduced by the conversion of Constantine and his wonderful Imperial influence, which he everywhere so potently wielded in his enthusiastic effort to get all the Pagans to turn Christians, which, as a normal consequence, brought a great apostasy into the Church, and actually prepared the way for the Pope, who is none other than Antichrist, the *anonmos, i. e.,* the lawless one, because, claiming the Vicarage of Christ, and Vice-gerency of God, he actually verifies the definition of Antichrist, which means, "a substitute for Christ," *i. e.,* "one taking the place of Christ."

The Emperor fell from his throne when the barbarians took the city under the leadership of Attila, the great Hunnish conqueror (A. D. 476), and thus clearing the way for the pre-eminence of the Roman Bishop, whose prerogative, authority and majesty continued to develop more and more, till Boniface III. actually received the Papal crown from the hands of Procas, king of Italy, (A. D. 666).

APOSTASY.

Prophecies frequently have different stages and epochs in their fulfillment. During the long rolling centuries of the Dark Ages, when there were no civil governments on the earth, the Papal prerogative was pre-eminent, the Pope actually sitting upon the throne of the world, in the succession of fallen Cæsar; the Inquisition, with the flaming faggot having succeeded the Roman armies, kindling martyr fires on every hilltop, to enforce the Papatical *ipse dixit*. The great and universal apostasy now prevailing in all the Protestant churches, which has actually supervened within my recollection is the ominous precursor of the re-enthronement of Antichrist in greater power, majesty, autocracy, and availability than ever before.

He already claims the sole right to rule the world, as the Vice-gerent of God and Vicar of Christ, and is only waiting the fall of the thrones (Dan. 7:9), which are even now everywhere tottering under the accumulating mountains of moral deterioration, spiritual apostasy and political corruption. The awful crisis is hastening when the Lord shall take away His Bride, *"The thrones be cast down,"* and Antichrist rise, and the Tribulation proceed to do its work of illimination, hackling out of the world incorrigibles and unsavables, preparatory to the glorious reign of righteousness, peace, love and holiness,

"While He shall have dominion o'er river, sea and shore;
Far as the eagle's pinion, or dove's light wing can soar."

Those prophecies above quoted (2 Thess 2nd Chapter), about the lying wonders, are this day receiving their fulfillment, corroborated by the old prophets, *e. g.*,

Isaiah, who speaks of *"the wizards that croak and the spirit that chirp,"* fulfilled in the gibberish passed off on the people for the "Gift of Tongues," which is a glorious reality and of infinite value auxiliary to preaching the Gospel in all the earth; but now utilized by Satan in the most formidable fanaticism that has ever struck the Holiness Movement, fearfully prolific of apostasy, whithersoever it goes.

The leaders very adroitly and boldly tell the people, who have been witnessing to the incoming and abiding Holy Ghost in their hearts, that they never received Him, because His coming was not confirmed by an unknown tongue; whereas, He did give you the language of Canaan, which you had never before received and gave you two fiery tongues, *i. e.,* splitting yours in twain, and wrapping both in a Heavenly flame, qualifying you to speak the red-hot truth of God to all you meet; having the wonderful convenience of the two tongues, the one to preach Hell-fire to the sinners, to alarm and convict them, and keep them out of it, and the other to preach Heavenly-fire to Christians, to sanctify them and get them ready for Heaven.

He gave me this blessed experience in 1868, and I have been using these two tongues ever since. Yet, when, by invitation, I went to the "Tongues Meeting," in Los Angeles and preached to them, they did their best to get me to go back on my experience and conclude that I had never received the Holy Ghost, because, at the time I did not receive a language spoken by some foreign nation.

If I had acquiesed, thus going back on the blessed work the Holy Spirit had given me, after witnessing to

APOSTASY. 337

it thirty-eight years, I should not wonder, if he had retreated away, grieved over my unfaithfulness. Then an evil spirit was just ready to come in, as they are all well prepared to do, pass himself for the Holy Spirit, and give me all the strange gibberish I wanted, as in case of the Mormons and Spiritualists in this country from the beginning of this organization, and the devil-worshippers in India.

N. B. *"Try the spirits, whether they be of God."* (1 John 4:1.) Read on, and you will see how to try them if the Spirit is of God. He says Jesus is the Christ, and He is everything you need to save you to the uttermost, and give you the victory forever; meanwhile, as John says, *"All other spirits belong to Antichrist."* John says there were many in his day, yet, comparatively with their multiplying in our day, it was but the drop, preceding the pouring flood.

As *Anti* means, "instead of," therefore, "Anti-christ," includes any and every substitute for Christ, *i. e.*, any doctrine, device, or experience, that will take the place of Jesus, and His Spirit, *i. e.*, the Holy Ghost.

While His glorified person is in Heaven, interceding for us all, He carries on His mighty work on the earth, through His Omnipotent Agent, the personal Holy Ghost, Who is none other than His own Spirit, (Acts 16:6, 7; 5:3, 4).

Satan has all Hell marshalled and panoplied with heavy organic gattling-guns, rifles and revolvers, without number, in order to defeat the Holiness Movement; his great climaxterous tragedy, focalizing the combination of earth and Hell, in order to counterfeit it, and thus make people think they have the experience, when he actually superseded them by the chimera of his own strong delusion, inducing them to believe his lies, that they may all be damned. (2 Thess. 2: 12.)

Oh, how Christian Science, Spiritualism, Mesmerism, Hypnotism, Astrology, etc., through Christendom, are this day co-operative with jugglery, enchantment, necromancy, and witchcraft, and all sorts of magic, throughout heathen and Mohammedan lands, that Satan may hold his grip on the latter, and by his substitutes bring in an army of counterfeits, thus preparing all Christendom, along with the Pagan nations, for the reign of Antichrist. Oh, how he has his eye on the sixteen hundred millions of souls, now populating this earth! As the Tribulation will be Hell's great harvest, he is marshalling all his myrmidons, getting ready to reap it. He has achieved a wonderful victory in the last fifty years, in the apostasy of the great Protestant churches. But the Holiness Movement is his perpetual eye-sore, however, he has made great proficiency in his fight for its capture, and destruction; his *ad captandum* manoevre culminating in all possible efforts focalized to counterfeit it.

N. The Church, in all ages has been afflicted more or less with a heresy, popularly denominated, "Final perseverance of the saints." Like all other heresies. Satan, in this case, selected a beautiful truth, for his homocidal enterprise for the population of Hell. This specious dogma rests on the hypothesis that there is no backslider in Hell, as in case of its truth, every soul having once been a citizen of God's Kingdom, even though fortuitously lapsing ever and anon, will get reclaimed and finally make his way through to the realms of perennial bliss, forever to dwelll in the light of the Divine presence.

Let us put this hypothesis to a very simple test, by making an invoice of Hell. Therefore, let us begin with his royal majesty, King Diabolus. He was once a bright archangel in Heaven, under the beautiful and significant cognomen, "Lucifer," which means, "Light-bearer," brilliantly revelatory of the glory he enjoyed. Unfortunately he deflected from the Divine administration, as the sainted Milton, in his poetic visions tells us, yielding to ambition, the strongest tempter, he chose, like many of his followers in our day, to rule in Hell, rather than serve in Heaven. Isa. 14:12: *"How thou art fallen. O Lucifer, the son of the morning!" i. e.,* "morning star." Rev. 12th Chapter informs us, that Michael, with his angels, fought and defeated him, and his followers, and thy were all cast out of Heaven; thus becoming devils, myrmidons and demons.

They were a mighty host, as it says, *"The dragon's tail drew one-third of the stars," i. e.,* Satan's (which means adversary, and became his cognomen after his apostasy), influence drew after him one-third of the angels. Astronomy reveals one hundred and seventeen millions of suns. Our sun has ten great worlds revolving around him, of which our earth is comparatively a small one, as Neptune is sixty times her magnitude; Uranus, eighty times; Saturn, eleven hundred times, and Jupiter, fourteen hundred times the magnitude of this world. Now, as many of these suns are larger than ours, analogy concludes that they are all equally attended by worlds occupied by immortal intelligences and destined, so to be in coming ages. This simple calculation gives us the enormous number of one billion, a hundred and seventeen millions of worlds, speeding their precipitate flight through the void immense, responsive to His Sovereign mandate.

Astronomers have discovered that all of these hundred and seventeen millions of suns, with their vast retinues of worlds revolving round them, are also themselves prosecuting vast revolutions, through their appointed orbits around some infinitely distant primal center, which they have identified with Alcyone, of the Pleiades (the seven stars), which they believe to be the capital of the Celestial Universe, containing the City of God, so vividly described in Rev. 21st Chapter. Around this glorious center of the Celestial Universe, all of these suns, accompanied by their vast retinue of revolving worlds, are also revolving, thus making their respective peregrinations within the lapse of definite ages and cycles. All created intelligences were originally on probation, to be tried and tested, with perfect freedom to be loyal to the infallible Divine administration, serving forever, not only by choice, but with infinite delight, or to be disloyal and abide their destiny on the line of their own independency.

The fall of Lucifer, by which he was transformed into Satan, and became the devil, took place some time before Adam was created. Within the lapse of the last six thousand years we know not how many more created intelligences have fallen, and thus becoming demonized, as the normal result of their own disharmony with Divine Perfection, we can form no adequate conjecture. Doubtless the work of creation is still going on; new worlds preaching a state of adaptation to the occupancy of immortal intelligence, whom Omnipotence is still creating for the occupancy of the majestic worlds, all of which he has created in view of their occupancy by immortal intelligences.

o. Three things God never created, *i. e.,* the devil, a sinner, and a snake. He created angels, holy, and free to be loyal or disloyal. Some of them (Jude 6), *"Kept not their first estate."* 2 Peter 2:4: *"For if God spared not the angels who sinned, but having cast them down to hell, delivered them to chains of darkness, to be kept to the judgment."*

Hence you see, when we proceed to invoice the inhabitants of Hell, we find Satan, himself, to begin with, an old backslider, having once been a glorious arch-angel, standing at the front of the enraptured heavenly hosts, swelling the chorus of God's ineffable praise. All the devils, myrmidons and demons in Hell, were once angels, basking in celestial bliss and glory, but forfeited their probation and found their place in a backslider's Hell.

God created human beings upright and sinless; but, like all other created intelligences, free to be loyal, or disloyal. Misery loves company. Unfortunately, fallen Lucifer sought their companionship, and won them for his own irretrievable doom. Therefore, in the exercise of their freedom, they became sinners. But the mercy of God interposed in such perfect and glorious redemption that it reaches every human being in the pre-natal state; so every son and daughter of Adam's ruined race has actually been born into the world citizens of God's Kingdom, and only get out, like the Prodigal Son, by sinning out.

You see clearly, every sinner on the globe is a backslider, and what we call his conversion is simply his reclamation, bringing him back to his father's house, where he first saw the light of day. Therefore, every human soul in Hell is a backslider. Hence, you see, the very contradictory of Satan's hackniel dogma, "Once in grace, always in grace," involving the conclusion that no backslider ever makes his bed in Hell, is not true; the facts incontestibly demonstrating, and forever settling the conclusion, that the pandimonium is simply a backslider's Hell, made for his incarceration, and never would have existed had there been no backsliders.

When Satan goes into the lying business, he caps the climax and dumbfounds all competition. Oh, how adroit to have millions of preachers standing in the pulpits, and year after year preaching his doubled and twisted falsifications, lulling the poor backsliders into a perpetual deepening carnal slumber, from which only the deep-toned thunders of their own damnation will ever awaken them. The serpent has so prominent connection with the history of the fall as to justify a brief notice.

I said, God never created a snake. The Bible says He did create the nachash, and that he was the most intelligent of the animal creation, which is not at all true of the snake, which is far excelled by the elephant, the monkey, the ape, the gorilla, and the orang-outang, and other animals. The above mentioned bipeds, much resemble man, and in point of intelligence, rank at the top of the animal creation. This nachash occupied a position in the zoological column, above any of these or above any other animal on the earth, as the Bible says, he was pre-eminent. You see, he had the power of oral communication, conversing with mother Eve, and deceiving her. Therefore, when Adam laid the blame of the awful disobedience on Eve, she turned it over to the nachash, who had to stand before Jehovah and receive his awful judgment, which transformed him from the human position and similitude, into that of the ugly, odious, dyabolical serpent, which God had not created, but you see, he normally supervened from primitive transformation, resultant from the just Divine anathama, the consequence of his unfortunate Satanic manipulation.

P. The Holiness Movement is now seriously afflicted with another equally astute and detrimental Satanic heresy, in connection with the subject of this chapter. *i. e.,* apostasy. This heresy assumes that the apostate from justification, invariably simultaneously apostasizes from sanctification. It is but a *sub rosa* repetition of the famous Zinzendorfian heresy, which assumes our simultaneous regeneration and sanctification, *i. e.,* that the entire sin principle is destroyed by a single work of grace.

As Zinzendorf was a contemporary of Wesley, his heresy gave them more trouble than any other. It is this day playing sad havoc with the Methodist Church, desolating pulpit and pew with the withering sirocco of carnal security. Even a cursory analysis will enable you to see the untenibility of this dogma. As God's people had two crosses out of Egyptian slavery into a land flowing with milk and honey, and abounding with corn and wine, they must also have two crosses, if they retreat back into the land of bondage. But you say, they might go a straight shoot, and cross neither the sea nor the Jordan, but walk dryshod over the Isthmus of Suez.

N. B. Old Testament symbolism does not admit of any such procession. So far as that is concerned, God could have led them to Canaan, that way, without crossing either the sea or the Jordan, but He makes no mistakes. Therefore, what He does, is settled forever. You see He has taught us, in that unmistakable symbolism the two crosses out of Satan's bondage into the Canaan of perfect love. Therefore, if your Bible is any authority at all, you recognize two crossings retrogressively from perfect love, to Satanic slavery.

N. B. The name of this book is "Bible Theology;" because, "Theology," from *Theis,* God, and *logis,* "word," does not mean creedology, as the churches all construe it, but the literal and unmistakable word of God revealed in the Bible. If Satan can spoliate you of both works of grace with a single blow of his iron scepter, surely God could give you both at a single blessing. We certainly must admit the latter, as He is Omnipotent, but the trouble is on the human side; finite man is not competent to receive both simultaneously. Conversion empties and fills you to the extent of his infantile capacity, whereas, sanctification does the same, appertaining to his adult capacity, which is vastly greater than his infinite immense subterranean regions of hereditary depravity, having been revealed by the Holy Ghost, and with which he was utterly unacquainted antecedently to his supernatural birth, which brought him into the Kingdom of God.

Rest assured, simultaneous forfeiture means simultaneous reception, which is the Zinzindorfian heresy, therefore, you see its utter contenability, besides, all the environments appertaining to the forfeitures, entirely heterogeneous. You lose your justification, not by committing an overt act of outward sin, as is generally supposed, but by giving your consent to commit a sin, which circumstances may forever prevent you from literal execution.

A sanctified friend of mine, in one of our cities, gave me this argument to prove the simultaneous forfeiture of both works of grace. "A sanctified man, in this city, breaks into a house and commits burglary; does he not, in so doing, lose both blessings?" I responded, "Nay, he does not lose either." The man was astounded to think he could commit such a crime without losing either his justification or sanctification, when I proceeded to tell him: "The moment the man got his consent to commit the burglary and robbery, he lost his justification, and fell under condemnation; though vigilant policemen and infractible locks, might forever prevent him from prepetrating the diabolical crime." Then he observed, "When he got his consent to commit the crime, and fell under condemnation, did he not also lose his sanctification." I answered, "No; if he had been in possession of it when the temptation came, he would have died in his tracks, rather than consent to perpetrate the foul crime." The solution of the problem is actually double. We always lose our justification by doing something which we know to be wrong, not simply the outward act, *but inward consent to do it.* We do not lose our sanctification in this way, but by the reunbition of depravity, to whose liability we are constantly exposed, in view of our environment by evil spirits, who literally throng the air (Eph. 2:2), led by Satan, their *generalissimo*.

The question is often asked, if old Adam is crucified, and destroyed, in sanctification, which is true; then how can he ever get back? This old man of sin, which we all inherited from the fall, is simply another name for devil-nature. Though the old man is dead, Satan and his myrmidons are not dead, but full of life and activity, and always watching an opportunity to impart their own nature back into the heart and will certainly succeed, if we do not watch and pray incessantly. In a similar manner, the Antinomians are always asking how the people who have been born from above, can ever be unborn. They simply unwarrantably manipulate the English translation. The prevailing word used by the Holy Ghost, is *zooeepoieese*, from *zooee*, "life," recognizing the perpetual fact everywhere revealed in the Bible, that every sinner is a spiritual corpse till the Holy Ghost raises him from the dead. "Then how does he become a backslider?" Why, the devil shoots at him, and kills him, so he is a spiritual corpse again. "Is not the Holy Ghost still on hand to raise him from the dead? *i. e.*, to create the Divine life in his dead soul again. "He is Omnipotent, and that is His work. It is astounding how Satan can prevail on so many good religious people to do his dirty work. Preaching his lies, and discouraging people with the idea that they cannot be saved because they are not elected, but rejected with the non-elect, which is all true; but Satan's conclusion, that there is no hope for them is not true.

Well did Sam Jones laconically say: "The elect is the man that will, and the non-elect, the man that will not." Oh, how Satan lays under embargo all the hosts of Hell, to so hallucinate people by his lies, hatched copiously in the hot-beds of perdition, that they will not try. In that attitude he has a bill salable. Whereas, justification is forfeited and condemnation supervenes, the very moment you get your consent to do wrong, whether you ever carry it out or not. The reason why you yielded to the temptation and gave your consent, was because you had already lost your sanctification. So long as you really have it, the Holy Ghost is dwelling in you; while He is there, there is not power enough in Hell to down you, because He will whip the combined armies of earth and Hell, though they may all simultaneously march against you, rest assured, He will give you the victory and you will receive a great blessing in the conflict, as you will gain strength by the battle, and courage by the victory.

You lose your sanctification, not by doing something you know to be wrong, for you would actually suffer martyrdom, rather than yield to temptation, while the Holy Spirit is dwelling in you. You always lose your sanctification by the reunbition of depravity, which takes place through your unwatchfulness, inadvertencies, trivilities, frivolities, excessive levities, hilarities, etc., by which you grieve away the Holy Spirit, before you are aware, as in case of Samson, when Delilah put him to sleep and clipped his locks, the symbol of his Nazaritish vow of Holiness to the Lord, till his supernatural strength evanesced, and he became like another man. But he did not know that the Spirit of the Lord had departed from him till he got into a fight with the Philistines, and was so surprised that they whipped him, which they had been trying to do, all his life, and never had succeeded. Single-handed and alone he had often vanquished whole armies, heaping the battle-field with the slain, because Israel had so far gone into apostasy, that they never saw their opportunity, which God gave them in Samson, the last of the judges, with whom the hope of Israel evanesced.

All they ever did for him was, instead of utilizing his miraculous power, they simply betrayed him to his enemies. But as Samson knew not when the Spirit of the Lord departed from him, so it is now. When the holiness people backslide, they look to the time when they yielded to temptation, and did something which their conscience condemned, and there locate the loss of their sanctification. They make a great mistake. It was there they lost their justification. If the Holy Ghost had been abiding in the heart, He would have vanquished the temper, even if earth and Hell had combined, and given them the victory; so, instead of falling, they would have come out, like Samson, at the battle of Lehi, when formidable swords and spears, whereas, he had nothing but the jaw-bone of a donkey.

With the Holy Ghost dwelling in you, the most simple little word of truth will put to flight all of your enemies, and give you the victory.

Q. Satan directs all of his heresies especially against the formidable impregnable citadel of entire sanctification. So long as the Holy Ghost occupies it, there is not power enough in earth and Hell to storm it. Therefore, there is absolutely but one way to lose sanctification, and that is to grieve away the Holy Spirit, who alone can sanctify us, and He alone can keep us sanctified.

The train never starts without the locomotive, which is absolutely as necessary to keep it running, as it was to start it.

N. B. The new Jerusalem Railroad is up-grade all the way. Consequently, when the train begins at once to run back, it goes faster and faster, till it reaches the City of Destruction (from which it started), with awful and hopeless wreckage. Therefore, the great secret of keeping your sanctification is unfaltering obedience to the blessed Holy Spirit, and diligent loyalty to God's triple leadership. If you undertake to follow the Holy Spirit, a demon, dressed in angelic habitude, will come in, and pass himself for the Holy Ghost, and thus sidetrack and ruin you. When the Holy Spirit comes in. He crowns Jesus on the throne of your heart, so that you turn your eye to Him, and while true to the indwelling Spirit, never take it away. Really the only atitude of the sanctified is following Jesus, led by the Holy Spirit. and instructed by the Word. In that attitude, there is not power enough in earth and Hell, combined, to ever defeat, side-track, derail, strand, or ditch you. Abiding in that attitude, utilizing these fortifications, true to the indwelling Holy Ghost, you have the victory forever, as sure of Heaven as if you were in it, because there is not power enough in earth and Hell to defeat you.

Glaring mistakes are made even by holiness evangelists, *e. g.,* a noted evangelist recently in a powerful sermon on the Holy Ghost, said to the people, "God will not give you the Holy Ghost, unless you will use Him;" whereas, the very opposite is true; God will not give you the Holy Ghost, unless YOU WILL LET HIM USE YOU. This wonderful sanctified experience is simply *God the*

Holy Ghost dwelling in you. You will never lose your justification till Satan whips you, and makes you do something, which you know to be wrong; He can never whip you while the Holy Ghost abides in your heart, because He will give you the victory over every foe forever.

Therefore, when you yield to temptation and do what you know to be wrong you forfeit your justification, it is always because you had grieved away the Holy Spirit, and, consequently the enemy got the victory over you. The Holy Ghost is very and Eternal God. (Acts 5:3, 4.) "God is love." (1 John, 4:8, 16.) *Regeneration is first love; sanctification is perfect love.* More people lose their sanctification by the leakage of love, I trow, than any other way. (Heb. 2:1. My Version.) We should so watch and pray as to detect every leakage, our spiritual detriment, and depreciation, by which the Spirit is grieved away and, consequently, sanctification forfeited.

Just as it is graciously possible to receive pardon and purity in very quick succession, because with God a minute is as good as a month: yea, a second as good as a century: because He is not a God of time, but Eternity. Just as a person may get saved and sanctified in so short a time that in a discrimination between two works of grace, that they are not very clear; in a similar manner the two works of grace may be destroyed by our formidable foe, in such a continuous spiritual catastrophe that we will not discriminate between the two awful epochs. We have really a great consolation appertaining to the terrible ordeals through which we are liable to pass, in case the enemy should defeat us, and that consolation is that he actually has to whip us twice in

APOSTASY.   351

two regular decisive battles in order to capture us and lead us to Hell. It is God's super-abounding mercy and wonderful redeeming love, thus manifest, perpetuating our hope, however forlorn and despondent. When we suffer defeat, grieve away the Holy Spirit and lose our sanctification; oh, what a precious consolation, that we are still on Emanuel's land, treading the justification plane, and while Satan has robbed us of our holiness, he has not yet taken us captive. Therefore, these awful reverses should be utilized as profitable warnings to cry unto God for help, armed and equipped and again rally to the conflict, fighting as never before. Then God in His mercy will see the tears of the backslider (from sanctification), then the Heavens in mercy come down and give us back our Pentecostal experience, as we see graciously verified constantly in our holiness camp-meetings.

I was present at the battle of Perryville, the greatest of all in Kentucky, during the Confederate War. The Union Army having suffered signal defeat in Dixie-land, retreated before the triumphant Confederates, rendezvoused with great reinforcement and made another stand at Perryville, where a three-days' battle ensued, winding up with signal victory; the Confederates suffering so decisive defeat that they evacuated the State and never returned. Kentucky never having seceded from the Union was a loyal territory; therefore, they gave the enemy another decisive battle on their own ground, achieving the victory and regaining former losses, and continued the victorious trend till the war wound up, with decisive and universal triumph. It is exceedingly risky and injudicious for people who have lost their sanctification, not to seek at once for its recovery. The longer you remain without it, the stronger the carnality which you imbibe with its forfeiture will fortify itself in your heart and prepare to hold its ground and wage an exterminating war against your justification, fighting night and day to bring you under condemnation, which simply means the resumption of your Egyptian slavery and the eclipse of the last hope, but when you forfeit all and actually have fallen captive to the enemy, bound in the adamantine chains of her bondage. You should lose no time to repent, restore, cry to God to forgive you and take you back and never desist night nor day till you know he has delivered you again from Satan's brick-kilns and mortar-yards and reinstated you, a citizen of His Kingdom.

You cannot possibly live in Satan's kingdom, without suffering spiritual detriment, with ever-increasing calamity till the last hope is fled and the golden moments of probation evanesced and demons drag you into Hell.

N. B. It is utterly impossible to remain in Satan's kingdom without an awful combination of influences incessantly conducing to harden your heart, stiffen your neck, deaden your sensibilities, paralyze your will-power, enfeeble your judgment, depreciate your ratiocination, degrade your affections, actually diabolize and ripen you for Hell. Therefore, you should not let a golden moment fly away without crying to God with a broken heart and availing yourself with every means of grace in the way of confessing, restitution, humiliation, and every auxiliary, which you will find among the people of God to help you, to regain your lost ground; taking courage from the example of Samson, who was gloriously reclaimed from the very article of death, receiving back the Holy Ghost in his miraculous power and lifting up that great Temple of Dagon with three thousand people, when it all fell to pieces in crushing calamity and gave currency to the maxim, that, "Samson slew more in his death than in his life."

God's mercy endureth forever. Oh, what a victory if He only gives you back your experience in time to leave this world with a shout of victory, and in the end gain Heaven forever!

CHAPTER XIX.

Matrimony.

This institution is the only souvenir of Eden's glory, everything else having gone down in the terrible catastrophe when Satan bore away his Hellish banner in triumph from the first battle-field beneath the stars.

Matrimony is truly an Edenic institution which God gave humanity for an everlasting benediction. If it had gone down in the fall, it does look like this world would become a pandemonium.

The symbolic signification of this institution is very beautiful, as it typifies the indissoluble union of Christ and His Church; yea, their blessed and actual unification pursuant to the proclamation. "They two shall be one flesh."

Our Savior in person honored this institution with His presence at the marriage in Cana. where He wrought His first miracle, turning the water into wine.

The Apostle Paul, though waiving his own privilege. and living in celebacy, that he might be the more indissolubly wedded to the Gospel, and efficient in the service of Christ, speaks of it in the highest appreciation, commending it to all.

There is but one apology with which any of us can excuse ourselves in reference to this institution, pass it by, and live in celebacy; and that is simply for the sake of Christ and His kingdom. The primitive Bishops of American Methodism, Asbury, McKindrey and George, all lived and died in celebacy, travelling on horse-back throughout all this great wide Continent, carrying the Gospel to the pioneers, gathering hither from the ends of the earth, God wonderfully blessing their labors.

We here give you our Lord's exemption from this institution, as revealed through His Apostle Paul. (Matt. 19: 10, 11, 12.) His disciples say to Him, *"If thus is the cause of a man with a woman, it is good not to marry."* This has reference to our Lord's abrogation of the broad liberties which they had enjoyed under Moses, pursuant to which husband and wife might separate for incompatibility of tempers and other trivial causes. *"But He said to them: All do not receive this word, but to those to whom it has been given. For there are eunuchs who have been so born from the womb of their mother,"* i. e., people naturally deficient in the genital organs. *"And there are eunuchs who have been eunuchized by the people,"* i. e., in order that they might serve at royal courts. I have seen them. They are now in the city of Hydrabad, India. I have seen them in Egypt. *"And there are eunuchs who have eunuchized themselves for the sake of the kingdom of Heaven."*

Paul, himself, and those primitive Methodist bishops, above mentioned, with many in the Holiness Movement, this day, both male and female, belong to this class, who actually consecrate this privilege to the Lord and walking in the light He gives, pursuant to that light, willingly and gladly forego the privilege.

I had been one of that class myself, if sanctification had reached me before matrimony, and, consequently, I did not foresee the manner of my life, perpetually wandering from my earthly home, leaving my companion to dwell alone. While the Lord wonderfully blessed me in my matrimonial alliance; from the simple fact of my disqualification in the prosecution of His work to live with her, as she never had the physical ability to travel with me, I would certainly, like those above mentioned, have wedded the Gospel forever, and foregone the precious privilege of matrimony for the sake of Him, Who left all Heaven to die for me.

"Let him who is able to receive it, receive it."

This has reference to the privilege to eunuchize yourself for the sake of the Gospel. This is a matter in which God will always lead His true people. The simple fact that God in the perpetuation of mankind on earth keeps the sex numerically equal is an irreparable argument against Satan's awful polygamy, which is advocated by the Mormons in this country and the Mohammedans in Europe, Asia and Africa. And, of course, practiced by the poor heathen as they dwell in darkness throughout the earth. I see no authority in the Bible to excuse people of matrimony except the above, which is special in the interest of the Gospel. Society has been so manipulated as to arbitrate exclusively to man, which is very unfair to the woman, who have equal rights to negotiate matrimony, but is everywhere intimidated in so doing by this false and unfair interdiction of society, and especially the sterner sex. Consequently, many noble sisters live and die in celebacy who have a perfect right to the privilege of entering into matrimony.

All such should enter into the more exclusive wedlock with the Lord and live for His Kingdom, using their

MATRIMONY.

humble instrumentality to spread it over the earth. This great Holiness Movement now girdling the globe is presenting a wide, open door for all godly women as well as men to labor for the evangelization of the world. We are happy now in our peregrinations around the globe, preaching to the heathen nations, to see the wonderful fulfillment of David's latter-day prophecy. Psa. 68:11: *"The Lord gave the word and the women who published it were a great host."*

To the shame of King James' Translators, they left out the "women" in this passage, simply giving it, *"They who published it;"* whereas the Hebrew feminine gender of the pronoun is clear and unmistakable. They did their work almost 300 years ago, in the comparative dawn of our glorious Christian civilization; and the world was emerging out of the long night, so significantly denunciated the "Dark Ages," during which womanhood was degraded and many of her rights ignored and wrested from her. You see this prophecy describes great hosts of women going forth and preaching the Gospel. I have found it so fulfilled in my travels among the heathens; common thing to come to a Mission Station and find one man and several women preaching the everlasting Gospel, which alone can drive away the darkness and bring on the glorious Millennial Day.

It is pertinent for us to expound the subject of divorces, which has so much perplexed the Christian Church. The subject of matrimony, like almost every other great truth revealed in the precious Word; has suffered much from erroneous translators.

Matt. 5:32: *"But I say unto you that every one putting away his wife except for the charge of fornica-*

tion, causes her to commit adultery, and whosoever may marry her who has been put away commits adultery."

E. V. says: *"Whosoever may marry the divorced woman commits adultery."* It is utterly incorrect, and has done much harm, opening the door for fanatics to separate husbands and wives, which has actually been done in many instances.

The word here rendered "divorced" is *apalelunen*, the perfect passive participle from *apoluoo*, which does not mean divorce, but simple put away; *i. e.*, it is a case of incompatibility developing domestic troubles characteristic of brawls, quarrels, and in all probability pugilistic combats, in which the man proving the physical champion has driven the woman from home. In this case a man marrying her would be guilty of adultery, because she is still the lawful wife of the cruel husband, who has flagellated and driven her from home. If she were Scripturally divorced, she would no longer be the wife of that cruel husband, but perfectly free to enter into matrimony with another man, at their mutual discretion, and both in that case perfectly free from the sin of adultery, which is peculiar to the state of wedlock; the same transgression appertaining to unmarried people being denominated fornication. There is not so much as an insinuation in this case (Matt. 5:32) that the woman expelled by her husband has a Scriptural divorce or even a right to it. It is simply one if those innumerable cases of domestic troubles arising from incompatibility of tempers, which Moses relieved by granting divorcement. (Matt. 19:7; Mark 10:4; Deut. 24:1.)

The Mosaic dispensation was on the lower plain of

MATRIMONY. 359

justification, in which he in his godly judgment adjudicated the expediency of granting divorcements on account of incompatibility of tempers and uncongeniality of dispositions; concluding that separation was better than living together amid perturbations, quarrels, and perhaps fights. Consequently, with the Jews the matrimonial relation was very lax. Even the great historian Josephus, who lived and wrote in the Apostolic Age, moving along with his current chronicles, simply states, "This day I sent away my wife;" evidently treating it as a matter of no very serious moment, deserving only a cursory notation. The Gospel dispensation whose materials God used John the Baptist to inaugurate and Jesus to construct the grand evangelicalship, which the descending Holy Ghost launched on the Day of Pentecost through the instrumentality of the one hundred and twenty disciples preaching with tongues of fire; under the patent influence of the copious baptism of the Holy Ghost and fire which Jesus gave on that notable occasion. Matt. 3:11 is on the high plane of entire sanctification, perfected by the cleansing blood (Acts 15:9), and administered by the incoming and abiding Holy Spirit, the Executive of the Holy Trinity. Therefore Jesus restricts divorcements to the isolate sin of fornication. Matt. 19:9: *"I say unto you that whosoever may put away his wife except for fornication, and may marry another, commits adultery."* Mark 10:12 continues this revelation: *"And if a woman may put away her husband and be married to another, she commits adultery."*

R. The nature of the matrimonial institution is the unification of the parties. Mark 10:6: *"From the be-*

ginning God created them male and female." Gen. 1:27: *"On account of this a man shall leave his father and mother and cleave unto his wife; and they two shall be one flesh." "What God hath joined together let not man separate."* Matt. 19:6: *"They are no longer two, but one flesh."*

This unification of husband and wife in the kingdom of God is a beautiful and powerful symbolism, typifying the mystical unity of Christ and His Church. You see with momentary diagnosis the plausibility of divorcement for the isolated sin of conjugal infidelity; because this sin in its very nature, destroys the matrimonial unification, that they are no longer one but two.

The word translated "divorcement" is *apostasion*, which with slight modification has been adopted into the English language; *i. e.*, our familiar word apostasy. This word is plain and simple, all can understand it, and thus avoid the complications and perplexity which frequently involve the problem of divorces. The use of this word in the kingdom of God familiarizes it, so you will have no difficulty in understanding its application to the marriage relation. You lose ground spiritually the celestial flame cooling off, so that the fire gets low, much needing a supply of fuel; still the grate is not replenished; eventually the fuel is all consumed, the flame evanesced and the live coal is no longer seen; nothing but dark ashes. The visitor steps in, looks in the fireplace and thinks you have none; yet it is there and only needs stirring up and replenishing with fuel, and soon the bright blaze lights the room and warms the inmates.

This is an ordinary case of backsliding and reviving. Now, suppose we drop to the epoch in the transaction when the visitor came in, looked and saw no sign of fire, and feeling chilly, thought you had none; but you quickly uncovered and rekindled it. Now, suppose all efforts, stirring up those ashes had signally failed to find a solitary spark. In that case you would have known the fire was out, and proceeded to procure a new supply before you could warm the room.

As this word apostasy is plan, clearly defined and well understood in its Bible signification, it is by all exegetes admitted to signify a state in which spiritual life is utterly forfeited. It is often the ultimatum of backsliding.

The backslider is still a citizen of the kingdom; but living in a low state of grace, and much needing reclamation, lest he go on into apostasy. The great and only remedy for this bent to backsliding, which is peculiar to people in the regenerated experience, is entire sanctification, which destroys the man of sin, who was conquered and captured in the great work of the new creation, wrought by the Holy Ghost in the heart; but still surviving and under Satanic manipulations, always ready to unfurl the standard of revolt and press hotly the stygian war for the recovery of his lost dominion. Therefore, the only permanent settlement of the trouble is his crucifixion, destruction and interment. (Rom. 6:1-6.) Until that is done the most of Christians live an up-and-down life, ever and anon backslidng and getting restored.

Not so with the apostate. He has reached the ultimatum of this up-and-down life, and though once treading the plane of regeneration and electrifying the people with the shouts of a newborn soul; he is now a confirmed backslider, aye, a miserable apostate, no longer in any sense a citizen of God's Kingdom in days gone by; but a poor lost sinner as he was antecedently to his conversion.

s. A gross misapprehension of the literal signification and normal force of a divorcement, leads to much talk about Christians who have been divorced; exceeding detrimental to their spirituality and discouraging to their hopes.

E. G. "John Smith, the evangelist, has no right to preach and hardly deserves membership in the church, because he has two living wives." "What are the facts in the case?" "He was wedded to Miss W——, and afterward, for Scriptural reason, divorced; eventually he enters into a matrimonial alliance with Sister P——, a flaming evangelist. Their work is suffering much damage, because C—— has been divorced from her husband on Scriptural grounds, by Divine authority."

Oh, how Satan howls wherever Brother and Sister Smith spread their tent and hold a revival meeting. Many of the saints refuse to help them in their arduous labors to save lost people around them dropping into Hell. Oh, how the "Burning Bush" exposes them and warns the people to keep away from their meetings, assuring them that they are both sinners, living in adultery and at the same time preaching the Gospel.

We frankly admit that Brother Smith and Sister Preston both made a mistake when they entered into matrimony either with the other. They should, like Paul, have eunuchized themselves in the interest of God's Kingdom (Matt. 19:10), and while we recognize their mistake, it is now too late to howl over it; espec-

Matrimony. 363

ially in view of the fact that they are both perfectly innocent and had an inalienable right in the sight of God and all the world to enter into matrimony. As they are both preachers, they felt that they would be mutually helpful either to other, and in the Apostolic succession going out two by two; *e. g.*, Aquila and Priscilla. "Now, Brother Godbey, do you not think they are actually incompatory, the one having two living wives and the other two living husbands?" In that take notice once for all, you are utterly mistaken and actually bringing false accusation against that dear brother and sister.

Brother Smith has but one wife living on the earth, and she is the noble evangelist so efficiently helping him in his meetings. Miss M—— was at once time his lawfully wedded wife; but that divorcewent (*apostasion*) which was given by authority of our blessed Saviour (Matt. 19th chap., Mark 10th chap) forever annihilates the marital relation between them, so that henceforth she is no more his wife than mine or yours.

It is equally true that Sister Smith has but one living husband, namely, Brother John, the powerful preacher of the Gospel, whom God is so wonderfully using. Mr. Preston was at one time her husband, but legally and Scripturally divorced. Consequently, though he still lives in Cincinnati, he is no more her husband than that of Mrs. Emma Godbey, or some other woman. Will you not take warning and desist from slandering Brother and Sister Smith, grieving the Holy Ghost and impeding the work of God in the salvation of the multitudes who, magnetized by their powerful preaching *"with the Holy Ghost sent down from Heaven"* (1 Pet.

1:12), would yield to their conviction, crowd the altar and get saved, were it not for the perpetual clamor of those unfraternal cruel criticisms, whispering and vociferating: "These people will not do because the man has another living wife and the woman another living husband;" which is a downright falsification and contradiction of God's Word—*apastazion*, which literally means the dissolution of the matrimonial alliance, the nullification of the covenant and the relegation of the parties back into celebacy where wedlock found them.

"What God hath joined together, let not man separate." The divorcement is not the separation, but a recognition of it in order to protect the innocent party as God's institution of matrimony unifies the parties so they are "no longer twain, but one flesh." The transgressor who commits this sin which *suigeris* (destroys) the nuptial unity is responsible for separating what God has joined together. Therefore the unity already destroyed by the flagrant sin is siwply ratified by the divorcement and the parties relegated back to the celibacy in which matrimony found them.

It is gratifying to recognize all the Protestant churches with us in this attitude; the Roman Catholics only dissenting and refusing to grant divorces.

In my personal observation, a bright young preacher in the Holiness Movement entered into matrimony with a beautiful young lady, also an evangelist, quite gifted, the daughter of a Baptist preacher, who had in her teens been captured by a brilliant young man, who seemed all right, but soon proved himself an incarnate demon, treated her like a dog and utterly abandoned her, disappearing, and never after heard from him.

MATRIMONY.

When Brother C—— knocked for admission into the Louisville Conference, the objection was raised that his wife had another husband. A committee was appointed, consisting of the elderly preachers, to investigate and report. In due time they read the report before the Conference, pronouncing the case all clear and nothing in the way, assuring them that Sister C—— has no other husband but the Brother knocking for admission; at the same time stating that another man had once been her husband, but sustains that relation no more, because she had been Scripturally divorced from him.

N. B. God's Word is not shoddy like man's when he grants a divorcement, as you see clearly provided in Matt. 19th chap., Mark 10th chap.; it settles matters forever, utterly and eternally nullifying the matrimonial relation between the parties.

We should be very careful how we talk, accusing people of having two living wives or husbands when it is not true. Wherever there is a Scriptural divorcement, the matrimonial relation evanesces as if it never had existed, leaving the parties perfectly free to enter into wedlock at will, "only in the Lord." (1 Cor. 7: 39.) God's people should always be willing to subordinate their matrimonial privileges to the interests of His kingdom, and live single rather than bring any impediment to the cause of Christ. But when in the exercise of their Gospel rights, they have injudiciously entered into wedlock, we should all forbear all criticism calculated to damage their efficiency as soul-savers. "We should be wise as serpents and harmless as doves," ready to bear all things for Christ's sake.

T. Divorces as given by the civil courts are utterly

worthless unless in harmony with God's Word, which authenticates them only for the one sin, which *per se* annihilates the matrimonial unity. In case that they have a right to the divorcement according to Scripture and through modesty do not present it, but procure it upon some other allegation admitted by the civil law, of course it is equally valid and all right, as we are not transacting business in the sight of men, but God. Is it the duty of the innocent party always to sue for a divorcement? We certainly answer this question emphatically in the negative. It is not the duty, *as it is no commandment, but simply a privilege,* which should not be utilized so long as there is reasonable hope of saving the sinner. Christian patience should have its perfect work, bearing suffering and toiling for Christ's sake. Then after the last hope of saving the sinner has fled, oh, how commendable on the part of the sufferer still to forbear for the sake of the children, the peace and prosperity of the home. How commendable even ignoring the matrimonial relation to remain in the home, patiently praying and toiling to save the family, awaiting the reward of the finally faithful, even though suffering abuses, insults, and even flagellations, till from a human standpoint it would seem that forbearance had ceased to be a virtue; all the time looking to God for grace to bear all things for Christ's sake. While all Christians are certainly willing to obey our infallible Exemplar, who grants the divorcement for the solitary cause of conjugal infidelity, we must remember that we are surrounded by millions who are not Christians and therefore void of the Christian conscience which says "Amen" to the God of the Bible. The unsaved people of the world get into all sorts of matrimonial complications and tangled up till the disentanglement would be like untying the Gordian knot, which had dumbfounded all the heroes of the earth, till they turned it over to Alexander the Great, when he came, as it had been predicted that the one who untied it would conquer the world; therefore when he did his best and failed, he took his sword and cut it; moved on and conquered the world.

We find Gordian knots in the matrimonial complications as we go over the world, which would beggar the heroes and sages to solve if they were all here. Therefore the only thing we can do is to take the "Sword of the Spirit" and cut them.

Matrimony, the only survivor of Eden, is the greatest break-water against sin in all the world. We should all thank God and gratefully appreciate this institution and encourage the people, not prematurely, but duly, to enter into it. Among heathens it is awfully perverted by child-marriages from which floods of sin and misery inundate the country. I find in my travels many of these complicated cases among people professing Christianity, and even sanctification, involved in these inextricable complications, having been married and separated, perhaps two or three times amid the vicissitudes of Satan's kingdom; their former consorts either left in other lands or departed to regions unknown, lost sight of, long unheard of, and knowing not whether they are dead or alive; yet, in the good mercy of God, He has gloriously saved them, given them beautiful and promising children to bring up to preach the everlasting Gospel and bear aloft the blood-stained banner over many a battlefield.

Meanwhile the "Burning Bush" and other fanatical people tell them their marriage is not lawful, and they ought to separate. I tell them to walk in all the light God gives them, dropping the curtain over their former alliances with the ungodly, doing their best to make all wrongs right; putting everything on the altar, to be true to their companions and bring up their children for God and Heaven and live for the Judgment Bar.

In our missionary work, we are constantly meeting polygamists, as those countries abound in all such complications. We always tell them that they must do their best to take care of all their wives and children, but live with only one. As in sanctification you are actually wedded to the Lord Jesus Christ, all carnal lovers having been forever discarded. Therefore the important point in the whole problem is to be true to Him and let all worldly lovers go forever.

CHAPTER XX.

The Church.

Floods of idolatry this day inundate the whole world like seas, emanating from a false apprehension of the church problem as an old prophet speaks of the fishermen who offer sacrifices to their drag. This peculiar form of idolatry is pertinently denominated ecclesiolatry. This form of idolatry is so subtle, clandestine and occult and at the same time so apological and plausible, as to fortify itself in the mind and actually beguile the affections of the herd and building a wall of ignorance and superstition around it, bids defiance to investigation.

The Roman Catholic believes his church is holy, though every member in it be ever so wcked and the priest a drunkard. The only reply is that he has idolized a chimera, which he calls a church. Millions worship a fine edifice, a pipe-organ, Corinthian columns, frescoed ceilings, and a high steeple glittering in the sunbeams and the loud-sounding bell.

All these things they invest with sacredotal dignity and sanctity, and conclude that God is in them. The word translated church is *ecclesia*, from *ek*, "out," and *keleoo*, "to call," and therefore it literally means "the called out." The Holy Spirit in mercy calls every human soul to repentance and salvation. Some respond, leave sin and Satan, come to God and get saved, while others hold on to their idols and cling to their sins, abide with Satan and sink with him into Hell. The whole number of the former constitute the Church of God, by far the greater wing having already passed through the Pearly Portals, tread the Golden Streets of the New Jerusalem, while every regenerated soul on the earth, is beating his march that way, Heaven-born and Heaven-bound.

There are three administrations in the spiritual universe; Heaven, the glorious unmixed, containing none but the good; Hell, the punitive, unmixed, containing none but the bad, while the earth is mixed, containing good and bad; *i. e.*, the kingdom of Heaven and that of Hell, extending into this world with their respective votaries.

Church joining is really a heresy which is doing immense harm. In that way you can become a member of a sect or denomination or a congregation. But it cannot possibly make you a member of God's Church; which is the exclusive prerogative of the supernatural birth. John 3:5,7: *"But you must be born from above. Except any one may be born from above, he cannot see the kingdom of God."*

Verily the supernatural birth of the Holy Spirit and the Water of Life, alone can admit you into the kingdom of God, *i. e.*, His Church, *i. e.*, His family. While the members of God's Church are in all sects and denominations, more or less, it is equally true that there are some of them in all nations, kindreds, tongues, peoples, throughout the whole earth.

v. John 1:9: *"He is the true light, which lighteth every person that cometh into the world."* The Holy

Spirit, who is none other than the Spirit of Christ is omnipresent, and actually signing on every human being that wonderful Scripture (1 John 1:7), *"If we walk in the light, as He is in the light, we have fellowship one with another, and the blood of Jesus Christ His Son cleanses us from all sin;"* His truth in its application, through every human being that ever lived on the earth or ever will. In the final judgment, as you see (Matt. 25:31-45), while all nations are gathered before the Judge of the living and dead, sitting on His throne; He places the sheep, *i. e.*, the saved people, on the right, and the goats, *i. e.*, the wicked, on the left and proclaims to the former: *"Come, ye blessed of my Father, inherit the kingdom prepared for you before the foundation of the world, for I was hungry and ye fed Me; thirsty, and ye gave Me drink; naked, and ye clothed Me; sick and in prison, and ye ministered unto Me."* Then there is found, *"Lord, when saw we Thee hungry,"* etc., *"and ministered unto Thee. Then will He say, As much as ye did these things unto the least of My brethren, ye did them unto Me."*

You see here from the responses of these people that they had never heard the Gospel, never become acquainted with Him historically, but acquainted by the Holy Spirit, alluminating their minds and consciences; they yielded the best they knew and actually received through Him the redeeming and adopting love of God in Christ, so they passed the judgment scrutiny with the approving welcome of the infallible Judge.

Meanwhile, turning to those on the left, we hear Him say: *"Depart, ye cursed, into eternal fires, prepared for the devil and his angels; but I was hungry, and ye gave*

Me no meat; thirsty, and ye gave Me no drink; sick and in prison, and ye ministered not unto Me. Then they respond, Lord, when saw we Thee hungry, thirsty, sick, etc., and ministered not unto Thee. Then He responds, Inasmuch as ye did not these things unto the least of My brethren, ye did them not unto Me."

Here you see these people had never heard the Gospel, but the real trouble with them was, they had not walked in the light of the Holy Spirit, corroborated by nature and their own consciences, and, consequently, lost their souls, because they did not walk in the light they had; but lived like irrational animals, for self alone, and, consequently, forfeited all the redeeming grace of God in Christ which the Holy Spirit would have dispensed to them.

The judgment of the people who had the Bible and enjoyed the blessings of the visible church are included in preceding parables of the Virgins and the Talents; while hearing this final paragraph beginning at V. 31, *ehtnee,* "nations," literally means heathens or Gentiles. Hence it includes all the people of all ages and nations who pass through this world with the blessing of the written Word and the visible church.

v. The Church has no visible body, *i. e.*, nothing that is cognizable by the senses, but the nuptical spiritual body of Christ, has, as it is frequently denominated His body. (Eph. 1:23.) As He is a Spirit, His body must be *homogenour* and, consequently, spiritual.

The Visible Church of God will never be seen or known till the manifestations of the sons of God. We think we see, hear and know them, but are liable to be mistaken, as Satan and his myrmidons are greater, stronger and wiser than we, and doing their utmost to deceive us. Rom. 8:18: *"For I consider that the sufferings of this life are not worthy to be compared to the glory which is to be revealed in us. For the earnest expectation of the creature awaiteth the manifestations of the sons of God."*

This body, with the finite animal soul dwelling in it, is looking forward and longing for the manifestation of the sons of God, which will take place in the transfiguration, when this mortal puts on immortality. Verily these transfigured bodies, including all the varied saints and all who shall be living on the earth when the Lord comes for His Bride and all the balance who hold membership in the family of God by the supernatural birth wrought in the heart in regeneration, and all who ever shall be identified with the kingdom of grace and received their transfiguration in the final resurrection will constitute the Visible Church of God indeed and in truth without defaultation or mistake.

Mark this truth and do not forget it, as there is so much cavil and confusion about the Visible Church of God; ranting ecclesiastical demagogue, crying, *"Lo, here, and lo, there,"* bewildering and deceiving the people till they troop after them in platoons like the roaring rabble on the streets of Ephesus. Acts 19th chap., shouting, *"Great is Diana of the Ephesians."* In this chapter the word translated "assembly" is the very word which throughout the Bible means "church;" as it was the church of Diana having a big revival and shouting praises to their goddess.

N. B. As our glorious Christ in this world is an Invisible Spirit, *i. e.,* the personal Holy Ghost, His Church is invisible and spiritual, and will so remain till these bodies are transfigured and glorified, like that of our Lord, our great and blessed Federal Head. Therefore, we must all be content, as the word here says, to await the manifestation of the sons of God, which will take place in the transfiguration. Hence the folly manifest in the arrogant claims of any sect or denomination to be the Visible Church of God in contradistinction to others, as the members of God's Church are simply His regenerated people in all organizations, and some of them in none at all; and if you would aspire to be a member of God's Visible Church, you can only reach it through the transfiguration which will invest this body with the glory, similitudinous to the glorified body of our Lord, of which Peter, James and John saw a prelude on the Mount of Transfiguration.

Rom. 8: 20: *"For the creation has been subordinated to mortality, not willingly, but through Him that subordinated; therefore pursuant to hope, truly the creation itself shall be liberated from the bondage of corruption into the liberty of the glory of the children of God."* This is a wonderfully inspiring truth. Most electrifying and thrilling to our anticipations; to think these poor mortal tenements are going to be delivered from mortality and transformed into that beautiful and glorious spirituality similitudinous to the transfigured body of our Lord. This will demonstrate forever your identity to the Visible Church of God, whereas the matter must rest short of the experimental certainty till this mortal puts on immortality.

I can know it for myself here by the indisputable witness of the Spirit. (V. 16.) But no one else can know it. In this we are graciously fortified against spiritual pride, which would likely supervene in the event that other people could know this glorious truth in reference to us; but we cannot reveal it to them and never will till this mortal puts on immortality, and thus the transfiguration glory demonstrates to all the world our identity with the family of God.

This side of the transfiguration we must leave them to their own conjectures, and whereas we may think our dear fellow-pilgrims are members of the Church of the Firstborn, but we do not know it, and never can till the transfiguration glory truly manifests their sonship in the Divine family.

V. 22. *"For we know that all creation groans together and travails together until now."* This transcendent glorification is not only going to reach their mortal bodies, eliminating away all mortality and investing us with the immortality homogenous with that of our Lord's glorified body, but it is going to reach this whole world, which God created after the heavenly similitude and gave to the human race for a delightful heavenly home through all eternity. Whereas Satan, with the combined host of Hell, have fought heroically to assimilate it to the dark regions of woe, add it to Hell to augment the restricted territory of the lost, the Son of God, having espoused the lost cause, has already perfected the wonderful redemption and sent into the world the Omnipotent Holy Ghost to carry it into availability in behalf of every soul, thus so gloriously triumphing over the devil and Hell that His wonderful redemption is destined to reach this world, and, as Peter reveals, thoroughly sanctify it by the purgatorial fires of the last days, and as John (Rev. 21st chap.) so gloriously reveals, He will actually resume the work of creation, renovate and make it all new (V. 3), and finally reannex it back to Heaven, where it belonged before Satan broke it loose, to add it to Hell, thus not only sanctifying and recreating the whole earth, melting the frozen poles, restoring all the deserts, consuming the oceans and seas by the purgatorial fires, as it says, *"There shall be no more sea;"* thus augmenting the superficial magnitude of this earth ten times; meanwhile the River of Life abundantly irrigated and ambrosial fruits of celestial species will here superabound, when the redeemed shall walk the earth, our wonderful Christ, who vacated Heaven to rescue it from Satan's dark grapple, will abide in our midst and abide forever.

Here inspired Paul beautifully describes all of this world groaning and travailing together awaiting the glorious parturition which will not only transfigure all the saints living and dead, but actually sanctify, recreate and celestialize this poor, fallen earth, which has six thousand years been deluged with blood and heaped with the slain, while the heavy tread of Satan and his myrmidons has crushed the last lingering hope of the lost millions. V. 23: *"Not only so, but indeed we, having the firstfruit of the Spirit, truly ourselves do groan within ourselves, awaiting the adoption of sons, the redemption of our body."* The firstfruit of the Spirit is the wonderful salvation we already have in our immortal spirits, giving us membership in the Church of God, which is His family. But here, even these material bodies are apostrophized as groaning within ourselves, while we await the adoption of sons, *i. e.,* the redemption of the body, which is none other than the transfiguration of the body which forever confirm and reveal to all created intelligencies in all celestial worlds, whithersoever we shall wing our flight through the roll of eternal ages, thus exploring with adoring wonder the boundless celestial universe; meanwhile our membership in the Divine Family and in the Church of the Firstborn will be revealed by the ineffable glory of this transfigured body, so perfectly spiritualized that it will be eternally divested of all ponderous matter, so it will never weigh the amount of a feather, and can move with angelic velocity through the realms of celestial ether, thus winging our precipitate flight from world to world.

It is very important that you get this truth clearly fixed in your mind, as it is the only effectual fortification against the ecclesiastical demagogery which will confront you through this mortal pilgrimage, resorting to every conceivable stratagem to proselyte and manipulate you, conservatively to their poor little sect, which they are preaching, instead of the glorious Christ, who is all and in all to the people who know Him in the happy experience of redeeming grace and perfect love. Just turn them over to this paragraph on the glorification of these bodies in Rom. 8th chap., and you can read to them the plain Word, that the transfiguration alone can incontestably reveal the members of God's Visible Church, who are the sons of God, however not manifest to mortal eyes till the transfiguration glory that flashed from the radiant bodies of Jesus, Moses and Elijah on the Mount of Transfiguration shall transform the body of our humiliation similitudinous to the body of His glory, according to the working of Him who is able to subordinate all things to Himself. (Phil. 3:21.)

The preceding verse says: *"For our citizenship is in Heaven, from which we are indeed expecting our Saviour, the Lord Jesus Christ."* All the children of God are citizens of Heaven, sojourning on the earth, during our probationary order, that we may help our Lord save this lost world, ever ready even to add our blood to His. Carnal people do not know us, consequently we are misunderstood, misjudged and persecuted; false prophets and anti-christs doing their best to spoliate us, that we may serve them, who are vividly described in Vs. 18 and 19: *"For many are walking round, of whom I have frequently spoken to you, and now indeed I tell you weeping, that they are the enemies of the cross of Christ."* The cross means crucifixion of sin and its destruction, *i. e.*, entire sanctification, which they despised. *"Whose end is destruction, whose god is their stomach, and whose glory is in their shame;"* *i. e.*, the things in which they glory are sectarian, selfish, proselytic enterprises, and ought to be their shame; who are minding earthly things, *i. e.*, they are really after the things of this world, blind to what does not jingle and serving their own stomachs, *i. e.*, after things that perish with their using, and doing their best to manipulate you so you will help them in temporal things; they only want you for what they can get out of you, and the moment they despair of making you serve them, they abandon you, and have no more interest in you. How signally have I seen those mournful verifications of these awful Scriptures manifested by people making loud professions of holiness, but thereby demonstrating to all luminous people the counterfeit gospel, which Satan has panned off in them and they are doing their best to peddle out to you for filthy lucre.

W. 1 Tim. 3: 14, 15: *"I write to thee, hoping to come to thee the more quickly; but if I tarry, in order that you may know, it behooves you to devote yourself in the house of God, which is the Church of the Living God, the pillar and foundation of the truth."* Here you see the Visible Church pronounced "the pillar and basis of the truth," i. e., the citadel in which the Divine oracles are deposited and preserved from the spoliation which would quickly overtake them, if not protected by this Divinely appointed custodianship. God is the greatest organizer in the universe. We see this fact revealed and copiously confirmed by the countless millions of world which His incontestable wisdom, co-operative with His omnipotence, has arranged in the most perfect order and stupendous mechanism; one hundred and seventeen millions of suns already having been discovered by the astronomers, and as our sun is accompanied by a retinue of ten great worlds, the logical analogy would give us the paradoxical number of 1,170,000,000 of worlds speeding their precipitate flight through their appointed orbits, each one revolving around his own sun with so perfect order as never to deviate one iota from its place in the plane of these ecliptic. Meanwhile all of these hundred and seventeen millions of suns, accompanied by their retinues of worlds, revolve in their perfect order around the great primal center of the celestial universe, which astronomers have identified to be Alcyone of the Pleiades, which is believed to be the capitol and metropolis of the boundless celestial universe, containing the New Jerusalem, so brilliantly described in Rev. 21st chap., the City of Gold, 1,500 miles in length, breadth and height. Such is the perfect of the Divine organization that there is nothing abnormal in the universe of God. Every planet is held in its place by the centripetal and centrifugal forces, which perfectly balance each other, holding the great and pondrous worlds in their orbits, through which they speed their flight with the most perfect harmony, varying not an iota in an age. Of course, He has not failed to organize His Church, which is really the climax of His creation, infinitely superior in importance to all these great material worlds. This organization consists of the bishop, *episcopos*, from *epi*, "over," and *scopeoo*, "to see;" therefore his office is the spiritual oversight of the flock, as the phraseology is pastoral similitudinous to the shepherd leading his flock and providing them with food and water, at the same time protecting them from wild beasts and robbers.

(1 Tim. 3.) See God's definition of this most important office in His Church: *"It is a faithful work; if one desires the pastorate, he is seeking after a beautiful work."* Certainly the leadership of God's flock is a work so important and delightful that every angel would lay aside his golden harp and come down to enjoy the honor and glory. *"Therefore it behooves the bishop to be blameless, the husband of one wife,"*—*i. e.*, polygamy is here forbidden,—*"temperate, prudent, orderly, hospitable,*—*i. e.*, always ready to entertain strangers,— *"competent to teach."* This is exceedingly pertinent, as he is *ex-officio* the teacher of his people; *"not a wine drinker; not a controvertent, but gentle, peaceable, not*

a money lover." Oh, what a snare the love of money, and how fatal to the preachers! It ruined one apostle, world without end. It is awful to contemplate the great following poor fallen Judas has this day among the preachers. *"Ruling his own house in subordination, with all gravity."* If this were obeyed, the proverb appertaining to the reckless incorrigibility of preachers' children never would have found currency. *"But if any one does not know how to rule his own house, how will he take care of the Church of God."* Example is more influential than precept. God has ordained the preacher's family lead the way in the exemplification of all saintly virtues, domestic and social decorum, and thus co-operate with their father in the leadership of all the people, in the ways of truth and peace and everlasting life. *"Not a novice, lest being puffed up he may fall into the condemnation of the devil."* Young people may be used with the greatest efficiency in the evangelistic work, especially in the neglected fields; but you see here the Divine interdiction to their occupancy of the pastoral charges, thus invested with authority to rule over people who are old enough to be their parents and even their grandparents.

I have known terrible detriment inflicted on the Kingdom of God by the inflation, egotism and consequent maladministration of juvenile pastors. The old Methodist economy of always sending out a young man with an old one is Scriptural and should be universally observed. We not only see much detriment to the cause of God by the promotion of juveniles to the responsible office of pastors, but an auxiliary maladministration fearfully prevalent in the premature superannuation of the old preachers. It is a common thing now to superannuate them at the very time in life when their matured experience is so much needed in the pastoral work. If the charge is too heavy for the failing physical ability of the father in the Gospel, his deficiency should be supplied by a young man sent along with him, whose youth and vigor would be equal to supply every deficiency.

x. While the bishop is the supervisor of the spiritual interest, the deaconate was instituted in order to relieve the pastorate of all incumberance with temporal interests. (Acts 6:1-7.) We see here that the deacons are required to be "full of the Spirit and wisdom," pursuant to this special provision for the temporal interest. *"They select Stephen, a man full of faith and the Holy Ghost, Philip, Procorus, Nicanor, Timon, Hormenus, and Nikoloos the Antiochan proselyte, who they placed before the apostles, and having prayed, they laid hands on them. And the Word of God continued to increase and the number of the disciples were multiplied exceedingly in Jerusalem, and a great crowd of the priests were becoming obedient to the faith."*

We see here that they ordained these seven brethren deacons in the Jerusalem Church, and God set His seal on the institution, wonderfully blessing their labors, and building up the Church, even reaching many of the priests, despite the inveterate opposition of the high priests. 1 Tim. 3:8: *"Likewise let the deacons be grave, not double-tongued."* The double-tongue is the normal concomitant of "the double mind," (Jas. 1:4 and 4:8). The sinner has but one mind, and that is carnal; the sanctified have but one mind, and that is spiritual, *i. e.*, the mind of Christ, having been created in the heart by the Holy Ghost in regeneration. Consequently, the inward conflict so prevails that we cry out with Paul, while seeking sanctification, *"When I would do good, evil is present with me."*

In the great work of entire sanctification, the carnal mind, *i. e.*, the old man, is crucified and destroyed (Rom. 6:6), and buried into the atonement by the baptism which Jesus gives, (V. 4,) *"And the new man raised up to walk in newness of life;"* thus the double mind is taken away, and with it the double tongue.

"Let them not be given to much wine, not fond of filthy lucre, having the testimony of faith in a pure conscience. But, indeed, let them first be proven, then being irreprovable, let them execute the office of deacon."

This office is exceedingly important for the fact that it not only takes in all the temporal interests of the Church, *i. e.*, the place of worship, financial interests, the support of the ministry, widows, orphans, and the poor, but you see they preached the Gospel heroically, as verified by Philip the evangelist, and Stephen the martyr, who were chosen deacons along with the other five. When people are "full of the Spirit and wisdom," as you see it is required of the deacons, they are flaming preachers of the Gospel, as abundantly illustrated in the ministry of Philip in Samaria. Therefore, you see the Holy Ghost commands that they must be proven, *i. e.*, tested, tried and found competent and worthy; then let them exercise the office of deacon, being irreproachable. The deacons are really competent to carry on the Church in the absence of the pastor, as they not only attend to the temporal interests, but preach the Gospel.

V. 11. *"Likewise, let the wives be grave, not tat-*

tlers, temperate, faithful in all things." The poet well says:

> "Of earthly goods, the best is a good wife;
> A bad, the bitterest curse of human life."

Therefore, it is pre-eminently important that a deacon's wife be competent to adorn the doctrines of Christ and efficiently help her husband, not only in church work, but dispensing the living Word.

V. 12. *"Let the deacons be husbands of one wife."* As polygamy is so prevalent among heathens, it was important to make this specification. *"Beautifully ruling their children and their own houses. For those having administered the office of deacon beautifully, procure to themselves beautiful progress and much boldness in the faith which is in Christ Jesus."*

Oh, how we need the good old-time deacons all over the world this day, to preach the Gospel to the ends of the earth, and at the same time so look after the temporal interests as to provide places of worship, holiness literature, build up Sunday-schools, lengthen the cords, strengthen the stakes, defend the outposts and enlarge the borders of Zion.

Y. We now reach the eldership, which is contradistinction to the episcopacy, looking after the spiritual interest, and the deaconate, the temporal interest; have charge of the general interest, *i. e.,* they are really the seniors in the school of Christ. While they normally include the membership, enjoying spiritual seniority, and are obligated by the Word of God, even in case there should be no official election, yet in order to strengthen their hand and the more efficiently bring them into availability the apostles in their peregrinations ordained elders in every city. (Acts 14:23.) Doubtless in Jas. 5:14, where we are commanded to call the *"elders of the Church and pray over the sick, anointing them with oil in the name of the Lord,"* we are to understand simply the people enjoying spiritual seniority in the things of God, as in our peregrinations over the world, finding the sick everywhere, it would be always convenient to secure the service of the official elders, whereas, the positive commandment of our Lord to the twelve when He sent them out two by two, and to the seventy, when He sent them out, specifies that they were to heal the sick and cast out the demons wherever they went. Therefore we understand the ministry of healing in the normal economy of the world's evangelization to accompany that of soul saving, as an illustration of the broad prerogative committed to the elders. We refer you to Paul's last visit to Ephesus, when he called the elders of the Church to meet him at the seaport of Miletus, where he bade them adieu, breaking their hearts by the mournful information that they will see his face no more in this world. Then he proceeds to give them their charge, exhorting them to heroically verify their momentous responsibilities. Acts 20:26: *"Therefore, I have witnessed to you this day that I am pure from the blood of all."* Now he gives them the reason why he enjoyed this glorious exemption from all responsibility: *"For I have not shunned to declare unto you all the counsel of God."*

Let us all take heed and govern ourselves accordingly, resting assured that it is only in this way that we can be pure from the blood of all the people. That is the reason why you find so many things in my writings that you think should have been left out. Everything you see is necessary to the instruction and warning of some souls, who, without faithful ministry at that point would be in jeopardy. *"Take heed to yourselves and to the flock, over which the Holy Ghost has appointed you bishops."* Here we have the regular word for bishop, *episcopos*, from *epi*, "over," and *skopeoo*, "to see." The eldership is ordained of God to look after the general interest of the Church, including the office of pastor and deacon, as well as their own, in case that those places should be vacant. In this case there is no mention of the bishop separate from these elders, who are all called bishops as you see, the presumption is the pastoral office was at that time without a personal incumbent. Now he tells these elders what their work is, to shepherdize the Church of God, which He purchased with His own blood. The E. V. says: *"Feed the Church of God,"* which is an inadequate translation. The verb here, *poimaivein*, from *poimeen*, "shepherd," literally means, "to shepherdize," which not only includes feeding the flock, but protecting them from wild beasts and robbers, and every other peril. Oh, how important this charge! How the sheep are devoured on all sides, both by wild beasts and robbers! And how they are stinted and dwarfed for the want of sufficient food and vitiated by unwholesome food, and actually killed by feeding on poisons!

V. 29: *"I know that after my departure grievous wolves will come in unto you, not sparing the flock, and* men from you yourselves will rise up, speaking perverse things in order to lead disciples after them."

Paul saw these things in the clear light of the prophecy which the Holy Ghost gave him. Who would have thought that those elders who were kissing him good-bye and bathing him with their loving tears, would ever have fulfilled that prophecy. Yet they did it. Ambition to leadership is the strongest temptation. It ruined Lucifer, the archangel, and we see that it played awful havoc with the Apostolic Church of Asia Minor. God said to this same Church after this awful prophecy was fulfilled (Rev. 2:6), *"But you have this, that you hate the works of the Nicolaitanes, which I also hate."*

Those Nicolaitanes, as that word is from *nikaoo,* "to conquest," and *laoo,* "the people," means these very men, whom Paul looked in the face and prophesied that they would rise up, speaking perverse things, in order to lead disciples after them. It has been the bane of the churchism in all ages, and is now the demon of terror to the Holiness people; these elders among us, who ought to shepherdize the flock, rising up and "speaking perverse things, in order to lead disciples after them." Terrible has been the havoc already in that way, and the end is not yet. Who would have thought that any of those Ephesian elders would have turned traitors; and yet it was so, tempted by the desire for leadership and filthy lucre. The world is flooded with people who want a human leader, because they are not willing to follow the Divine. Consequently every one who so aspires can have a following. Jesus said (John 5:43): *"I came in the name of My Father, and you will not follow Me; if any one may come in his own name, ye will follow him."* The same people who rejected Jesus and killed Him, followed those false christs who arose after Him, till the Romans came and desolated their land, selling into slavery every one who escaped the sword, pestilence and famine. That was the awful Jewish tribulation, which lasted seven years (A. D. 66-73). Ours is fast hastening, in which many led away by these false prophets and antichrists will perish. As I am the oldest evangelist in the South, I might have had a following if I had accepted the urgent call of the Holiness people, when the churches were turning them all out who professed sanctification, and they pled with me hard to come and organize them into an independent church. That was a call I never answered. God has called me to do nothing but preach the Gospel by speech and pen, therefore, all other calls will have to reach somebody else if answered. I shall never have any following. If the people are not willing to follow our Leader, they will have to paddle their own canoe. Like Barnabas (Acts 11:24), I am adding people to nothing but God. When they want the Gospel, I am their humble servant, preaching both by speech and pen; but if they want a human cause conserved, they will have to excuse me, as I am utterly bill-of-saled over to the Lord and lost in His Divinity, and only longing to sink deeper and be more like Him.

V. 31: *"Therefore, watch, remembering that three years night and day I cease not to warn each one of you with tears. And now I commend you to the Lord, and the word of His grace, who is able to build you up and give you an inheritance among all the sanctified.* You see from this interview of the beloved apostle with the elders at Ephesus and his touching valedictory, how he recognizes them the custodians of the Church in the providence of God, separating the flock, which means supplying all their needs appertaining to food, water and protection. When we contemplate the importance of soul pabulum, to the maintenance, prosperity, availability and efficiency of the Lord's people in their great and responsible work of saving the lost millions on all sides thronging the broad road down to endless destruction; not only the spiritual nutriment, which they must have or dwarf, famish and die, but the sheep must be protected by the fold from the depredations of wild beasts and robbers, roaming abroad on all sides, seeking whom they may devour.

The Presbyterian Church seemed to have learned the art of utilizing the ruling elders more efficiently than any other Church. It is a common thing for their Churches to remain years together without a pastor and seem to suffer but little detriment; whereas Methodist churches would dilapidate, distintegrate and fall to pieces.

Every Church ought to have a substantial board of elders, perpetuated on the ground, serving as the *locum tenens,* holding the fort while pastors and evangelists come and go. If they would verify the commandment in this Scripture, to shepherdize the flock of God which is purchased with His own blood, they would really have to do the work of lay preachers, which would certainly prove a great means of grace to their own souls and secure to them a crown that will never fade away.

See Peter's beautiful valedictory (ch. 5:1-5): *"Therefore, I, an elder and a witness of the sufferings of Christ and a communicant of the glory about to be revealed, exhort the elders among you, feed and shepherdize the flock of God which is among you, not by constraint, but willingly for God's sake, not for filthy lucre, but of a ready mind, not as those domineering over the heritage, but being examples of the flock; and the Chief Shepherd having appeared, you shall receive a crown of glory which will never fade away."* This exhortation to the elderly members of the Church is slow, replete with wisdom, truth, heroism, holiness, and victory, would without end. All Christians should commit it to memory and assimilate its salutary efficiency as a perpetual souvenir of our glorious privileges in the family of God and the momentous responsibilities encumbered on us to do our utmost to not only shepherdize the flock, but bring them all into the greatest possible availability for the salvation of the world. Oh, what an inspiration—the constant anticipation of the Chief Shepherd coming in His glory, with a crown for every faithful elder, which will never fade away, but accumulate new luster and shine on forever and ever.

z. It is pertinent here to give cursory notice to the subject of ordination. While viewed from a practical standpoint, it is very simple and eminently useful, separating us from the world with its fascinations and encumbrances.

As you see (Acts 6:6), the simple *modus operandi*, praying and putting the hands on them, thus by the imposition of hands symbolizing their removal from worldly enthrallments over to God, to be used for His glory forever, meanwhile all ordained people are recognized as having the power to transmit it to others, thus rendering the problem of succession very simple and easy. It is pertinent that we should be ready to meet the advocates of the famous apostolic succession, both in popery (Roman Catholic Church) and prelacy (Episcopal Church), who stoutly contend for the exclusive privilege of ordination, under their arrogant claims of succession all the way down from the apostles, in an unbroken chain, and the invalidity of all other ordinations, and, consequently, repudiate the claims of all the Protestants to the apostolic succession, and, consequently, invalidate all of the ordinances administered by people who have not received the ordination of the apostles, transmitted through all of the intervening generations. In some localities great concern, investigation and solicitude, with even tearful eyes and broken hearts, have supervened from the conviction that the ordinances they have received are all invalid, because not dispensed by a legitimately authorized administrator. Against these, or against claimants, whether under the shibboleth of popery or prelacy, we make two protests. Firstly, they have to carry us through the bloody centuries of papistical persecutions, while they burnt millions of martyrs, in order to make connection and secure the apostolic succession. In that case Satan must have put in so many links in the chain that you know it is utterly worthless. Even one link from him breaks the succession forever. Secondly, it is impossible to take the New Testament and establish the essentiality of ordination in order to the validity of the administration where it says (Mark 3:14) of our Saviour, when He called His apostles, *"He ordained them."* The Greek is *epoiese,* "He made them twelve," *i. e.,* He made them just what He wanted them to be, as He does you and me when we let Him have His way with us. Again (John 15:16), "*You have not chosen Me, but I have chosen you, and ordained you.*" The word there is *etheka*, "I have placed you in your positions"—just as He puts you and me and all willing hearts in the place where we can most efficiently glorify Him. Acts 14:23: "*And having ordained unto them elders in every church, praying with fastings, he commended them to the Lord on whom they had believed.*" The word here translated "ordained" is *cheirotoneesantes*, from *chi*, "from the hand," and *tonto*, "to reach forth," simply means, "electing them by reaching up the hand;" however there is no doubt but that they ordained them by the imposition of hands and prayer. One of the straightest Scriptures for ordination which they use is Acts 13:2, 3, "*And they ministering to the Lord and fasting, the Holy Ghost said, Indeed, separate unto me Barnabas and Saul, to which work I have called them; then having fasted and prayed and laid hands on them, they sent them away.*"

Now this could not be used for ministerial ordination from the simple fact that both Barnabas and Paul had been preaching many years and actually were called apostles before that time. But it is simply a *consecration for the missionary tour* on which they were sending them, fasting, praying and laying hands on them, that God might pour on them the Holy Ghost and give them the endowment necessary to prepare them for their great and responsible work. So far as the administration of baptism is concerned, the Great Physician (Matt. 28:19, 20) certainly reveals that it is a privilege of all who are used by the Holy Ghost to make disciples, also to baptize them "*Therefore, having gone and discipled, all the Gentiles, baptizing them in the name of the Father and of the Son, and of the Holy Ghost, teaching them to keep all things as many as I have commanded you; and, behold I am with you all the days unto the end of the age."*

The only way to disciple any one is to get him truly born from above. You see from the connection here that the people who are so endued with the Holy Ghost, as to become His instruments in the supernatural birth, have a right to baptize the newly saved people as they go. This commission was given directly to the apostles who had neither received license nor ordination. Baptism is not an institution of the New Testament, but the Old; the Jews having a hundred times as much of it as the Christians, from the fact they lived in the symbolic dispensation. It is very clear that all the people who received the Pentecostal baptism of the Holy Ghost and fire had a right to go along and administer baptism and the eucharist to the people who received salvation through their instrumentality; meanwhile, ordination by the imposition of hands and prayer, may be given wherever the blessed Holy Spirit has so wrought upon the heart as to get the people ready to anoint themselves fully and unreservedly to His work; then the ordained people of God have a perfect right, as in the Apostolic Age, to gather around and ordain them to the service of God, by the imposition of hands and prayer, without going back through a corrupt priesthood and centuries of martyrs' blood, shed by the enemies of God, and receive our ordination through them. It is really superstitious because we cannot possibly know that we even make the connection after we consent to go through thousands of bloody links.

A. The simple solution of this succession problem is quick and easy; instead of running through myriads of dark, bloody links, in order to pass through the Dark Ages, while the proud, worldly Church of Rome, with her lecherous priesthood, claimed to be the true Apostolic Succession, meanwhile the bloody Inquisition was everywhere burning the faithful martyrs; all that is the Boss and Buncombe of Satan, whereas the chain of the Apostolic Succession has but one golden link, and that is the supernatural birth of the Holy Ghost, which brings us into God's "ecclesia," which is the only true Church. Of course we are in the Apostolic Succession, just like Taft is in the succession of Washington and Jackson, simply because he occupies the same chair as their successor in office; yet he is in no way dependent on his predecessors for his right to preside and for the validity of his administration. Therefore, your membership in the Church of God and the validity of your administration as such have but one essential antecedent, and that is the supernatural birth. You have nothing to do with the sepulchers, bones and ashes of your predecessors. If the Spirit bears witness with your spirit that you are supernaturally born of God (Rom. 8:16), ecclesiastics may criticise and devils may howl and abnegate and ridicule your claims, yet you have nothing to do but shout on and be true. Amen.

B. The problem of Christian fellowship demands a faithful exegesis. Some Holiness people make the mistake of restricting to the sanctified; that means to put all the sheep into the fold and leave the lambs out for the wolves to devour, whereas the latter for two reasons ought to have special attention; the one, because they are the most valuable and the other, because they are the most needy.

I have had regenerated folks complain to me of the non-fellowship of the sanctified. We have Holiness Churches on the Pacific Coast, really their first independent organization in the Movement on the basis of entire sanctification, making that the *sine que non* of membership, and closing the door against all who have not received it. That is really a mistake above mentioned, *i. e.*, housing the sheep and leaving the lambs out in the cold, a prey to the lions. Regeneration, and not sanctification, is the *basis of membership*. A babe in Christ is a truly a member of God's family as a father or mother in Israel, and the younger the person the more attention is needed; babies in every case having the preference. In this respect people who have survived their physical, and perhaps their intellectual vigor, are entitled to extraordinary attention, pursuant to the maxim, "Once a man, and twice a child." Therefore, from the simple fact that the *"ecclesia"* is the Church of God, to the exclusion of all counterclaimants, and there is but one way to get into it, and that is the supernatural birth of the Holy Ghost, therefore all who have been born of the Spirit and not fallen by apostasy are *bone fide* members of God's Church, entitled to the communion of the holy eucharist and the full fellowship of the saints. Really those living on the lower plane of regeneration should receive a special attention and fellowship by those dwelling on the heights of holiness, for two reasons; the one, because there is so much danger of lapsing into Satan's kingdom, since there, and the other, simply in order that we may enjoy the better opportunities to throw our arms around them, asking the Holy Spirit to use us as a Jacob's Ladder on which, by His merciful sanctifying power, they may climb to the altitudes of Beulah Land, and walk with us on the heights of holiness, bordering on the celestial clime.

c. We should in this connection by way of elucidation give you a word on close communion. That is easily explained. Its advocates frankly admit that it hinges entirely on the ordinance of baptism, which they claim to be the door into the Church. We do not enter the Church by joining, as is generally supposed, but by the supernatural birth of the Holy Ghost. Jesus forever settles this question about this door into the Church. John 10:7: *"Truly true I say unto you that I am the Door of the sheep."* He repeats it also in verse 9. Hence you see water baptism is not the door, but Christ Himself. The moment He saves you, you are a member of His Church. All the saved are members. All outsiders are lost. He is the Ark; He is the Life-boat; all who do not fly to Him for refuge go down in eternal wreckage.

Close communion on the basis of immersion baptism is an awful mistake. It is really a double summersault, landing its votary flat on his back. In the first place, water baptism has nothing to do with Church membership any more than the mark has to do with the sheep. It is all right to mark the sheep if you see proper. Yet the mark does not make the sheep. You must have it on hand before you can mark it. No one but a Christian has a right to water baptism, because it is simply God's mark by which He designates His people in the eyes of the world, thus differentiating from those who are not Christians. So there is the first mistake, *i. e.*, making water baptism the door into the Church. The Church is but another name for God's family, and all of His children only become such by *the supernatural birth of the Holy Ghost.*

The second mistake consists in the fact that there is no immersion baptism in the Bible, being utterly unknown in the Apostolic Age. While, of course, it was sufficient for water baptism, valid and not to be discounted, yet, because it was never practiced by John the Baptist or the Apostles or their contemporaries, and is really unknown in the Bible, therefore it is a great mistake to exclude the children of God from Church membership, the holy communion and Christian fellowship simply because they have been baptized with water by effusion, or like the godly Quakers that never had conviction to receive it any way.

"Brother Godbey, you are shooting at the Baptists." You are certainly mistaken. The leading Baptists of the world are bold free communionists; *e. g.*, the great C. H. Spurgeon, the cosmopolitan preacher, and Samuel Randall, the founder of the Free Baptist Church. The strongest arguments against close communion I have ever seen in print have been penned by the Baptist's Christian fellowship communion. The brotherhood of Christ is all simply on the basis of sky-blue regeneration, witnessed by the Holy Ghost. (Rom. 8: 16.) The greatest mistake ever made by Christians is to divide up over non-essentials, *i. e.*, church ordinances, creeds, sects and denominations, which never did have anything to do with salvation. The great battle-cry of Christendom should be "One in Jesus." While we must all be perfectly free to study the Word of God, and in love teach the truth and correct errors, so far as we can; yet we must not magnify that which does not effect the plan of salvation. On the great work of Christ, the vicarious substitutionary atonement which He made for the sins of the whole world, and whose benefit all are free to receive by simple faith, after genuine radical repentance, accompanied by veritable conviction and restitution, has put us on believing ground, a life of humble obedience, proving our faith to all the world, and the supernatural birth, wrought in the heart by the Holy Ghost. (John 3:5,7), followed by entire sanctification, the cleansing blood applied by the blessed Holy Spirit; thus having completed this wonderful radical expurgation, He comes in to abide forever, giving us the victory over the world the flesh and the devil. Jesus says, *"Ye must be born from above."* (John 3:5.) God says, *"Without the sanctification, no one shall see the Lord."* (Heb. 12:14.) We cannot afford to take any risk on Heaven. We dare not make any compromise on these essential truths, lest we lose our own souls and in the Judgment Day not only are found wanting, but actually guilty of the blood of others, because we did not duly warn them.

D. What is our attitude toward the sects and denominations? While none of them are the Church of God, yet numbers of the *ecclesia* abound more or less in all of them, including regenerated people exclusively; not according to any creedistic standard, but the people who experimentally verify the *ipse dixit* of Jesus to Nicodemus (John 3:5-7), *"Ye must be born from above."*

THE CHURCH. 399

Of course, there are many more Christians in the orthodox, *i. e.*, Methodist, Friend, Baptist, Presbyterian and Congregational Churches, than the heterodoxical, *i. e.*, Greek and Roman Catholic, Unitarian, Campbellite, Mormon, etc. As the Holy Spirit is omnipresent, shining on every soul in all the earth (John 1:9), and offering all salvation, if they would only walk in the light He gives (1 John 1:7), there is a gracious possibility of universal salvation, not only among the orthodox, but the heterodoxical and even the paganistic. In case of all outside of the orthodox, He has to save them despite the devil and the doctrines of their church. His omnipotent grace is equal to the emergency, and does save all who in the integrity of their hearts, and the candor of their judgment and the verdict of their conscience walk in all the light they have; ready gladly to appreciate brighter and stronger light, should the good providence of God send it in the Gospel of His Son.

The orthodox Churches all began the glorious revival of genuine spiritual proof and glorious experimental salvation; *i. e.*, the Congregational Churches with the Pilgrim Fathers, who fled from the persecutions in Europe, and found an asylum among the wild Indians of the New World.

The Baptist Church in her modern organization from the clear, bright light, which God gave the world through the instrumentality of John Bunyan, who spent twelve and a half years in the Bedford jail for preaching the true Gospel of holiness to the Lord; meanwhile he wrote the "Pilgrim's Progress" and the "Holy Wars," which have been shaking the world ever since. The Presbyterian Church, in the providence of God, developed out of the holiness bands in Scotland, called the Covenanters, because they had made with God, a covenant of holiness for which they were anathematized by the Pope and hunted with bloodhounds and burnt at the stake during the reign of "Bloody Mary," till John Knox, their wonderful leader, prayed her down from the throne of England, to vacate it for Queen Elizabeth, the friend and protector of the Protestants and the founder of the British Empire, the greatest Christianizing power on the earth. George Fox, in the providence of God, the founder of the Friends Church, preached entire sanctification in England with great power, and wonderful demonstration of the Spirit, a hundred years before John Wesley, whom God so wonderfully used to dot the British Isles with the Holiness bands, out of which the Methodist Church was organized, after he went to Heaven.

E. Whereas these great Orthodox Churches all originated in the current Holiness Movement; as the veterans wound up the battle and passed away to the Mount of Victory, their successors gradually depleted, meanwhile carnality by intriguing demons was initiated till especially in these latter days it has so predominated, as to lamentably disspiritualize and degospelize these great denominations.

In the Providence of God the Friends' Church has retained primitive simplicity, spirituality and power more successfully than any of her sisters, and has done much to rekindle the fire in the present Holiness revival girdling the globe.

Of course, Methodism is by pre-emption simply a Holiness organization, but having accumulated the teem-

The Church. 401

ing millions, is awfully burdened with the carnal element. Unitarianism in the East, Campbellism and Mormonism in the West never had a spiritual history, having originated in heresies incompatible with spirituality; in the former repudiating the Divinity of Christ, and the latter, the personality and work of the Holy Spirit, and really deifying immersion in water, thus actually propagating hydrolatry, *i. e.*, water-worship, positively violating the first commandment of the decalogue, *"Have ye no other gods before Me,"* and the same time utterly minifying the work of Christ, who had to come from Heaven and die for us all, from the simple fact that it was impossible for us to be saved by legal obedience. (Gal. 2:21.) As in that case, Christ would have died gratitudously, *i. e.*, for nothing.

We had the commandments from the beginning, and there was as much water in the world in which to immerse people before Jesus came as afterward, for they had Noah's flood. Therefore, these heterodoxical churches have never fallen, from the simple fact, they were launched on Satan's bottom, whence there is no place to which they can fall, till they pass out of this world. Yet, we should be full of love for all the people who have been caught by Satan's delusion, under the cognomen of Christianity, and pray for them.

I am aware that those people take the statement, *"Except any one may be born of water and the Spirit, he cannot see the kingdom of God,"* construcing it the physical water in which they immerse the body.

Nicodemus, though a great theologian, because he was still spiritually dead and though having eyes did not see, drifted to that same conclusion, that our Savior meant that His body should be born again; but Jesus corrected him. *"That which is born of the flesh is flesh and that which is born of the Spirit is spirit; then marvel not that I said, Ye must be born from above. The Spirit breathes on whom He willeth, and thou hearest His voice, but canst not tell whence he cometh or whither he goeth, even so is every one who is born of the Spirit."*

This, you see, showed Nicodemus his mistake in thinking that something had to be done to this body, and here reveals in wonderful beauty and force, the pure spirituality of the birth, having nothing to do with physical water, but the Water of Life. This is abundantly confirmed in the next chapter, meanwhile He is preaching to the woman at the well and mentioned water several times. She, thinking He meant the water in the well till He told her positively that He did not, but that He was talking about the Water of Life, which He alone can give. This supernatural birth is wrought by the Holy Ghost, who is the Spirit of Jesus (Acts 16: 6, 7) and gives to all the Living Water.

The Church that does not preach the regeneration and sanctification of the Holy Ghost, constantly, urgently and explicitly, is beneath the Bible standard, to say the least, and when, as in case of the above mentioned, they ignore these mighty works of God, and preach vain substitutes; they are actually doing the work of anti-christ and the false prophet.

Every counterfeit is a false prophet, and every one who preaches a substitute for Christ is undisputably anti-christ. I have known members of the heterodoxical churches gloriously saved and sanctified and all

The Church.

right. *"Man looks on the outside, but God looks on the heart."*

r. In case of the Orthodox Churches, so long as they are ruled by spiritual people, they do noble work, preaching the pure Gospel and saving souls. But when carnal people get the control of them, their doctrine of "Holiness to the Lord" becomes a dead letter, and the people perish, just like they do in the heterodoxical churches.

"When people get saved, should they not withdraw from the carnal church in which they hold membership?" If you are truly saved, sanctified and wholly given up to God, He will answer this question. Go to Him, and let Him settle it for you, lest you make a mistake.

N. B. God loves all the people in that carnal church (even though her doctrines may be heretical) enough to die for them, because He has come from Heaven and laid down His life to save them. He suffered martyrdom in the Church because He preached the truth. Amen. Perhaps He wants to give you a crown of glory for walking heroically in His footsteps, witnessing to His power to save to the uttermost and preach the Gospel to the lost people in that Church, who are blinded by Satan and led captive at His will. I do not want to sail to Heaven

> "On flowery beds of cease,
> While others fight to win the prize,
> And wade through bloody seas."

No, but give me the hottest of the battle and the thickest of the fight.

"I'd rather be the least of them,
    Who are the Lord's alone,
Than wear a royal diadem,
    And sit upon a throne."

But you say: "If I stay in my carnal, icebergy church, I am sure to lose my experience." Then run with all your might and *join the hottest Holiness Church you can find.* But if you go to preaching with all your might, there where you are so much needed, you will not lose your experience.

"But they will not let me preach." They cannot hinder you from preaching from house to house and on the streets, where you are so much needed, in order to reach multiplied thousands in our Christian land who never do go to church and are fast sinking into heathenism. While you are concerned with the heathens in Africa, do not neglect them at home.

"But I have no invitations to preach." Then you ought to shout loudly, because you are in the happy succession of Jesus; yet His weary feet never found rest; walking everywhere over mountain and plain, and preaching as He went. Do not yield to Satan's temptation and become a church fighter.

N. B. It is his diabolical trick to turn away your sword from his own head. If he can get you to fight the churches, or the lodges, or the doctors, or anything else, then he wins the victory, for you have already turned your back on him, and as you have no armor to protect your back, he has nothing to do but plug you with his bullets, and kill you. We have no fight with churches, lodges, nor physicians; but all we can possibly do to fight devils, heresies and diseases. We should ever keep in view the fact that all regenerated people are really members of God's Church abiding in spiritual infancy, till entire sanctification gives them adultage. This qualifies them to hold office and preach the Gospel. Therefore, we must learn to discriminate between sin and sinners, heresies and heretics. While we dare not make any compromise with sin or heresy, we must be full of love to all sinners and heretics; by wisdom, patience, forbearance, meekness, brotherly kindness, charity and the perfect love which is not provoked (1 Cor. 13:5), to win and save them.

Amid all of our efforts, if we do not watch and pray Satan will slip in like a weasel and drop vinegar into our honey. We must, absolutely, at every cost, keep sweet; otherwise our defeat is inevitable, and the cause of God in our hands will bleed at every pore. While we must have unity in essentials, *i. e.*, regeneration and sanctification by the Holy Ghost, we must allow liberty in non-essentials, ever remembering the proneness of man to look on the outside, while God looks on the heart. *"Love beareth all things, believeth all things, hopeth all things, and endureth all things."* (1 Cor. 3:8.) Hence you see we must bear with all their infirmities and mistakes, believing and hoping for their salvation, remembering that there is nothing hard for God to do, and that He is infinitely more merciful than we are.

On the street of Oakland, Cal., I heard a Mormon prophet preaching with all his might. As I listened to him laboring to convince the people that God is still making revelations to the world, by sending prophets on the earth, thus laboring to authenticate his Book of Mormon and the inspiration of Joseph Smith, Brigham

Young, and others of his church, while I was ready (D. V.) to suffer martyrdom for the Truth, my heart was flooded with love for the preacher, that love taking the form of sympathy, pity, kindness and philanthropy. *"The weapons of our warfare are not carnal, but mighty through God unto the pulling down of strongholds, casting down reasonings and every high thing that exalteth itself against the knowledge of God, and bringing into captivity every thought unto the obedience of Christ, and holding yourselves in readiness to fight off every disobedience when your obedience may be perfect."* 2 Cor. 10: 4-6.

This is a grand revelation, setting forth the triumphant attitude of the Christian soldier, heroically fighting down every inward trend to disobedience, even bringing into captivity every thought to the infallible knowledge of God.

The word here is *aichmelotizoutes*, which means "taking our enemies captive on the battlefield, and leading them away in perfect subjugation at our discretion." The wonderful experience of Christian Perfection so cleanses the heart, that we can truly say, like our great Exemplar, *"The prince of this world cometh, and findeth nothing in Me."* Our Lord came and suffered and died to make us all like Himself, free from sin, having our fruit unto sanctification and the end eternal life. (Rom. 6: 22.)

John Wesley illustrates it: "A man insults me grossly, as Satan can inspire him. Instead of feeling resentment, I feel nothing but love. The people eulogize me; instead of feeling pride rise, I feel nothing but humility; their eulogies only serving contrastively to remind me of the opposite, which I feel to be true and am, consequently, humble in the dust. They make me a liberal contribution, instead of stirring up love of money, it only arouses aversion to think of filthy lucre, reminding me how evanescent are all transitory things."

While listening to my Mormon prophet flatly contradicting the Bible, which certifies in the last chapter the completion of the prophecies and pronounces a woe on all who shall add to it or take from it, meanwhile my thoughts reverted to God's own definition of the New Testament prophet. 1 Cor. 14:3: *"He that prophesieth, speaketh to the people to edification, exhortation and comfort,"* showing up clearly and explicitly the office of the prophet in our dispensation, simply under the illuminations of the Holy Ghost who inspired our predecessors, during the Bibles Ages to reveal its wonderful truths, now in condescending mercy, shining into our minds, filling our hearts, irradiating our spirits, electrifying our sensibilities, using our humble instrumentality to elucidate the precious and wonderful Word, ages ago revealed by our noble antecedents; exhort the people to believe and obey with all the fervency of the Holy Ghost sent down from Heaven (1 Pet. 1:12), and when the lightning bolts have done the work of conviction, then it is our glorious privilege to give them precious infallible promises enforced by all the burning pathos and tornado vehemence He in condescending mercy inspires; till having prayed through and struck bottom-rock, they rise with shouts of victory.

Yet, amid all, I did not stand by with a critic's cap on my head; but there beneath the twinkling stars my heart was lifted up in fervent prayer for the salvation of him and his audience. Reader, have you the glorious liberty characteristic of the sainted Origen, the greatest scholar in the Church of his day, whose maxim is exceedingly pertinent to us all: *"Love the Lord with all your heart and do as you please."* The fact is, if you love the Lord with all your heart, you will not please to do anything that is not right; you will actually be lost in God's will.

G. Since the Holiness Movement has spread out her wings like a great eagle and folded the nations in her ungracious pinions, it has become the dumping-ground for all sorts of heresies. Consequently, you should pass no one under the simple chibboleth "holiness evangelist," but bring all to the standard of the law and the testimony. Take nothing for granted, but diligently obey the Lord's commandment (1 John 4:1), *"Try the spirits whether they be of God."*

Under the Christian cognomen, even at that early day, John assures us that many anti-christs were going over the world, *i. e.*, people preaching a substitute for Christ, whose mighty experimental works are wrought by the Holy Spirit, His own omnipotent Agent, and these great and stupendous works are regeneration for the sinner, and sanctification for the believer. You are actually to take the *ipse dixit* of none; but rigidly test all by the unimpeachable criterion of God's Word. The Divine Leadership is threefold, homogeneous with the Trinity of humanity, *i. e.*, spirit, soul and body, which are in perfect harmony. The Holy Spirit leading the human spirit; the Word, the intellect, and Providence, the body. In every genuine case, these three are in perfect harmony. This follows as a logical sequence, from the fact that the Holy Spirit, who is none other than Very and Eternal God, created this body and the material world. Therefore when the spirit comes along out of harmony with the Word of God and His Providence, set it down and rest assured he is an evil spirit doing his best to deceive you by playing the Holy Ghost on you. Consequently, if you follow him, you are going into fanaticism, as that is precisely the solution of all fanaticism; an evil spirit plays off on you for the Holy Ghost, and leads you astray. We have now much fanaticism denominated "Holiness." You can detect it every time simply by bringing it to the test of the Divine leadership, which is transcendently beautiful, magnetic and charming in the extreme. In these last days of counterfeit, while the *ignis fatuus* of wild fanaticism is beguiling thousands and leading them away into the dismal swamps of Spiritualism, Christian Science, Hypnotism and all sorts of magic arts, oh, how we need the effectual fortification of this triple leadership. Whenever you find yourself out of harmony with God's Word or Providence, rest assured you are already side-tracked and must have the compass and chart of God's Word and Providence to get you back. When Sanford forced his own little boy of only two years old to fast from food and drink two days and nights, and with the authority of the autocrat, ordered all his people to get immersed in mid-winter, and they had to cut the ice, see how he violated the Providence of God. When Dowey proclaimed his Elijahhood, in the face of the testimonies of Jesus (Matt. 17; Mark 9; Luke 9, all giving the honor to John the Baptist), he shows clearly that he was out of harmony with God's Word. Of all the obvious and unapologizable disharmonies with God's Word, the so-called Tongues Movement caps the climax. You must not be shaken by good names and Scripture epithets; *counterfeits and heretics always use them.* (See chapter 21, "Divine Healing," in connection with this chapter; also turn back and read No. 4, in "The Gifts of the Holy Spirit," *i. e.,* that of bodily healing.) While this is not essential to salvation, because it is only our Lord's merciful repairing of the tenement, till we can finish the work He has given us to do; whereas, the perfection of physical healing is postponed till the resurrection Morn, unless He should honor us with the Translation, in which we will receive it simultaneously with the glorification of the soul and spirit, in the twinkling of an eye. (1 Cor. 15:51.) If our healing were perfect, we would be saved from mortality that very moment, yet, you know that is not true; however, we have the blessed consolation that it will be true, when the resurrection trumpet sounds, and, *"Many who sleep in the dust will awake."* (Dan. 12:2.)

H. We do not wonder that Divine Healing is given by our Savior, both to the twelve and to the seventy; when we consider its potent inspiration and concomitant of Entire Sanctification. You remember how Satan afflicted Job, and terrific were the ordeals through which he passed. His affliction, though administered by Satan, was not for him, but for us in order to give us an example of patient suffering and a confirmation of that wonderful Scripture (Rom. 8:28), *"All things work together for good to them that love God."* That wonderful Scripture enables us to unravel all the mysteries in the Divine administration. You could not have all things and leave Satan out; because he is not only a thing, but a big one. Yet, whereas, all sickness originated from him and is to this day the work of his hands; yet, you must remember that he cannot do anything to God's people without His permission and as you see in the case of Job, God permitted him to afflict him, that through it, showers of blessings in the dispensation of patient, longsuffering have accrued to God's people in all ages.

In a similar manner, this day, and throughout all generations, God permits Satan to afflict His people in order to their humiliation, that they may the more copiously receive the profitable enduements of patience, forbearance and longsuffering, that He may the more abundantly magnify His mercy through their instrumentality. The reason why Christians suffer so much sickness, is because they do not fully consecrate their bodies to the Lord to be used for His glory forever; but through the chicanery of the enemy, they use them for selfish enterprises and aspirations, and even for the gratification of their appetites, predilections and passions. Consequently, God permits the enemy to castigate them by disease and diversified, distressing physical maladies in order to their profitable chastisement, so they cannot only be more useful in their day and generation, but bring Him greater glory in the world to come and receive a richer reward in Heaven. The Jews have no physicians, but look to Jehovah to heal their diseases.

1. We would not raise the war cudgel against the doctors; as they have their work to do, and are so much more competent than we. When I got my arm broken at the age of seventy, I went at once to a physician, who

braced and bandaged it, putting no medicine on it, and then joined me in a prayer of commitment to God, to execute the healing, which He did. Meanwhile, I carried my sling and went along preaching three months. Then returning to him upon removing the bandage he found it healed without leaving a scar or ridge, or a bend, as he much feared, and which would certainly have supervened in case I had not secured his medical service. We frequently need a physician for more profound diagnosis than we are competent to administer; again we need him for the hygienical wisdom in which his opportunities have given him the pre-eminence over all others.

Jan. 13, 1901, I lost my life in Fresno, California by the inhalation of gas escaping in my bed-room, and was found dead the next morning at ten o'clock, the fact of my habitually taking no breakfast having prevented an earlier discovery. In the providence of God, I was enjoying the hospitality of Dr. Meux, an excellent physician, and a holiness man, believing in Divine Healing. At ten A. M., the good sister knocking at my door and receiving no answer, venturing to look in, saw my shoes under the bed, and meeting the gas, took fright, darted down the stairs and notified her husband, who, leaping up the stairway grabbed me in his arms, carried me out of the gas, at the same time calling aloud, gathers around him an ample force to render the needed help in resorting to artificial respiration; one taking each hand, and another each foot, and another my head, and another holding my mouth open, and another throwing water on my face, and fanning me, while they threw me around with great violence, giving me a number of boils, developed from bruises, where they had struck me against the furniture in the room. In the midst of these violent manipulations, the doctor saw me catch my breath; of course I only know what they told me, as I was unconscious forty hours. The doctor said when he found me, my breathing had entirely ceased, but upon an immediate diagnosis, he found the very slightest lingering symptom of heart-action. If he had not been there, he said, the last hope would have fled before a physician could possibly have been reached.

The argument that we have no case of resurrection in the present age, I regard as untenable. I do believe I was then out of the body. After convalescence the most delicious memories lingered in my spirit. I heard music and utterances and realized a sweetness in my soul, which no tongue can tell; much reminding me of Paul's testimony (2 Cor. Chapter 12), when they stoned him to death at Lystra, and he testified that he was carried up to the third Heaven, *i. e.*, the home of the glorified angels and saints and the mansions of our Heavenly Father, when he saw and heard things impossible to tell, not "unlawful" as the E. V., because there was certainly no law against his telling everything he saw and heard, but mortal language can never describe immortal verities. Therefore, in Heaven we will speak, not simply the language of mortals, but of immortals, indispensably needing the latter in order to communicate realities, replete with Heavenly rhapsodies and celestial glory.

I read a book thirty-five years ago, giving the apparant death of Mary Etta Davis, of Elmira, N. Y., who went to Heaven and saw wonderful things, came back and dictated them. The affadivit of her Baptist pastor and physician who certified to it all, *i. e.*, her comatose nine days, and revival and living on the earth. I have seen people who have read a book circulated over Dixie Land, entitled, "Letters from Hell," dictated by an English nobleman, who apparently died, thinking himself a Christian, but went to Hell, and stayed a number of days, came back and re-entered his body, lived on the earth again, profited by his opportunity, sought and found the Lord and afterward died in glorious triumph. I've seen the tomb of Dorcas in Joppa, whom God used Peter to raise from the dead. She had been dead but a few days and kept till the arrival of Peter. The two above mentioned were kept, the young woman nine days, and the man several Doubtless, premature interment has prevented the revival in many cases I shall always believe the testimony of that physician that my breathing had entirely ceased, so they would have proceeded with my interment, if he had not ministered to my restoration.

Similar results frequently obtained in case of people who had been asphyxiated by drowning or electricity.

J. I have consulted physicians through out the continent, relative to their power to heal diseases, and they have uniformly assured me that they did not claim it, but simply the ministry of helping Nature, meanwhile they frankly admitted that God is the only Healer. In the recognition of this fact, it does not follow that we should discard physicians, because we need them to assist Nature and all know that their competency far surpasses ours Even in the capacity of nurses, in which they certainly are competent to excel, they are calculated to render valuable service. The imputation of healing power to them is simply a popular superstition and they are not to blame for it, as they do not claim it.

The Church. 415

The doctor who ministered to my broken arm applied no medicine to it whatever, but simply performed the needed mechanical labor and then joined me in turning it over to the Great and Only Physician to heal it.

Dr. Kelly at Portland, Oregon, an eminent physician, having been educated in this city (Cincinnati), when upon examining a troublesome sore upon my body, pronounced it a cancer and sent me to the Medical College in this city (Cincinnati) for its amputation, at the same time writing to them a letter of introduction and turning me over to them for the needed surgical operation, which he pronounced the only hope of saving my life; whereas, I had often tried in vain to protect it from the friction of my clothing, but could not make the bandage stay on it; he had no trouble to put one on that stayed till it wore off, administering no medicine at all, as he put nothing on it, but raw cotton. But you see it was very important to my comfort and I had not the mechanical skill to do it. However, I never did deliver the letter of introduction in Cincinnati, as I had a considerable slate of appointments on the Coast and in the Interior, which I much regretted to disappoint; therefore, instead of coming to the surgeons for amputation, I on the spot turned it over to the Great Physician with these words of consecration, prayer and faith, "Now, Jesus, this troublesome sore, which has given me much affliction, has finally been pronounced a cancer; I know that cancers do their work quickly, therefore, if you have more work for me to do, You must speak to this cancer; I know it is bound to obey your mandate. If You tell it to leave, it is certain to get away, and that quickly." Then my faith was imbargoed to the very utmost. With no sign of healing, but all the symptoms of the contrary, I just had to take the bit in my teeth and by simple faith say, like Peter told Eneas in Lydia, *"Jesus heals thee, take up thy bed and walk;"* the thing he had not done in eight years, because he was prostrate with paralysis. In a similar manner my heart was enabled to say, "Jesus heals my cancer." I observed that the pain evanesced, but did not remove that bandage, letting it alone until it wore off. When I looked in vain for my cancer; I had only the scar, which I have this day, though a decade of years have flown. The surgeons could have cut it out, but in many cases of that kind, the cancerous virus surviving in the blood, has broken out in another place and all hope taken its flight. While we have no war to make on physicians any more than we have on the churches; they all have their work to do, let us turn them over to God, and pray for them, and do them all the good we can, meanwhile recognizing the fact that Jesus is all we need for soul and body.

In my humble way, I have been preaching fifty-four years; meanwhile serious lung trouble brought me to death's door, where physicians all abandoned me to die, and Jesus healed me suddenly, so I have none since, though that was thirty-five years ago. He also healed me of terrible Sciatic rheumatism, so that I could not walk—twenty-three years ago, and I am perfectly free of all trouble of that kind.

In 1906, in Vienna, on the other side of the Globe, He healed me of Cholera. In these fifty-four years with these severe ailments, and many others attacking me ever and anon, I have lost almost no time out of the pulpit, and from labor in the Lord's vineyard, because

He has healed me so quickly. Glory to His wondrous Name forever

Matt 8:16, 17: *"And it being evening, they brought to Him many demonized people: and He continued to cast out the spirits by His word, and healed all those who were afflicted; in order that the Word spoken by Isaiah the prophet might be fulfilled, saying, Himself did take our infirmities and carried our diseases."* This clearly covers all the ground and settles the question of its place in the Atonement. Here you see it goes right along with soul-saving, actually all revealed in the same sentence, showing us clearly it is concluded in the Atonement. We may observe, however, that in this probation we only receive the temporary healing, until we can finish our work, so the completion of bodily restitution will take away mortality. Therefore, the Lord speaking from a human standpoint, has availed Himself of the convenience of simultaneous restitution in the general resurrection of the bridehood immediately antecedently to the tribulation (Rev 1:6), and all the remainder of all ages and nations in the final resurrection, subsequently to the Millennium, and immediately antecedently to the general judgment. (Rev. 20:11.) While our healing is simply accommodately to our probate labors, it is a glorious blessing and free-for-all who consecrate themselves fully to God, to be used for His glory, and receive it by faith. as it is the gift of the Spirit. (1 Cor. 12:9.) When our work is done, we will have no faith to be healed any more, then we will get to go to Heaven. It is not at all necessary that we have disease in order to die. It is our precious privilege in utter abandonment to God, to be kept until our work is done and then pass away by invitation, without sickness or suffering, the translation coming on in the sweet realization of an unearthly rapture, finding ourselves on the other side among the angels and redeemed spirits.

www.ingramcontent.com/pod-product-compliance
Lightning Source LLC
Chambersburg PA
CBHW032057090426
42743CB00007B/154